MASTERING AS/400 PERFORMANCE

Alan Arnold • Charly Jones
Jim Stewart • Rick Turner

A Division of
DUKE COMMUNICATIONS
INTERNATIONAL

Loveland, Colorado

Library of Congress Cataloging-in-Publication Data

Mastering AS/400 performance / by Alan Arnold ... [et al.].
p. cm.
Includes index.
ISBN 1-882419-49-9
1. IBM AS/400 (Computer) 2. Electronic digital computers--Evaluation. I. Arnold, Alan, 1960- .
QA76.8.I25919M38 1996
004.2'545—dc20 96-25347
CIP

DUKE COMMUNICATIONS INTERNATIONAL
Loveland, Colorado

It is the reader's responsibility to ensure procedures and techniques used from this book are accurate and appropriate for the user's installation. No warranty is implied or expressed.

This book was printed and bound in the United States of America.

ISBN 1-882419-49-9

1 2 3 4 5 VG 9 8 7 6

Thank you to my family: Jeannine, Allison, and Andrew, whose love, patience, and support always keep me going and keep life in perspective.

Alan Arnold

About the Authors

Alan R. Arnold

Alan Arnold has been working in the IBM midrange systems industry for the last fifteen years. He has worked as a programmer, case tool analyst, consultant, systems engineer, regional SE manager, national director of technology services, and most recently as a senior manager for Ernst & Young LLP in the Management and Consulting Information Technology Group. He has spoken throughout the world on the subject of midrange technology and performance and has written numerous articles that have appeared in many of the IBM midrange newsletters and magazines. He has also been active in the COMMON user group. As a member of COMMON, Alan was a member of the System/36 to AS/400 Strategic Task Force that worked with IBM Rochester.

Alan is a graduate of the University of Redlands, Chapman University, and Orange Coast College, where he studied both advanced business and computer systems methodologies. He can be reached at 71410.2276@compuserve.com.

Charly Jones

Charly Jones is the president and owner of Merlyn and Associates, a company he founded in Seattle to address midrange issues. His company consults throughout the world on advanced midrange performance and work management issues. Charly has been very active in COMMON over the last ten years and was a technical editor for *NEWS/400* magazine specializing in advanced midrange techniques and issues. Charly has worked very closely with IBM Rochester on a variety of AS/400 issues since the system's inception. Charly can be reached at (206) 851-9876.

James C. Stewart

Jim Stewart is president of Stewart & Associates of Rochester, Inc., a Minnesota-based AS/400 performance consulting company. Before his retirement from IBM, Jim spent 17 years in the Rochester Development Laboratory working on AS/400 and System/38 development. He was the development manager for the AS/400 Performance Tools Licensed Program Product, where he managed the initial release of the AS/400 Performance Tools. Before that assignment, he worked in the System/38 Performance Technical Support area where he was responsible for the S/38 external performance tools, new enhancements, maintenance, field education, and documentation. He has presented various performance analysis seminars at COMMON, IBM Technical Conferences, and regional user groups.

Jim is a graduate of Moorhead State University with graduate studies in Mathematics and Computer Science at the University of Minnesota. He also attended the IBM Systems Research Institute and completed an SRI course of study in Computer Science. He can be reached at (507) 253-9563.

Rick Turner

Rick Turner is president of Rick Turner & Associates, Inc., an AS/400 performance consulting company based in Rochester, Minnesota. Before retiring in 1993 after 29 years at IBM, Rick's most recent assignment was with IBM's AS/400 Competency Center in Rochester working on system performance issues, solving customer performance problems, working with the development lab on future system performance-related items, assisting in the training of other technical people to perform performance analysis contracts, and designing and teaching part of a five-day AS/400 Performance Analysis Workshop in Rochester.

Rick has worked in the IBM Rochester Development Laboratory on AS/400 and System/38 systems architecture and design since 1973. He has been involved in a number of system development areas, including hardware and software design, system performance planning, and performance instrumentation and tools on AS/400 and S/38 systems; he also managed a performance department. He is a co-author of several patents on the S/38 and AS/400 system tasking and control structures, inter-task communications, and queue management. Since 1980, he has specialized in system performance, leading the development of the S/38 Performance Tools, serving as a key architect for the AS/400 Performance Tools, and working with customers to solve performance problems. He has presented many performance analysis seminars and workshops to COMMON, IBM SEs, agents, and customers in the U.S., Europe, and Australia. He has also published a number of AS/400 performance articles in *NEWS/400* magazine and currently writes a bi-monthly performance column. Rick can be reached 73602.442@compuserve.com.

Table of Contents

Preface

Whenever we walk into an AS/400 site, we hear the same two pleas: "Make our system perform better" and "Help us figure out why our system is not performing well." The size of the site makes no difference—the question of performance applies to small B-model systems as well as the largest Advanced Series RISC models.

Unfortunately, solutions to performance problems are not always straightforward. Sometimes solving a request to make an AS/400 perform better is simple; however, the solution is often complex. Nevertheless, whether your system is small or large, whether you have a large staff or are a one-person shop, you have the same questions and many of the same problems.

Tuning your system for performance is a matter of finding answers to your questions. Many answers are in the IBM documentation (e.g., *Performance Tools Guide*, *Operator Guide*, and *Work Management Guide*), but they can be well hidden. There is no straightforward road map to better performance. The challenge of performance tuning is understanding the workings and interrelationships of multiple parts of the system, such as communications, database, and hardware, as well as your end users and your business. In other words, having a good grasp of the big picture of performance tuning is a large part of finding a satisfactory solution.

Most people can tune their own systems with some help and direction. Our intent is to help you tune your AS/400 when needed, but also to give you insight into monitoring and correcting performance problems before they become severe.

You can use the material in this book regardless of whether you have a CISC or RISC machine. The primary difference is in the way the Timing and Paging Statistics Tool (TPST) and Sampled Address Monitor (SAM) are presented. On RISC machines, they're now part of the Performance Explorer; CISC machine users can simply follow the book.

Performance Management Methodology

Analyzing performance can involve working with large amounts of very detailed information. To help you avoid getting wrapped up in too many details, our approach in this book is to focus on a performance management methodology (Section I). This methodology describes a way to stay aware of performance levels by evaluating performance information against the end users' objectives and tracking and analyzing trends in system resource utilization. The basis for comprehensive performance analysis is understanding where the bottlenecks are, what is causing them, and how to eliminate them.

The Components of Performance

After establishing a methodology, we look at the components of performance by examining the resources each request for work requires. The key AS/400 performance components are:

- Communications line resource
- Activity level
- CPU resource
- Disk access
- Memory
- Object contention
- Error handling

These performance components are the basis for analyzing performance problems and give you a way to communicate the problem and the reasons for your recommendations for solving the problem. You can attribute most performance problems to one or more of these components. They are useful for narrowing the scope of a performance problem and identifying the specific resources causing the problem. We will discuss these components in detail in Section II.

Analyzing performance data may suggest solving a problem by changing the application. Though this book is not about designing applications for optimal performance, we do mention some key application considerations related to each component of performance.

Tuning Your System

The next subject we will examine in detail is performance tuning. First, we will demonstrate ways to tune your system without using the IBM Performance Tools (Section III). This discussion addresses options that use only the standard OS/400 interfaces. The various system status displays, combined with performance data collection, job accounting, and error and history log facilities, give you significant analysis ability without requiring an investment in the Performance Tools.

Our examination of the IBM's Performance Tools in Section IV identifies the reports and the sections of the reports you will find most useful. It also looks at the specific performance guidelines that apply to the report data and mentions other tools that help isolate specific application performance problems.

Because the Performance Monitor is the heart of any performance monitoring and improvement program, we give instructions for using the Performance Monitor both with and without IBM's Performance Tools.

This book will show you how to observe what is happening inside your system and how to control it. The goal is to optimize the performance of your system. We will show you ways to achieve better performance without hardware upgrades or application changes. Shops frequently run bigger systems than they need to mask application performance problems. Of course, if your organization has extra money, this solution may temporarily provide the results you want. But if you are like most companies, you probably can't spend any more money than is necessary on computer hardware.

Many application performance problems appear suddenly and without warning. For example, a file might grow to a critical size, or the number of users of a particular program might increase. We will give you basic information that will prepare you for a sudden performance problem so you don't have to respond to a problem quickly without the necessary background.

Because modifying applications is usually your most expensive option (unless you happen to have extra programmers sitting around), we usually consider optimizing application performance as a last resort. This subject is too complex to give it justice in one chapter, so we do not cover application changes for performance in this book. However, it is important to realize that if you have followed all the suggestions and rules in this book and are still having performance problems, you may have no choice but to look inside your applications.

If you are new to performance management and analysis or are looking for new insights to improve your AS/400's performance, this book is for you. You don't need any previous knowledge about AS/400 performance tuning or experience with the IBM Performance Tools licensed program and other system interfaces for collecting and analyzing performance data. However, you do need some familiarity and experience with AS/400 operations and work management.

If you're not a performance-tuning newcomer, you'll also find lots of important and useful tips and advice. In talking to people in the AS/400 world, we've found that most AS/400 professionals can pick up a lot from our experiences. These experiences are based on many years of performance analysis work on the AS/400; its predecessor, the S/38; and many other systems. We've included sidebars that give examples based on our own experience in performance tuning. In addition, you can also find some background material or detailed information about particular topics under the "In Depth" heading. We hope our experiences prove useful to you.

One last point: Remember that your system is different from every other system. The guidelines and advice in this book are here to help you, but they may not help your particular situation. For this reason, we strongly recommend that you fully document your system's environment and performance issues before making any changes that we recommend. If you fully document your system, you can always change it back. Your documentation can also be a road map for any improvements you make. Appendix A consists of a checklist to document your current system configuration and performance.

Good luck and good tuning!
Alan, Charly, Jim, and Rick

CHAPTER 1

Defining and Managing Performance

Before we dive into finding solutions to performance problems, we need to consider the question, "What is performance?" Although this question has several answers, most definitions of performance focus on concrete, practical criteria by which you can judge your system's productivity and speed.

PERFORMANCE CRITERIA

We can say that performance involves response time, throughput, batch work, capacity, and resource use. To get *good* performance, we need to make the most of each of these criteria. So, as we look at performance criteria, we will keep in mind what's necessary to improve performance.

Minimizing Response Time

On an AS/400 that supports interactive applications, interactive response time is typically the primary criterion for defining and measuring performance. The system must respond quickly enough that users don't perceive delays. To meet this requirement, programmers often assign very high priority and separate storage pools (ensuring each job has an activity level and sufficient memory whenever it's needed) to highly visible interactive functions, such as customer service.

Maximizing Throughput

In some cases, the AS/400 must respond quickly enough for each user to complete a specific amount of work in a certain period. For example, a department store clerk doesn't want customers to wait a long time while the system is verifying their store credit card. You can configure your system to ensure that every transaction gets into the system and starts working immediately, even though interactive work already in progress is using the available CPU and storage. In such cases, the definition of performance is maximizing throughput.

Optimizing Batch Work

When you have an end-of-day processing requirement (as, for example, at a brokerage house), the primary performance concern might be optimizing your batch work. The time necessary for batch jobs to run is often directly proportional to the amount of interactive work that preceded it: Usually, batch cycles are low-priority work and get only the cycles left over from high-priority interactive work. However, enough processor cycles must be available for batch work to run. You really have two performance criteria here: reducing individual job runtime and getting all the work done in time.

As in the interactive environment, you reduce batch job runtime through system configuration settings that give the job its own storage pool and, possibly, higher priority than other batch work. Increasing its priority, however, might cause inefficiencies in using the disk. Normally, I/O is FIFO (first in, first out), whereas the CPU resource is prioritized. When all batch jobs compete for the I/O resource from the same priority level, each can put I/O tasks into the queue equally, the disk works on each task in the order in which it came in, and all the jobs can be completed. However, when one batch job has higher priority than other batch work, its I/O resource requests tend to be queued ahead of other jobs, and batch jobs with lower priority will have less chance to access the CPU to get their I/O tasks in the queue. If your objective is to get everything finished in time, you should keep the priority level equal for all of the batch jobs but still give each job its own storage pool to reduce main storage contention.

Ensuring Adequate Capacity

On unpredictable occasions, such as after earthquakes and hurricanes, an insurance company can expect its AS/400 to handle unusually high claims processing loads and still maintain an adequate level of throughput and a satisfactory response time. To prepare for acceptable performance in the aftermath of disasters, the insurance company must give this system more resources than it needs for its regular workload. In such cases, the definition of performance is adequate capacity at all times.

Maximizing Resource Use

On the other hand, some systems have to stay busy all the time and use all resources to the fullest to maximize the use of expensive computer hardware components. (Some AS/400 shops run their systems this way without even realizing it.) Such demands probably aren't a problem if the workload is consistent

Documenting Changes

A common problem I see occurs when people install a new operating system release. Immediately after they put on the new release, I'll get a call saying that performance is suffering. Often, this problem happens because the users did not save subsystem descriptions, and when they install the new release, they lose all their adjustments, and performance suffers. ■

Charly Jones

from one day to the next and all users are satisfied. However, if the workload grows or the processing varies from day to day, continually operating on the edge is a dangerous proposition.

AS/400 system design and programming sometimes push resources to the maximum to get the greatest return on the dollar for high-cost hardware. For example, when data isn't in main storage, the processor (the most expensive component of any system) may have to wait for the data to be brought in from disk (the least expensive component). In this situation, the system makes run-time adjustments to move data quickly in and out of main storage to keep the processor working as close to 100 percent as possible. In this case, you define performance in terms of appropriate resource use.

These five areas of concern require five definitions of performance — and you can probably find others. Performance means different things to different people, and even for one person at different times. Another reason it's hard to pin down "good" performance for a single system is that performance varies in a nonlinear fashion as the system load increases; that is, performance can get really bad really quickly.

Because "performance" is such a multi-faceted term, you need to assess your own performance situation and develop a performance plan by which you can judge how well *your* system is meeting *your* needs. You must do more than simply monitor performance. You must manage it.

PERFORMANCE MANAGEMENT

Performance management *is the ongoing process of ensuring that a business's work is done on time and within budget.* As part of that process, performance management takes into account that business volume, needs, and available resources may vary from one time to another. Performance management helps you prevent surprises by providing criteria for estimating in advance what resources you will need and then periodically giving you updated information to ensure that you don't exceed your estimate.

We want to stress that performance management is a continuous process, not something you do only to react to a specific performance problem. Because performance management is a process, someone — maybe you — needs to spend time attending to performance management issues. Your organization should have a designated performance person to whom managers, end-users, and other IS people can turn for information, analysis, and guidance. This person is the performance focus for the organization and is aware of and involved in various performance activities, such as requirements, objectives, collection, analysis, and feedback.

Performance management is an important element in managing any business's data processing resources. People in large systems environments have realized the importance of performance management for many years. AS/400 professionals, on the other hand, often wait until they have an obvious performance problem before they take action to manage performance.

You can justify performance management in many ways. Some obvious benefits are that performance management maintains business efficiency, provides a smooth transition when business conditions change, increases user satisfaction, improves change management, and provides rapid response time. Each of these areas is worth consideration.

Maintain Business Efficiency

More than ever, business systems are running mission-critical applications. A slowdown in such applications represents a slowdown in business. By providing the means to maintain a given level of efficiency, performance management directly affects how successful a business can be: Better performance equals more business equals higher revenue, and, we all hope, an increased revenue-to-cost ratio.

Provide Smooth Business Transitions

Given normal growth within a business and the consequent ever-increasing application demands, computing professionals frequently face changing system requirements. One goal of performance management is to project the need for system changes and plan a response to them. This process is known as capacity planning and modeling and uses performance measurements and trend analysis. However, performance management must look beyond system hardware and performance data analysis to incorporate the whole business environment. The designated performance person should also be involved in business planning. Because of the lead time required to acquire and test new resources, this person needs an early awareness of plans for the business's growth.

Increase User Satisfaction

Users tend to perceive the system as dedicated exclusively to their tasks. As a result, users have clear expectations for performance. If the system doesn't meet those expectations, you can expect little appreciation or tolerance for delays for any reason. For example, if your end users expect their batch work to run in less than an hour and it takes two hours, you will not be meeting their expectations. Effective performance management reduces resource demand conflicts, thus maintaining user satisfaction. Performance management also gives you the means to prioritize user tasks to help establish proper expectations.

Improve Change Management

You must be able to measure changes to your system. These changes could include adding new applications, modifying an existing application, going to a new release of the operating system, or changing the number or type of users.

Simple Sampling

I find that long-term tracking, or trend analysis, is most useful when I have set objectives, such as average transactions per hour or average response time. With trend analysis, my experience teaches me to be careful that I'm comparing apples to apples.

For example, if you're tracking average transactions per hour over several months, be careful of what time of the day you're sampling for your analysis. If you use a 24-hour day, you may have long periods (such as at night) when the level of transactions is low. If you attempt to even out the sample by averaging this low level with a high level during the day, the results may be misleading. Your system may be beyond capacity during the day, but the averaging can mask this problem.

For trend analysis, I suggest you break down your analysis periods into units such as morning processing, afternoon processing, and nightly processing. This way, you don't let averaging skew your results. ■

Alan Arnold

You can assume that any significant change to the system will cause some aspects of performance to change. To evaluate and correct a performance problem, you must measure the system both before and after the change so that you can see the change's effect. You can make such measurements only if you are periodically monitoring the proper performance data. Therefore, you need a performance-data collection plan that will give you both "before" and "after" data.

Provide the Economic Benefits of Rapid Response Time

If you work for a service-oriented business, performance management is especially important. Rapid response time lets your users provide better service. When users are confident that they have plenty of available system resource, they work much more efficiently because they don't have to worry about bad response time or anticipate long waits.

A Performance Management Methodology

Achieving the benefits of performance management is much more likely if you have a performance management methodology. When you start working on performance, it is very easy to fall into the trap of blindly monitoring performance numbers and making changes to get them within some magical guideline. Though guidelines based on performance testing and user experiences can be valuable, each system environment is unique. You need to base changes on careful analysis of the specific system to which you apply them. A better use of guidelines is as a starting point or as a flag to signal potential problem areas that deserve closer analysis. But to use guidelines in this way, you must have a performance management methodology that puts your performance numbers in a context that is meaningful.

The goal we want to achieve in this book is an important one: to help you establish an ongoing performance management process, based on a widely accepted performance methodology, supported by an understanding of the components of system performance.

Performance management consists of the six steps shown in Figure 1.1. Let's briefly consider each step.

1. **Understand business requirements**: You must understand the business requirements the system is meant to address. Besides these requirements, your system's operation likely must stay within certain constraints, such as budget limitations. These business requirements and constraints are directly related to system requirements. For example, any change in your business will have an impact on your data processing requirements. You need to understand your business requirements to establish system performance objectives and to know your options for meeting those objectives.
2. **Establish performance objectives**: Setting objectives establishes a set of goals and expectations for measuring system performance. The objectives focus attention on particular issues. Your attempts to improve performance can become an exercise in shooting at moving

FIGURE 1.1
Performance Methodology

Understand business requirements
Establish performance objectives
Determine measurements needed to track objectives
Periodically measure the system
Evaluate the measurements
Provide feedback to operations development, and management

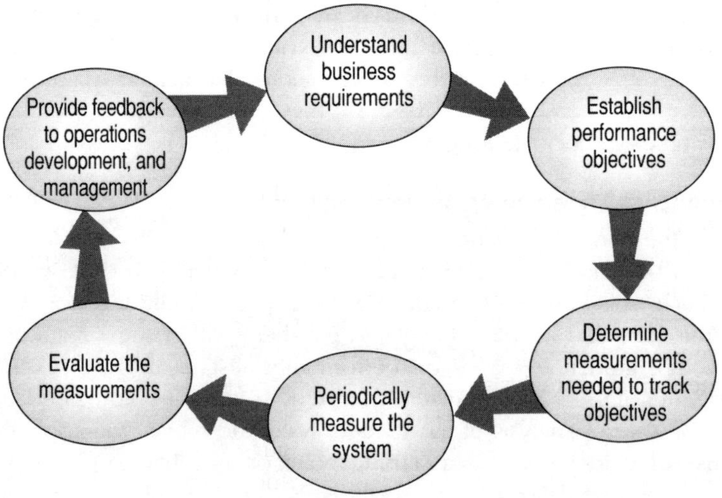

targets unless everyone involved — the end users, the systems people, the programmers, and management — agrees on a set of performance objectives. You don't want to start out trying to get better interactive response time and be directed to pursue some different objective, getting caught in an endless performance tangent in which nothing seems to get accomplished. An agreed-to performance objectives document will keep you and your organization focused on the goal and remind you of what you are trying to accomplish.

It is important to be as specific as possible when you set a performance objective. For example, if your users are getting three-second response times and you want subsecond response times, your performance objective is subsecond response time. We recommend you focus on meeting one objective at a time.

The key to success with any performance objective is to have a clear definition of management's and users' performance criteria and to accomplish the objective with minimum expenditures of time, people, and money. So please, before you start any systems tuning, sit down and figure out exactly what your performance objectives are. Once you have identified objectives, you are well on your way to solutions.

3. **Determine the measurements needed to track the objectives**: After you have set your objectives, determine how you are going to collect performance data. There is a direct relationship between your performance objectives and the way you collect data. You have several data-collection options. For example, you may use the AS/400 Performance Monitor, OS/400 job accounting, interactive performance commands, or other methods. The method you choose depends on what you are looking for. Chapters 8 through 14, which consider performance tuning with and without tools, discuss each collection option in detail.

4. **Periodically measure the system**: You need to measure the way your system is performing. A simple set of graphs showing system resource usage and workload will help you track your progress while tuning your system. Using your defined objectives, you can determine how often to measure your system and how complex the measurements need to be. Measurements can be as simple as producing a print screen once an hour, or as detailed as running the Performance Monitor with specific period collection parameters. The more measurements you collect, the more options are available once you begin your performance analysis.

   A dynamic and complex environment — for example, with many changes to applications, system configuration, and end user activities — will also influence the frequency and types of measurements you will want. This kind of environment calls for more frequent measurements and requires data that enables more detailed problem analysis, such as Performance Monitor data with the Trace option active.

5. **Evaluate the measurements**: Evaluation of your measurements is the analysis component of the performance methodology. The analysis work is based on the type and amount of data you collected. Your performance analysis depends on which collection method and tools you use. For example, if your objective is a certain response time, you can examine the performance reports included in the Performance Tools for all fields related to response time. Or, if you do not have performance reports, you can look at the output of the interactive commands that provide data about response time. You should use the data to perform long-term analysis (weeks or months) and produce a trend analysis report.
6. **Provide feedback to operations, development, and management**: When you complete all the analysis work, it is vital to deliver the findings to the people who can make the decisions to improve the performance. Therefore, you must give the analysis results to the key decision makers in an easy-to-understand format.

After you finish the performance methodology cycle, you sometimes discover that the objective you defined in Step 1 based on business requirements was not the correct objective. You must then redefine the objective and repeat the performance methodology cycle. It is not uncommon to repeat this cycle many times, depending on what you uncover during your analysis.

For example, you may decide that once you have better interactive performance, you need to work on the performance of your batch jobs. Once you meet batch and interactive job performance objectives, you may decide to work on system performance for remote users. So you may have to repeat your six performance steps often until all your performance objectives are satisfied.

Performance analysis is a continuous process. You can make this process work for you by ensuring that you know what performance means, that you have definite objectives, and that you have a methodology that lets you measure performance in a meaningful way.

In Depth: Performance Information Flow

Operations Versus Applications

Most Information Systems (IS) departments separate the operations and applications groups under different management. Often the levels of management or simply the cultures of the two groups leads to poor communication between them, which can have numerous impacts on the performance of the system.

I recently worked with a customer whose operations group was struggling to get a handle on the company's business growth so they could project system resource requirements. Because I was also working with the application group on performance issues in an application, I learned that one of the developers had included a function in the application that gathers workload statistics — exactly what the operations folks needed, but they didn't realize it existed.

The function provided by the applications group was the measurement of business volumes. For instance, the A/R phase of the sales order update recorded the number of invoices created. Other statistics, such as the number of sales order lines and the number of warehouse requests, were also gathered. These business statistics, combined with system performance statistics, enabled the operations folks to gain a much clearer view of how the projected business growth would impact their system resource.

As these functional requirements are gathered for enhanced and/or new applications, it is important for the *entire* IS department to use the information. It can bring significant advantage to managing the performance and growth of the system.

Jim Stewart

The Flow of Performance Information within the Organization

Let me expand on Jim's observations. The flow of performance information within the organization is important. In Jim's example, communication between the applications and the operations groups was the issue. Let's look at the four primary groups — Jim's and two others — I see in an organization: the Performance Management Group (operations or a group within the operations department), the Applications Development Group, the End User Group (not necessarily a coherent group but simply the users of all of the applications), and the Executive Management Group (the people with the money, final decision-making authority, and responsibility to direct the strategic vision for the organization).

The larger the organization, the more formal the process of communicating performance information must be. Figure 1.A shows an example of performance information flow for an organization.

The Performance Management Group encompasses the performance expert(s) within the IS department. All performance information for the organization flows through this group. The End User Group communicates all performance issues directly to the Performance Management

continued

In Depth: *continued*

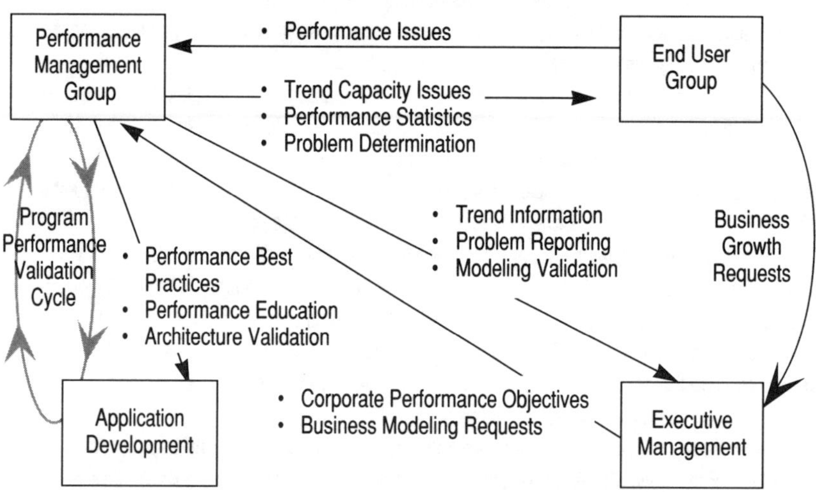

FIGURE 1.A
Performance Information Flow

Group. In turn, the Performance Management Group returns trend and capacity information, performance problem statistics, and problem determination information back to the end users.

The Applications Group can be critical to the success of the performance management effort. It is important that programs placed in your company's production environment meet certain minimum performance objectives. For example, a change in an application program can create a performance problem. If a customer service program is producing sub-second response time, and a change to the program creates five-second response time, your programmer has just created a new application performance problem.

These kinds of performance problems can be avoided if the Performance Management group benchmarks performance of applications before and after changes. The Performance Management Group should also be proactive about performance management, setting minimum performance guidelines for the organization's applications and educating the application development staff about ways to optimize the performance of their programs.

The Executive Management group must set corporate performance objectives and supply business growth estimates so that the Performance Management group can ensure that there is sufficient capacity for the systems to handle the company's growth. As part of the capacity planning for the organization, the Executive Management Group must work closely with the End User Group to understand, or drive, their growth plans for the future. In turn, it is important for the

continued

In Depth: *continued*

Performance Management Group to validate all modeling and trend information and report this information to Executive Management in a manner they can understand, which usually means graphs and summarized performance numbers. ■

Alan Arnold

CHAPTER 2

Performance Management: Methodology and Components

Having defined performance, examined the benefits of performance management, and introduced a performance management methodology, we are ready to consider in detail specific aspects of the performance management methodology and the components of performance.

PERFORMANCE MANAGEMENT METHODOLOGY

Understand Business Requirements

As we discussed in the previous chapter, your system's performance objectives are closely tied to your company's business requirements. As you look at a system's performance, you need to focus first on the business requirements the system must address. These business requirements provide the rationale for the system's performance objectives.

You must clearly understand your company's business requirements and, in particular, the priority of these requirements. At the same time, you should realize that a system designed to address a given set of business requirements can easily evolve into one that is doing work unrelated to these initial requirements. As the system evolves, you need to reconsider old requirements, assess new requirements, and integrate evolving expectations into the original business plan.

In addition, as you provide AS/400 solutions to business needs, users realize the power that computer solutions bring to daily work. Suddenly, the demand for system solutions increases. As you consider business requirements, you have to anticipate and adapt to such demands.

Besides understanding what the business requirements are, you need the following detail about the requirements:

- A statement of each business requirement
- A list of business volumes associated with the requirement
- A history of the business volumes and growth expectations
- A list of justifications for expenditures related to the requirement
- A list of budget constraints
- A list of operational aspects of the requirement (people, applications, and machine resources). This list expands into such considerations as
    - System availability requirements

- Data access needs
  - online: the user needs fast access to data; data should be on disk
  - Nearline™: the user doesn't need access to data as quickly; data could be on a remote system
  - archived: the users seldom needs the data; data could be moved to tape
- Application and user documentation (scheduling options, end user experience/education levels, end user expectations, etc.)
- Future application strategy
- Business plans for centralized vs. distributed growth

These business requirements relate directly to system requirements. Any change to the business requirements will have a corresponding impact on data processing requirements. Understanding business requirements is necessary for you to establish system performance objectives and to know what options you have for meeting those objectives.

Establish Performance Objectives

As the various definitions of performance imply, a typical performance objective may be to maintain average response times or maximum transaction throughput. Your performance objectives establish expectations for measuring system performance. Objectives also help you focus on particular issues.

Your system performance objectives must grow out of business needs, focusing on the business objectives the system is addressing. For example, a hospital sets business objectives for the time required to admit a patient, for the number of patients admitted, and for the number of beds filled. To measure any one of these business objectives, the hospital's business staff thinks in terms of *business transactions.* Business transactions are expressions of real-world business units: Each patient admission, for instance, is a business transaction. Similarly, you express your system objectives in terms of measured data on the system. The system work units for such measuring are called *system transactions*. An example is the work that results each time a user presses the Enter key. The Performance Monitor tool can measure how many times a user presses Enter to send a work request from a workstation.

All applications are different and are based on the requirements of a particular business transaction and the user. In the case of a patient admission at a hospital, the single business transaction of admitting a patient entails entering demographic and insurance information and may also involve assigning a room and scheduling initial laboratory tests. Thus, this single business transaction requires multiple system transactions. And the number of system transactions may vary widely from one admission to the next, depending on whether a patient has been admitted previously or is a new patient, or on the number of tests ordered for this admission — to name just a few factors.

The performance manager's job is to identify a system performance objective for the system transactions necessary to complete the business transaction. For the patient admission, that system objective could be interactive response times for the transactions in the typical patient admission. The system performance objectives can determine whether the hospital will meet its definition of an acceptable amount of time for the admissions process. Fifteen minutes may be acceptable. If a 15-minute admission time is possible only with a 1.2-second or better average response time, then the performance objective for this hospital's system is a 1.2-second or better average response time. To further restrict the scope of this objective, the business requirements may indicate that the critical response time is the period between 7 A.M. and 10 A.M.

Management, on the business side, will understand and state objectives in terms of business transactions. You need to be able to relate these business transactions to the underlying system transactions so that you can manage the growth in system resource requirements. By tracking this relationship over time, you will gain accuracy in your estimates of what that relationship is. The link between system transactions and business transactions is generally not an easy one to establish. However, establishing that link enables business management and systems management to communicate effectively.

Once you've defined the relationship between business transactions and system transactions, you can start thinking about system objectives. The first step will be to consider both batch and interactive needs.

Combining Business and Performance Data

As far back as the first release of the AS/400 Performance Tools, we at IBM discussed how to enable a user exit function that would allow the Performance Monitor database to incorporate business transaction data. We abandoned the idea because we could not find an approach that did not cause timing problems in the monitor's normal data collection or an approach that would generalize across a wide set of customers.

It seems that an application could use a journaling approach to record business transaction data. With the STRPFRMON (Start Performance Monitor) command, you can use such an approach. This command provides a new exit program function that lets you invoke a user program when the Performance Monitor ends. You can use a user-written analysis program that correlates the application's journal data with the performance data from the same period. A summary report relating the business transactions to the system transactions and resource costs could result from this program. ■

Jim Stewart

Batch and Interactive System Objectives

Batch and interactive processing involve quite different performance considerations. Frequent interruptions characterize interactive work, as end users key data for a request or read the results from a request they've entered at the workstation. The individual work requests that interactive users enter can be the transactions that you measure and that go into your statement of the system objectives.

Batch processing, on the other hand, is continuous and at first may not appear to have separate transactions you can measure and use for setting your objectives. The examples that follow will show that, indeed, you can measure batch units of work and use them to establish system objectives. Table 2.1 provides a sample sheet for recording batch and interactive performance objectives.

Let's consider a batch example from the insurance industry. In this example, information was gathered and charted to establish a correlation between the number of claims and services adjudicated (business transactions) and the batch job runtime and/or CPU resource used (system transactions). Figure 2.1, which plots the data from individual batch runs, demonstrates that a correlation exists. The raw data for Figure 2.1 is in Table 2.2, on the following page.

Figure 2.2 shows the relationship between the number of claims and services processed and the batch runtime. The analysis behind these two figures

TABLE 2.1
Sample Performance Objective Worksheet

PERFORMANCE OBJECTIVES

Interactive Objectives

Local transaction response time	time (seconds)	percent of time
Order entry	0.5	90%
Purchasing	1.5	90%
MIS	2.0	75%
Remote response time		
Customer inquiry	4.0	60%
Remote sales staff	6.0	60%

Batch Objectives

Picking slips	10/hr
User-submitted reports	< 0.25 hours
Batch sales processing	< 1.5 hours
Upload of sales information (nightly)	< 5.5 hours
Nightly backup	< 3.5 hours

TABLE 2.2

Data for Batch Runs of Claims and Services

Job Run Date	3/11	3/11	3/6	3/6	2/14	2/14	2/12	2/12	2/10	2/10
Claims	7,044	6,358	12,813	12,486	9,721	9,271	8,456	7,313	16,821	15,291
Services	11,172	9,943	22,640	21,819	16,620	15,543	13,695	11,946	28,679	26,470
Run Time (Minutes)	256	243	524	471	349	336	267	246	517	472
CPU (Minutes X 10)	285.5	266.33	590.67	571.33	388.67	381.67	327.17	305.67	706.50	671.67

FIGURE 2.1

Correlating Business and System Transactions

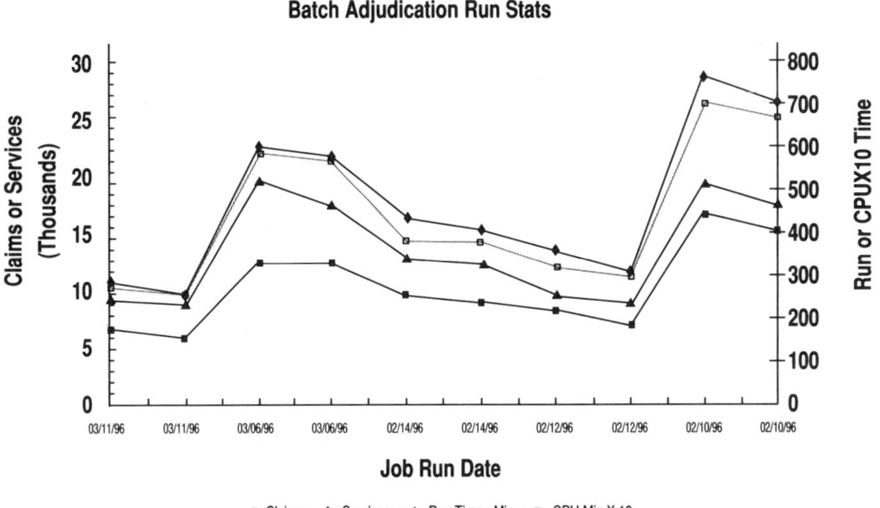

shows what current processing methods and system resources will be able to do in a given batch window. If the number of claims and services is projected to increase significantly — beyond the capabilities of this batch window — this analysis can be used to clearly communicate the need to increase resources or change processing methods to meet the new business objectives.

FIGURE 2.2
Relationship Between Claims and Services and Batch Runtime

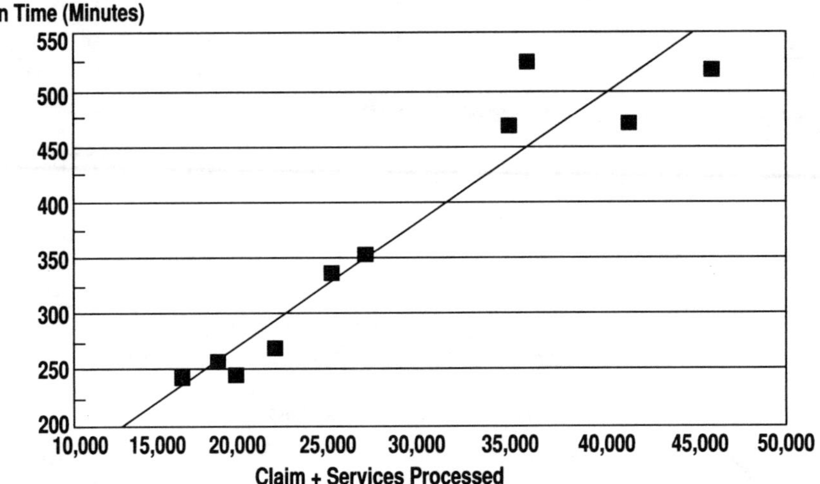

Interactive Objectives

Your business objectives might state that the system must handle 30 phone orders per hour or that a given set of batch jobs must run in one hour at the close of each business day. You need to translate these business objectives into system objectives that you can measure.

Some ways to specify interactive system objectives are to set a maximum response time for a percentage of all local transactions, to have different response-time criteria for different groups of users, and to determine how long or when an objective is valid. These objectives can also be used in combination with each other. We can examine each of these methods.

Specify that 90 Percent of All Local Transactions Have a Response Time of Less than 1.7 Seconds

Notice that this objective does not address remote response time. It also allows 10 percent of the transactions to exceed these guidelines. You may wonder why you would want to set up objectives this way. Well, this approach gives you an achievable objective without requiring excessive hardware expenditures. It also allows for extremely long transactions that you can't ever accommodate, no matter how much hardware you throw at them. Remember, you never want to set up unrealistic objectives.

Have Different Response-Time Criteria for Different Groups of Users

Although you may have an objective for total system average response time, you may want to set up a more restrictive response time objective for individual groups of users. For example, your order entry users may need 0.5-second response time, while your programmers can make do with 2-second response time.

Determine How Long or When the Objective Is Valid

Meeting certain performance objectives during certain hours of the day, week, month, or even year may be critical. An example of an appropriate time to set a yearly objective is a department store's inventory operations during the Christmas rush.

Batch Objectives

For batch jobs, tracking the number of logical records processed per unit of time defines a throughput objective that you can measure by collecting information such as the number of logical disk I/O operations per second. Stating a throughput rate lets you evaluate the job in the future to see what, if any, changes hardware or software alterations may have caused. (For more details, see the section on Physical and Logical Disk I/O in Chapter 5.)

Other batch objectives include how much time a specific job has to complete, the number of batch jobs completed per hour, the number of records transferred to another system in a certain time, how long all batch processing must have to complete, how much CPU capacity you need to reserve for unscheduled batch, and how much time is necessary for backup processing to complete. It's important to understand each of these objectives.

Time to Complete a Specific Job

If a specific batch job must finish before you allow your interactive users back onto the system, the amount of time it takes to complete your batch work may be a batch objective.

Batch Jobs Completed per Hour

Suppose your company is running a batch program that generates picking slips. If you are getting out only two picking slips per hour instead of the six you need, you have an objective to reach.

Records Transferred to Another System in a Specific Period

A company running dual systems may need to transfer records between the two systems. The record transfer between the systems must be fast enough to satisfy the users. Or, with Distributed Data Management (DDM) files, which allow you to access remote files as if they were on your local system, communications lines must be fast enough to keep up with a remote system's request for data. In both cases, you have an objective.

Period for Completing All Batch Processing

You must decide how much time your batch processing has for completion. If your shop has an eight-hour window for completing all batch work and your batch work takes nine hours, you have an objective to reach.

CPU Capacity Reserved to Handle Unscheduled Batch Jobs

Many companies have batch jobs that end users can submit any time. If these are critical reports and you don't have any CPU cycles available to get such unscheduled batch jobs through your system, you have an objective to reach.

Period for Completing Backup Processing

If your backup takes six hours every night, you have six hours of unavailable system time every night. If you have other work to do during this time, you have a batch performance objective to reach.

Cost Objectives

In addition to workload (throughput) objectives, you want to track system resources by establishing cost objectives for the resources that a given workload requires. In this context, "cost" refers to physical resources instead of money, although determining resource usage can help you determine whether you need to buy additional resources. The key hardware resources that you need to monitor are CPU, disk, memory, and communications usage, as you can see in Table 2.3.

Your performance management methodology should allow you to review the workload and cost objectives periodically in both normal and peak load situations.

As you will see when we consider the components of performance in the next section, you can measure other, more detailed resource items that are often candidates for other resource objectives. Though you normally don't report to your managers at this level of detail regularly, we suggest you have the data available that provides this level of detail if it's necessary. This information is especially useful as a basis for comparison in any future problem analysis you might need.

Your system performance objectives are critical to the success of your business. Experience shows that, generally, a system's workload grows over time. As business growth and new applications consume additional system resources, the system will no longer handle the workload with its original level of performance. In this growth process, most likely, the deviation from the system resource objectives will be your early warning that your business objectives may

TABLE 2.3
Hardware Resources

KEY HARDWARE RESOURCES TO MONITOR

CPU Use

Total CPU used

Average CPU used per interactive transaction

Average CPU used per batch logical disk I/O

Disk (Auxiliary Storage) Use

When total disk space use reaches 80 to 90 percent or higher, disk I/O performance can degrade. At high disk occupancy, the disk space allocated to objects can be fragmented, resulting in the need for increased physical disk I/O to access objects.

Total DASD arm use (expressed as a percentage of arm utilization)

Average number of database I/O per logical disk I/O

DASD space used

Memory Use

Database and nondatabase faulting rate in each storage pool

Effectiveness of the activity level setting assigned to each storage pool. (The activity level setting should result in an occasional wait-to-ineligible transition.)

Communications Use

Line utilization

IOP utilization

not be met. To know that your system objectives are sliding, you will need to have the appropriate data.

Determine the Measurements Needed to Track the Objectives

Regular performance measurements, combined with summary reports and archived performance data, will let you determine your current workload and its resource costs; variations in workload and resource costs over time; amount of resource capacity reserved for growth; effects of operational changes, tuning adjustments, and application design changes; effects of anticipated workload changes; and what upgrades you will need and when. Let's consider each of these issues.

Your Current Workload and Its Resource Costs

First, you need to understand your current workload and how much resource it is costing you. For example, you can determine that you are running 35,000 transactions per hour, your CPU utilization averages 92 percent, your disk IOP utilization averages 28 percent, and your disk-space capacity is at 82 percent.

The Variation in Your Workload and Resource Costs Over Time

It's important to measure how your workload and resource costs vary over time. If you were running 30,000 transactions per hour last month and you are at 35,000 transactions per hour this month, your CPU utilization, disk IOP, disk capacity, and other resources would also change by some percent. An explanation for this increase and the expectations for future workload increases are key issues related to your ability to meet future resource requirements.

How Much Resource Capacity Remains for Growth

Once you know these first two pieces of information, you can figure how much resource capacity you have left for growth. If any ad hoc work appears, is your system going to grind to a stop? Always try to have some excess capacity so that you can handle unexpected work. Knowing how much capacity you have can help you plan for these situations.

The Effect of Operational Changes, Tuning Adjustments, and Application Design Changes

We have been in many AS/400 sites where the staff make daily changes to programs without going through their development-support system. Of course, they have some data integrity problems, and their actions force their performance people to work with a changing base from one set of measurement data to the next. You need to be able to determine how alterations such as operational changes, tuning adjustments, and application design changes will affect your system before anyone makes such changes.

For example, if you release to production the new programs that your staff has been working on for the past six months, you need to know how this change will affect your overall system performance. Maybe your performance will improve because you are replacing some inefficient applications. Maybe it will degrade because you are adding a lot of new function. You can predict these changes if you have been collecting appropriate data, such as CPU records per transaction or database I/O associated with each transaction, and can compare the data after the changes with your records.

The Effect of Anticipated Workload Changes

Once you can predict workload changes based on business factors, you need to anticipate how such changes will affect your system. If you work for a store, do you know how your system will perform during the Christmas rush? You need to understand what resources are being pushed at your peak periods. When these peaks occur, you will need to know information such as the CPU utilization level for high-priority work on the system, the memory paging rates in key memory pools, and the disk arm utilization.

What Upgrades You Will Need and When

If you know your business is growing at 10 percent per quarter, you need to ensure that your system will keep up with the company's growth. Tracking system workload in relation to resource capacity and using that information to project hardware and software needs will allow you to recommend appropriate upgrades before performance suffers — and will give you the data you need to back up your request.

Periodically Measure the System

After determining what you need to measure and considering how often you need the data, you're ready to set up and follow a measurement schedule. As we mentioned in the section on batch and interactive objectives (page 16), performance information from both peak workload times and average workload times will be important for some of your objectives, so take both times into consideration when you're setting your performance measurement schedule.

Another important consideration in scheduling your performance measurements is the need to make valid comparisons between subsequent measurements. For a trend analysis to be accurate and valid, your measurements must allow for comparisons between like collection periods. For example, if you intend to project a valid trend, you don't compare data from a normal day's processing with that from an end-of-month processing day. Regularly scheduled data collection over the same periods (same workload) is necessary to generate valid trend analysis.

The data collection process, as well as many of the other steps, can be automated. The ADDPFRCOL (Add Performance Collection) command allows you to

Gathering Complete Data

The AS/400 Performance Tools were originally designed to focus on finding performance problems. These tools collect too much data for simple trend analysis. Now, IBM has introduced some summary functions for the Performance Tools, and another good option for trend analysis is IBM's PM/400 Service Offering. However, you really need to establish your own measurement plan.

As part of your measurement plan, periodically measure and keep a set of complete data (including trace data). This data can be especially helpful if you save it just before you make major changes in the system environment (new release, application change, added workload, etc.). If problems develop, this data is invaluable as a basis for comparison that can tell you what the change has affected. ■

Jim Stewart

Trend Analysis with PM/400

IBM's PM/400 is an excellent tool for doing trend analysis. The hardest part of trend analysis is the amount of data you must save and process to have a meaningful analysis. One nice feature of PM/400 is the ability to compress the history data and send it to IBM's machine in Rochester; IBM then stores the data for you and provides the trend analysis charts. IBM ships PM/400 with the operating system. You may choose which options to activate. The fee is small when you consider the analytical service that it provides. ■

Alan Arnold

set up a weekly schedule that specifies when the Performance Monitor will run. (For more information about using the Performance Monitor, see Chapters 10 and 12.) Basic job scheduling functions are also provided on the system — see the Schedule Entry Commands (GO CMBSCDE) menu for commands that allow you to create and work with schedule entries. And, of course, third-party job scheduling applications can automate the steps involved.

IBM also has a service offering, Performance Management/400 (PM/400) that provides automation software to collect, analyze, maintain, and archive performance data. The service also provides PM/400 reports and graphs that assist you in capacity planning for your AS/400.

Systematically collecting, analyzing, maintaining, and archiving performance data takes time and system resources. To properly manage this process, you need to allocate as much as one-third to one-half of a technical person's time to perform these functions. As a rough estimate, the performance data collected by the Performance Monitor uses approximately 10 MB to 25 MB per day, depending on the amount of activity on the system. If you keep five days of performance data online and archive it on the weekend, the amount of disk space used will range from 40 MB to 100 MB.

Because evaluating your measurements is closely related to deciding what to measure, we will consider other measurement issues as we look at the data evaluation process.

Evaluate the Measurements

Evaluating your performance data is a two-part process: trend analysis and problem analysis. Trend analysis is a continuing part of the performance management process that shows how your system and its performance change over time. You should always do trend analysis.

You may or may not need to do problem analysis. You can determine whether you need it either from trend analysis that reflects future resource constraints or from current measurements (or user complaints) showing that today's objectives were not met.

Trend Analysis

Trend analysis is at the heart of performance management. The value of trend analysis is that it lets you understand the current performance characteristics of your system's application environment, realize the impact of workload growth on system resources (allowing you to respond before future resource requirements and possible conflicts or constraints become problems), and understand and plan for workload growth on the system.

You need to do trend analysis regularly — typically, monthly is adequate. More frequent analysis might be necessary if growth is causing your system to approach specific resource capacity guidelines.

Decide what parts of your system to include in the trend analysis. All systems have multiple environments — interactive, batch, groups of users, and programs — that require you to analyze multiple trends. Be sure you separate trend analysis of interactive and batch jobs. Trend analysis for a specific application may also be useful. Many companies track key applications because such applications and their associated files may be used by 80 percent of the users (or

Comparing Apples to Apples

Trend analysis is very important, but I can't overemphasize that it will work only if you're doing an apples-to-apples comparison. Be careful to verify your results. The easiest trend analysis approach I've found is measuring over consistent intervals. Collecting three samples a day is my personal style. I collect a morning sample (e.g., 7:00 A.M. to 12:00 noon), an afternoon sample (e.g., 12:00 noon to 6:00 P.M.), and a night sample (e.g., 6:00 P.M. to 7:00 A.M.).

Also, be aware that sometimes, even when you think you're using consistent measurements, you aren't. Let me give you an example. I work with a very large store. This store's MIS staff has been on a performance methodology plan since I met them four years ago. Every couple of months, I review their trend analysis with them.

An interesting thing happened: They added two stores to the system. I expected the increase in transactions per hour to be at least twofold. When we reviewed the performance reports for the first month of business with the increased activity level, we noticed that the transactions per hour had increased only by a couple of thousand. "How can this be?" my customer asked. "We have been swamped." On closer investigation of the performance tools reports, I noticed that several TPH (Transactions Per Hour) fields on the reports maxed at 99,999 transactions, so the true number of transactions per hour was not being reported.

The point I'm trying to make is that whenever you do trend analysis, be alert to how reasonable your data is. ■

Alan Arnold

account for 80 percent of the transactions, or account for 80 percent of the resources used, or all of the above). The end-of-month processing is often another special environment that may be important to track.

Your plans for trend analysis will influence the type of data you collect, when you need to make measurements, and how to retain the data (how much data and for how long). As you begin practicing the performance methodology we're prescribing, try to keep your measurement and analysis as simple as possible. Getting too detailed in your trend analysis can quickly become complicated. As you gain experience, your ability to recognize the key environments and resources that you want to track will improve. As a starting point, we suggest measuring data related to your interactive and batch objectives plus the key hardware resources we listed under "Cost Objectives" (page 20). This information represents a good basic set for your trend analysis.

Problem Analysis

One of three factors usually triggers problem analysis. These factors are

- trend analysis that shows significant or unexpected changes (for example, your transactions per hour changed drastically)
- observation of excessive resource utilization (for example, disk arm utilization is 45 percent, or disk IOP utilization is 65 percent)
- an end user complaint (for example, a number of users call and say response time is bad)

The problem analysis process involves understanding the symptoms, collecting data, forming a hypothesis, testing the hypothesis (by changing one thing at a time and determining the effect), and repeating the cycle until you see improvement. As you will see in the next section, the goal is to apply this process to find the contribution of each performance component, identify which components are causing a problem, and try to reduce their effect.

Following this performance management methodology and retaining your regular performance measurements greatly enhances the problem analysis process because it gives you comparison data. You can base your hypothesis on data collected before the problem existed. This method doesn't promise to cover 100 percent of the problems, but it does cover most situations and gives some insight into the remainder.

To solve a performance problem, you may consider system tuning changes, workload scheduling, application changes, or hardware additions. Though the scope of this book will not allow an exhaustive treatment of application changes for performance, the sections on the components of performance will deal with those changes to applications that are usually necessary and that can significantly influence performance.

Keep Data for Comparison

You often need comparative measurement data to find the reason for acceptable and unacceptable performance for a system.

Rick Turner

I can corroborate Rick's comment with an experience I had in performance problem analysis. The customer had gone to a new release of the operating system and was experiencing reduced performance. The customer viewed the new release as a potential cause, and we were very interested in researching the problem.

I struggled to find some measurement data from the customer's system from the old release. This shop was not following a performance methodology, which would have provided me with the data I needed. However, I was able to find some old history files. Comparison of the data showed a tremendous increase in signon/signoff of their terminals. Further analysis also showed that users were powering the terminals on and off.

The increase in the number of these signon/off and power on/off transactions was significant enough to explain the reduced performance. When I asked why this increase had occurred, I learned that the company had experienced a fire at one of their locations. A problem with an electrical appliance was suspected as the cause of the fire. This resulted in a company policy that required any employees leaving their office for more than 10 minutes to power down all electrical appliances in their office.

I was lucky to find the comparative data in this case. It pointed to the change that had caused the performance problem. ■

Jim Stewart

Provide Feedback to Operations, Development, Management, and Users

Once you have successfully solved a performance problem or designed a solution to a performance objective, you should present your findings or recommendations to the people who will be affected. Your presentation should provide the appropriate level of technical data in a clear and concise form. Using PC tools, such as Harvard Graphics, PowerPoint, Persuasion, or any graphics package, can help you organize and present your feedback to management.

The appropriate level of technical data will vary for every shop. We all work with different people who understand technical data in different ways. For example, your manager may not have the same level of technical expertise you have about performance (especially after you have finished this book). If you walk into your manager's office with a stack of Performance Tools reports and try to justify a CPU upgrade, he or she will probably look at you as if you're crazy. You need to translate the numbers to the level of expertise of your audience.

A pie chart, like the one in Figure 2.3, that pictures the percentage of interactive users getting subsecond response time is much more readable than a column of numbers. Everyone understands it. Of course, you may also have to define "response time" if that level of information is needed.

Figure 2.3
Sample Pie Chart

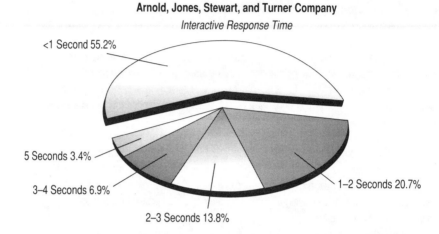

Arnold, Jones, Stewart, and Turner Company

Interactive Response Time

<1 Second 55.2%
5 Seconds 3.4%
3–4 Seconds 6.9%
2–3 Seconds 13.8%
1–2 Seconds 20.7%

The Components of Performance

Now that you have a systematic method for improving performance, we can consider the components of your AS/400 to which you can apply your methodology. Business and system transactions, important aspects of the performance methodology, are also critical to an understanding of the components of performance.

You can think of all work on the system as being made up of multiple transactions. All user requests, both interactive and batch, make demands on your system's resources. Many of the resources required by an interactive request are also required by batch jobs, and the two can conflict with each other. Interactive requests (or transactions) require CPU time, main storage space, and disk I/O resources in addition to the communications line time and I/O processor resources necessary to enter the request and communicate the results to the user. In batch processing, a request (or transaction) is the time between successive reads of a primary input file. These transactions also require CPU time, main storage space, and disk I/O resources.

Because the system generally services multiple transactions concurrently, a transaction often spends time waiting for system resources, such as

Performance Components

When system performance is less than it should be, one or more components of performance are involved. The challenges are to find out which component is having the most severe impact on performance, determine how to make changes that improve it, and then learn the cost of these changes.

The solution to a problem may not be just adding hardware. Often, a change to an application or the system setup can significantly improve performance. After making those kinds of changes, adding hardware can improve performance that much more. ■

Rick Turner

communications line resources, activity level, processor (CPU) resources, disk access, memory, and data or other objects. The chapters in the next section will discuss these resources, but they are not the only components of performance. Error handling, although not a physical resource, is another component that we'll consider because it can consume a significant amount of system time and impact performance.

You can appreciate the many factors that influence transaction response time if you consider the components as servers. Transaction response time depends on how long it takes to acquire and use each server. This amount of time, in turn, depends on how many servers there are, how fast each server is, the arrival rate for the server, and how the requests are selected for service. Each performance component has its own characteristics in connection with these factors.

The chapters in the next section cover the performance implications of the line, activity-level, processor (CPU), disk, memory, object-contention, and error-handling components. Before we get into the details, here's a brief overview of each component.

Line Component

Communications requires special performance considerations. Line speed, communications I/O processor utilization, device-controller and line utilization, and line errors all affect how much time a transaction takes to get through the line component.

Activity-Level Component

When a transaction needs access to the CPU, it must first wait for an activity level. The activity level determines how many jobs in a particular storage pool are eligible to access the CPU. How long a transaction waits for the CPU depends on the activity level, the number of other requests already waiting, and the amount of higher-priority work that goes ahead of the transaction.

Lowering the activity level keeps the system from overloading, because it limits the number of jobs that can access the CPU. However, an activity level that is too low will cause more jobs to wait for the CPU. If the activity level is too high, the utilization of the CPU and other servers can increase to levels that cause higher memory demand, resulting in high paging and disk utilization.

Processor (CPU) Component

Again, all jobs compete for CPU time. The system grants CPU resource in a priority sequence. Once the system gives CPU resource to a transaction, no other transaction may share that CPU resource until the transaction waits on another resource or the transaction times out (a time-slice end occurs).

Although some AS/400 models have multiple CPUs, a transaction cannot request the service of a specific processor. The system allocates the CPU based on internal algorithms that you cannot control.

Disk Component

When a transaction needs access to disk, several considerations come into play. The time to process a disk request depends on disk I/O processor use, drive use, record blocking, the type of operation, arm contention, errors, file placement, cache hit ratios, and any protection schemes (mirroring, RAID 5, checksum) you may use.

Memory Component

A transaction requires memory to contain the necessary programs and data for the CPU to work with. If the programs and data are in main memory, the memory server doesn't delay the transaction. However, if the programs and data are not in main memory, the transaction waits while the system allocates memory and brings the objects into memory from disk. The paging rates for the various main storage pools indicate demand for memory. By separating work into different main storage pools, you can help keep different types of work from competing for the same main storage.

Object-Contention Component

Examples of AS/400 objects include files, records, and message queues. Object contention occurs when, to proceed with processing, a transaction requires control of an object that is already in use. You can measure and report the wait time for gaining object control. The busier the system gets, the more contention occurs and the longer each incident lasts. You can sometimes reduce the effects of contention by changing the design of an application or by rescheduling selected workloads.

Error-Handling Component

Error handling is different from the other components we're discussing in that it is not a server. However, the way your system handles errors can consume significant resources and have a large negative effect on system performance.

Error handling is often related to the other components. Line errors can have a significant negative effect on the performance of the line component as the system attempts recovery. Timeouts produced by object contention may increase the errors that applications report and process, thereby tying up resources and affecting performance. For this reason, we treat error handling as a component that needs close attention. You need to measure and report on the various types of errors.

Now that we've outlined the components of performance, we can get down to specifics. The following chapters will look at each component in detail.

CHAPTER 3

The Line and Activity-Level Components

THE LINE COMPONENT

Any data sent between the system and a device (such as 5250 workstations, PS/2s, and printers) must pass through the I/O processor (IOP), the line, the appropriate device control unit, and the attached devices. Points at which to evaluate performance are listed below.

- Line I/O Processor
  - I/O processor utilization
  - The number of active devices (affects available memory in the IOP)
  - Interference from other systems (e.g., on a networked system)
- Line
  - Line utilization, line speed, amount of traffic
  - Number and type of errors
  - Interference from other systems (network)
- Control Unit
  - Number of attached devices
  - Workload distribution
- Devices
  - Amount of data sent per transaction
  - Frequency of line turnarounds with each device
  - Printer data or other batch-type data flow concurrent with interactive work

As you can see, focusing on the line component gives you many opportunities to improve your system's performance. However, most performance problems caused by communications lines are usually the result of either a work overload or the number of communications errors on the line.

Identifying Causes of Line-Component Problems

If your communications lines are overloaded, either more devices are using the line than the system can properly handle, or line use has increased and you are experiencing peak loads more often than you originally anticipated. If your system is experiencing a large number of line errors, the system may be trying to recover by retransmitting data; timeouts may be prohibiting the system from transmitting any data at all.

The AS/400 Performance Monitor can give you a variety of communications performance data. To gather this data, use a special option, the default DATA(*ALL) option on the STRPFRMON (Start Performance Monitor) command, and set the sampling interval on STRPFRMON to five minutes (the smallest value possible). Although you do not need the Performance Tools (which must be purchased separately) to use the Performance Monitor, the Performance Tools reports can be helpful in analyzing your data. (For detailed information about using the Performance Monitor and its options, see Chapter 10. For more information about Performance Tools Reports, see Chapter 13.)

The Performance Tools Advisor Report and the Resource Interval Report show line utilization and error information. The Advisor records instances when online utilization is greater than 40 percent and instances when error percentages are more than 5 percent. A good approach is to use the Advisor to signal possible line error and utilization concerns and then use other Performance Tools reports for a broader view of what's happening during the intervals the Advisor finds.

For example, the Performance Tools System Report provides a Communications Summary that shows average and peak line utilization over the report period. Also, the Performance Tools Resource Interval Report provides, for each time interval you select, information about line utilization, error percentages, and the percent of time spent waiting for a poll response. This information lets you evaluate parameter changes that affect communications and determine whether error recovery is involved in line performance problems.

Although the Performance Tools reports can be helpful, they are not comprehensive. You can gain even further insight into communications performance problems by querying the data. Examples of helpful data queries are in the IBM Redbook *AS/400 Performance Management* (GG24-3723). Appendix H in this Redbook has sample X.25 queries that can be used to determine if either the AS/400 or the X.25 network itself is congested, thus helping diagnose poor X.25 performance.

Creating your own queries of the data for the specific protocols you use in your environment is a good approach. For a comprehensive list of the Performance Monitor files and the data they contain, see Chapter 10. IBM's *AS/400 Communications Performance Redbook* (SG24-4669) contains many sample queries and helps identify the important fields in these files.

The STRSST (Start System Service Tools) command can also be used to your advantage when analyzing your system's communications performance. It provides a line protocol trace that can show formatted SNA-level data. With this trace and a knowledge of the protocols involved, you can verify what is actually happening on the line as well as determining the actual frame sizes used and line turnaround frequency.

A protocol-level line trace can provide output with time stamps for Send and Receive frames. The time stamps are in 100-millisecond increments and can be used to tell how long it takes for application and system processing to respond to incoming data. The time stamps are not correlated with the system's time-of-day clock, but they can be used to determine the time differences between various data transmissions and receptions.

The *AS/400 Data Collection Guide* (SC21-8253) contains information about using STRSST to collect communications trace data.

Special Error Considerations

When temporary communications line errors occur in the IOP, the system usually takes care of error recovery, thus reducing the impact on response time. The system must retry these temporary errors, however, and that increases the line time — sometimes by a lot! If you are experiencing many temporary errors, contact your line provider to get the problem fixed.

Although temporary errors are not logged, permanent errors are. When the system considers an error serious enough to log, OS/400 invokes the ERRLOG task. ERRLOG is an LIC (Licensed Internal Code) process that can use significant CPU resources when many errors occur and must be logged in a short period. Using the Performance Tools' WRKSYSACT (Work with System Activity) command, which shows LIC tasks in addition to OS/400 jobs, you can tell whether this ERRLOG task is active when you are experiencing communications line performance problems. If the ERRLOG task is active, you need to find out what work is causing the errors. For more information about the WRKSYSACT command, see Chapter 11.

Another indicator of a serious error rate is the number of communications errors and threshold messages coming to the QSYSOPR message queue. When the number of retries exceeds the number you specified on the line description, the system sends messages to QSYSOPR. Threshold messages to QSYSOPR indicate that errors are occurring and that retries are successful, but the error rate may be serious enough to degrade performance.

If the number of errors in your system is affecting performance, use the STRSST command to get the error log entries and review the error log information with your IBM service contact.

Influencing Line-Component Performance

The four basic ways to improve communications performance are to maximize line speed, minimize the amount of data sent and received, minimize the number of turnarounds per unit of work, and minimize unproductive line time (error recovery). To make these improvements, you can change parameters for timeout/retry values, frame sizes, and the frequency of frame acknowledgments for your communications lines. Generally, the more data you can send without turning the line around, the faster communications performance will be. After considering issues in line utilization, we will examine ways to improve line-component performance in LAN communications and in the applications environment.

Line Utilization

Line utilization rates can make the speed capability of any communications line especially important. In batch environments, line utilization should be as close to 100 percent as possible. In interactive environments, line utilization of up to 50 percent can deliver acceptable response times; however, sometimes performance will begin degrading at around 40 percent utilization. Because these two values are so far apart, it is difficult to set up parameters that work well for both batch and interactive environments. The easiest way to handle lines is to use separate lines or schedule separate times on the same line for batch and interactive applications.

When batch and interactive applications must run concurrently over the same line, line parameter values that are best for batch can degrade the performance of the interactive applications. Low-speed lines (and half-duplex support) aggravate this negative impact; however, as line speed increases, the negative impact decreases. Token-Ring speeds and lines with full-duplex support can also reduce this interactive degradation while maintaining good batch throughput.

In concurrent batch and interactive environments on an SDLC line, choose a pacing value of 1 and a MAXLENRU of 256 for the batch session. These values will give the best concurrent interactive performance.

For APPN connections, the general recommendation is to assign a low-priority Class of Service to batch applications and a high-priority Class of Service to interactive applications. Use *CALC RU length and 7 for pacing values on modes for each application. These values both provide reasonable prioritization of interactive applications over concurrent batch applications and retain good batch performance when batch applications run alone.

LAN Communications

For most LAN communications protocols, the rate of data transmission increases significantly as the frame size increases. Reducing the total number of frames by using larger frames also saves CPU and IOP resources. This approach improves the efficiency of the communications line by reducing line turnarounds and the amount of data contained in frame-overhead bytes; it works particularly well in batch communications, where the goal is to maximize the data rate for large file transmissions.

To configure large frame sizes for TRLAN, ELAN, SDLC, and ISDN, change the MAXFRAME parameter on both the line description and controller description to reflect the maximum value. For X.25, you must increase the DFTPKTSIZE on the line description to its maximum value. Also, make sure that the MAXLENRU parameter in the mode description (MODD) is *CALC.

One situation that requires qualification is a communications environment where errors are common: You may get better performance if you use smaller frame sizes, which limit the size of the retransmissions.

In a multiuser, interactive LAN environment, do not let line use exceed 50 percent, and maintain even lower percentages in Ethernet environments. However, in a large data transfer (batch) environment with few users contending for the line, higher line use may still offer acceptable performance.

Maximizing the frame size (MAXFRAME) achieves the best performance. You must configure both the AS/400 and the other link station for large frames; otherwise, the system uses the smallest value specified for either system in transferring the data. Note that the maximum frame size for TRLAN is 16,393; this is not the default for creating the line and controller descriptions. To change these values, use the WRKCFGSTS (Work with Configuration Status) command.

In APPC environments, the LANACKFRQ and LANMAXOUT parameters on the controller description govern how often the receiving system sends an acknowledgment and how often the sending system waits for an acknowledgment. Generally, LANACKFRQ should be about half the value of LANMAXOUT. Never allow LANACKFRQ on one system to have a greater value than LANMAXOUT on the other system. The parameter values on the sending system should match the corresponding values on the receiving system. To change these values, you can use the WRKCFGSTS command on the given controller description.

Usually, the value of *CALC for parameters LANACKFRQ and LANMAXOUT offers the best performance. However, for large file transfer environments, changing the value of these parameters may significantly increase performance. The following guidelines are in the *AS/400 Performance Capabilities Reference* document (ZC41-8166):

- With the newer LAN IOPs (2619, 2617, 2618, etc.), test the performance of a large file transfer with a LANMAXOUT value of 6. If the performance is better, leave the LANMAXOUT value there; if not, try the test again with a LANMAXOUT of 4. If the performance is still not improved, change LANMAXOUT back to *CALC.
- In using the older LAN IOPs, it is less likely that increasing the value of LANMAXOUT will improve performance. However, there are exceptions, so try it.

- When communicating with a PS/2 Model 50 or above, LANMAXOUT may be increased, but keep LANACKFRQ at *CALC. For smaller models of PS/2s or PCs, use *CALC for both values to limit buffer overruns.
- If you change the LANACKFRQ and LANMAXOUT values and do not notice a performance improvement, change the values back to *CALC.

If you specify a value of *CALC for the maximum SNA request/response unit (MAXLENRU parameter), the system will select an efficient size that is compatible with the frame size on the line description. If you make the MAXLENRU size larger than the frame size, use the CHGMODD (Change Mode Description) command to change the MAXLENRU value to a size slightly smaller than a multiple of the frame size. The newer LAN IOPs support IOP assist. Changing the RU size to a value other than *CALC may negate this performance feature.

Application Considerations

Application design and coding techniques play a major role in three of the factors that influence communications performance — minimizing the amount of data sent and received, thereby minimizing the number of turnarounds per unit of work, and minimizing unproductive line time (including recovery from error conditions).

Avoiding, or at least reducing, line turnarounds improves an application's response time; however, the workstation programmer does not always have explicit control over line turnarounds and may be using certain functions that affect line turnarounds without realizing it. So, keep in mind these programming considerations.

- Using the display file keyword RSTDSP(*YES) and full display file opens increases the number of line turnarounds — and the amount of data sent and received — sometimes dramatically! Avoid using these techniques whenever possible.
- Using CL's SNDRCVF (Send/Receive File) command and the RPG EXFMT (Execute Format) operation to write and read to a display file can eliminate a line turnaround until data is received or an error occurs. Equivalent Cobol support, using WRITE and READ statements, requires you to specify DFRWRT(*YES) on the display file.
- Specifying DFRWRT(*YES) on the display file typically can resolve the occurrence of a line turnaround by holding the output until the program issues an input operation. However, realize that with DFRWRT(*YES), the system will not display output data from a sequence of write operations until the program issues a read, write and read, or write format with the DDS INVITE operation. Whenever possible, use DFRWRT(*YES) for

the file and the FRCDTA (Force Data) DDS keyword for the write-only operations.

- A WRITE with INVITE, followed by READ, consumes more CPU than the typical use of WRITE and READ, so use it only if you need the functions it provides: additional processing before issuing the read operation, timing out on the read operation, and processing input data from multiple sources (consisting of display files, ICF files, and data queues). Some applications need to update a screen without user input; these applications perform best when no input operation, including DDS INVITE, is outstanding to the device. You should take this into consideration with applications that show frequent status changes, where operator input is optional.
- You can use the DDS record-level KEEP keyword to keep the system from clearing the display when the display file is closed. This keyword lets the application leave data on the display for use as input for subsequent programs; for example, a program that does not specify a record name on its first input operation can use the record you're keeping. This approach can reduce the terminal I/O during the transition from one program to another.

Overall performance, usability, and customer satisfaction will increase when applications include error recovery routines that react to communications error conditions. If your applications recognize an error and perform a simple recovery action, you can save significant resources. Otherwise, the subsystem monitor will terminate the job, put up a sign-on screen, and then create another job when the user enters the sign-on data. In fact, this factor is so important that you need to question and test the application's recovery techniques when you are evaluating a new application from an outside source.

The IBM Redbook *AS/400 Performance Management* (GG24-3723) is a good source for additional display workstation programming tips. Its section on choosing batch file transmission techniques deals with performance considerations for the many different AS/400 file transfer facilities.

The Activity-Level Component

Before a job can use the CPU, the system must first grant the job an activity level. The activity level manages eligibility for the CPU. You set the activity level for a particular storage pool by specifying a value that represents the number of jobs in the pool that can be active, or eligible for the CPU, simultaneously. A proper activity-level setting is a key AS/400 tuning adjustment that can help keep your workload within guidelines for other system resources, especially disk I/O and main storage.

Job States and Transitions

Job states define what a job is doing; that is, whether it's running or waiting. These states relate to many topics this book discusses and appear on many displays and reports related to performance. The three possible states are **active**, **wait**, and **ineligible**.

- **The Active Job State:** An active job is one that has an assigned activity level, which makes the job eligible to use the CPU. A job in the active state can use the CPU, or, if it needs another resource or more information, it can go into a short wait state for up to two seconds without losing its activity level.
- **The Wait State:** A job is in the wait state if it has completed its work request, or if it needs a resource that is not available to continue its work. The job does not hold an activity level in this state.
- **The Ineligible State:** A job will go into the ineligible state if that job is ready to continue its work but finds that no activity level is available. Of course, the job does not hold an activity level in this state.

A job can leave the active state in one of the following four ways.

1. The job reaches the end of the transaction and waits for more input from the user.
2. The job must wait a long time for some resource that is not available.
3. The job exceeds the two-second time limit for a short wait.
4. The job's CPU use exceeds the job's time-slice value.

When a job leaves the active state in one of the first three ways, the transition is from the active state to the wait state. In the first case, the transaction is complete, and the job waits for the operator to press Enter for the next transaction. In the second case, the job is waiting for some resource — for example, a database record another job has locked.

The short wait exceeded (case number 3) takes a little more explanation. Short waits occur on operations that ordinarily take very little time — typically, OS/400 operations that need a particular resource. The operating system calculates that the wait will be satisfied so quickly that it is not worth moving the job out of the active state. Some examples of short waits are low-level screen saves for RSTDSP(*YES), hardware responses on a write to a display with DFRWRT(*NO), and data returned from a receive-data-queue operation. If a job exceeds the two-second limit on a short wait, the system moves the job to the wait state. This movement from the short wait state to the ineligible state is called a **short wait extended**.

From the wait state, the job can move either to the active state or to the ineligible state. If no activity level is available as the job tries to become active, the job will move to the ineligible state.

In the fourth case, a time-slice end, the transition is from the active state to the ineligible state. When a job exceeds its CPU time limit, any job of equal or higher priority that is waiting for an activity level will become active. The job that exceeded the time limit will become ineligible and wait for a new activity level. However, if no jobs of equal or higher priority are waiting, the job will remain active. We will discuss changing time slice values in detail in Chapter 4, where we consider the CPU Component.

Influencing Activity-Level Component Performance

You can influence your system's performance by changing your activity-level settings, because they help control pool memory demand and paging. Constraining the activity level lets the old work in a pool finish before new work starts. When too many jobs in a pool are active, a job can spend much of its CPU time bringing data into memory. Before the job can use the data for productive work, the system gives the CPU to another job, which must then swap out the first job's data for its own. This unproductive use of CPU cycles is called thrashing. Limiting the number of jobs in the pool can avoid this overcrowding.

A good way to monitor your settings is to watch the number of wait-to-ineligible (W-I) transitions. The WRKSYSSTS (Work with System Status) command shows a W-I transition value (for more detailed information about using the WRKSYSSTS command, see Chapter 8). The Component Report in the Performance Tools also has a pool report section that provides a good way to monitor the effect of adjustments to the activity level. (For more information about using the Performance Tools, see Chapter 12.) The goal is to see occasional W-I transitions during peak periods in an interactive environment, because they demonstrate that control is being applied. However, when you change an activity-level setting, remember that the change may not produce an immediate change in system performance. To tune your system's performance, make minor changes and then observe their effect on wait-to-ineligible transitions over a given period.

In general, you should base your activity level value on workload requirements — subsystem throughput and response time — rather than on the memory size of the pool. Dividing the pool size by the estimated job size can result in an activity level set far too high, particularly for a large storage pool. However, setting the activity level so that you see an occasional W-I transition at peak periods will help you avoid overcommitting the pool and prevent the resulting excessive demands on memory, disk, and CPU.

One approach to adjusting the activity level is to start with it purposely high and gradually decrease it, monitoring each decrease with the Component Report for two to three busy days. If there are still no W-I transitions, decrease the activity level by another 10 percent and monitor again. Once you observe some W-I transitions in the Component Report, you can increase the activity level by 1 or 2 and then leave it at this value.

We do not recommend changing a pool's activity level to adapt to minor changes in workload. If you constantly need to adjust the activity level, something else is causing a problem; for example, *ad hoc* work, high-priority batch jobs, or resource-intensive transactions are running in the pool with the other work. Once you find the proper activity level value, set it and forget it.

Chapter 4

The Processor (CPU) Component

Waiting in line for a processor is an unproductive way for your AS/400 jobs to spend their time. However, all jobs compete for CPU time. Once the system gives CPU resource to a transaction, no other transaction can share that resource until the first transaction waits on some other resource or times out.

Although a certain amount of waiting for CPU time is inevitable, you can improve the performance of the CPU component by examining scheduling and priority issues, considering processor and system solutions, and checking your applications. In this chapter, we will consider each of these factors, as well as some tools you can use to analyze the performance of your CPU.

In addition to these issues, however, you should also consider how memory, disk, and error handling affect your CPU utilization. Your CPU utilization difficulties could be a symptom of other problems, such as excessive paging, a high number of disk I/O operations, or ineffective handling of errors.

Setting Priorities and Schedules

The most basic steps in controlling how long your jobs wait for the CPU are to assign the correct priorities to your jobs and to schedule your work effectively. The system grants CPU in a priority sequence, which you specify on the RUNPTY (run priority) parameter — the lower the number, the higher the priority — of each job's class description. This priority value determines which job gains access to the CPU first. It's often important, for instance, that interactive jobs run at a priority level that gives them access to the CPU before batch jobs.

Priority and scheduling issues revolve around two concerns: the number and complexity of your high-priority jobs and your workload. Two other related issues, the job's time slice and internal priority adjustments, can also affect your efforts.

First, you should examine your high-priority jobs; that is, jobs with a priority value of less than or equal to 20. How many transactions with high CPU per transaction are running at priority higher than 20? Are these transactions truly high priority? Are the programming algorithms (and structure of the data) causing problems?

Your CPU trend analysis should focus on total CPU utilization for high-priority work — including both the system jobs and user jobs. You can expect stable CPU service time for interactive work if the CPU utilization for all high-priority work is 70 percent for systems with a single processor, 76 percent for a two-way processor, 79 percent for a three-way processor, and 81 percent for a four-way processor. Running batch work concurrently with interactive jobs usually results in total system CPU utilization much higher than these values. This increase is not a problem as long as the high-priority work stays within these guidelines and the batch work is completing in the time required.

The system jobs mentioned above are OS/400 subsystem monitor jobs and LIC (Licensed Internal Code) tasks, including storage management, asynchronous disk I/O, and communications tasks. (Note that jobs that run below the machine interface are called tasks.) This work will generally run at between 10 and 15 percent of the total CPU time used.

After considering your high-priority jobs, look at your workload. Has the workload increased, or do you expect it to increase? Are jobs waiting too long for the CPU? Is the work scheduled to even out the CPU demand? The CPU usually becomes a major component of performance simply because of increasing workload demands. If you set priorities and schedule the work, you can even out the demand for CPU and extend the time between processor upgrades.

For example, extending the processing day can significantly benefit performance. Even if your installation does not have off-shift coverage, some system features can help extend your processing day. These features include unattended system shutdown/startup, auto-start jobs, unattended file save/restore, and job scheduling. Support is even available that allows the system to call your pager when the system sends specific messages. This support makes it possible for the system to run with minimal attention.

Job Time Slice

A job's time slice specifies how much processor time that job has before other jobs get a chance to use the CPU. The purpose of both the internal time slice and the external time slice is to prevent a job from monopolizing the CPU resource. As we discussed in Chapter 3, exceeding a time slice value is one way jobs can lose their activity level.

Depending on the model, an internal time slice interrupts a job after 0.2 to 0.5 seconds of CPU access. At this interruption, a job with equal priority on the queue is granted control of the CPU. The job giving up control goes to the end of the jobs of equal priority waiting on the queue but does not lose its activity level. This approach, which is called a round-robin allocation of the CPU, allows each job with an activity level a chance to use the CPU.

The external time slice differs from the internal time slice in that when a job's external time slice expires, the system considers all the jobs waiting for an activity level as candidates for the CPU. Thus, when the external time slice expires, the active job could lose its activity level if a job of equal or higher priority is waiting for an activity level. You specify the job's external time slice in the job's class description. The default class description for interactive jobs is QINTER, and its default time-slice value is 2,000 milliseconds (two seconds).

Interactive jobs that use enough CPU to exceed the external time slice are very complex. They are often like batch jobs in that they usually have fairly high I/O and high CPU utilization characteristics. In some cases, you may want to change the system value for QTSEPOOL to move these jobs out of the interactive storage pool.

If you set the system value QTSEPOOL to *BASE, the system transfers the job from the pool in which it is running to the *BASE pool at the end of the external time slice. The job returns to its original pool at the next long wait, such as a workstation input request. If complex interactive jobs that exceed the external time-slice are common, specifying *BASE for QTSEPOOL can improve performance by reducing the effect of those jobs on other interactive jobs. When you use this approach, you'll need to allocate additional memory and adjust the activity level in *BASE to handle the added work that will result there.

Job-Priority Adjustment

Although you have control over many aspects of your jobs' priority value, your system also adjusts job priorities. Although no OS/400 displays or Performance Tools reports show the effect of these adjustments, they can cause certain jobs to run at slightly higher priority than you have assigned to them.

Every time a job issues a disk I/O operation, the system inspects the job to see how much CPU time it has used over the previous eight disk I/O operations. If the job has used 5 to 10 percent of the CPU over that period, the system will raise the job's run priority (i.e., decrease its numeric priority value) to move it ahead of jobs with equal priority. If the job has used 0 to 5 percent of the CPU during the previous eight disk operations, the system adjusts its priority even higher. When the job has used more than 5 to 10 percent of the CPU during the previous eight disk operations, the system lowers the job's priority.

Time-Slice Values

The default AS/400 time-slice value of two seconds is usually too large for interactive jobs. It is also unrealistic to expect the same value to serve all system models. You want a smaller time-slice value as you move up to faster CPU models.

I recommend a setting of three times the average CPU seconds/transaction for the interactive work you are running. You can find the average CPU seconds/transaction for the interactive work on your system in the Performance Tools System Report.

My goal is to have 90 to 95 percent of all transactions complete within one time slice. Assuming a normal distribution for CPU time per transaction, this value should achieve this goal. ■

Rick Turner

Adjusting the job priority keeps a job from waiting too long for the CPU when that job uses more I/O than CPU resource and maximizes the amount of data flowing to and from the disk.

MULTIPLE PROCESSORS

If your jobs are still waiting for the CPU after you adjust their priorities and your schedules, you should consider upgrading to a faster processor or to multiple processors. Users often see improvements in their system's performance when they upgrade either to a faster processor or to multiple processors with the same speed as the original system — at least until the workload grows beyond a certain point.

In a system with multiple processors, the system allocates the CPU resource based on internal algorithms that the user cannot control; a transaction cannot request the service of a specific processor. Increasing the number of CPU servers reduces the average length of the queue of jobs waiting for the CPU, and reducing the time spent waiting for the CPU resource improves performance.

Although the processor to which a job is assigned is essentially random, the system does assign **cache affinity** to the processor that the job last used. OS/400 assigns a job to the processor for which it has cache affinity unless that assignment would cause another processor to remain idle. Cache affinity can accelerate overall processing because information that the job needs may still be available in that particular processor's high-speed memory (cache).

Doubling the number of processors on your system won't halve processing time; relating processor speed to performance is more complex. IBM uses relative performance ratings (RPRs) to represent the number of instructions one processor model can execute in a given period of time compared to another. RPR values are normalized to the AS/400 model B10, which has an RPR of 1. In comparison, the model F02 has an RPR of 1.9, which means it can run 1.9 times more instructions per second than a B10. That seems pretty straightforward, so far.

But what about AS/400 model 320-2052, which has an RPR of 71.5? The 2052's RPR means it can execute 71.5 times more instructions per second than a B10 — making it 71.5 times *faster*, right? You would think so if you didn't also know 2052 has four processors and the B10 has only one. While the B10's one processor does all the work the system is capable of, the 2052's work is spread out among four processors, each executing only one-fourth of the instructions the system is capable of (or 71.5/4 relative number of instructions per second). So while the 2052's relative system performance — its throughput — is 71.5 times that of a B10, each processor in the 2052 is only 17.88 (71.5/4) times as fast as the processor in the B10. Accordingly, an RPR 2 machine with two

CISC vs. RISC

Central Processing Units (CPUs) come in many sizes and flavors, such as Intel's Pentium and IBM's PowerPC. One CPU that hasn't had as much popular press is IBM AS/400's Internal Microprogramming Interface (IMPI) processor. The IMPI processor has a Complex Instruction Set Computer (CISC) architecture, as opposed to a Reduced Instruction Set Computer (RISC) architecture, which is used by the PowerPC chip in the Advanced Series AS/400s.

What are the differences between these two architectures? Basically, RISC performs many very simple instructions very fast, whereas CISC performs both simple and relatively complex instructions and thus doesn't run as fast as RISC. Many performance comparisons between the two architectures are based on the number of instructions per second (called millions of instructions per second, or mips) each can perform. What isn't always considered is that, even though CISC is slower than RISC, it takes many RISC instructions to accomplish the same work performed by one CISC instruction.

RISC systems do very well in processing environments conducive to parallel execution of multiple instructions (pipelining). But a major reason manufacturers build RISC-based machines is that it's cheaper to create faster hardware for RISC than CISC. This savings, however, may be offset by the complexity of the software functions needed to build programs that can exploit the RISC architecture. ■

Rick Turner

processors doesn't run any faster than an RPR 1 machine, but it is capable of doing twice as much work.

Queuing Comparisons

Let's consider some specific cases. Table 4.1 compares, for three scenarios, the average time a transaction spends waiting for and using the CPU. The first scenario, A-Load 1, is for a one-processor model with an RPR of 10. The second scenario, B-Load 1, is for a two-processor model with an RPR of 20 and the same workload as scenario 1. The last scenario, B-Load 2, is identical to B-Load 1 except that the workload is doubled.

You can obtain the information in the columns marked with asterisks in the Performance Tools' System Report (PRTSYSRPT) as well as the *SUMMARY option of the Transaction Report (PRTTNSRPT). For more information about these reports, see Chapter 13.

The CPU + Wait column represents the total average time a transaction will spend waiting for and using the CPU. As you can see from the CPU Time/Transaction column, the time spent using the CPU is a constant 0.5 seconds, so the variation in the total time (CPU + Wait) is in the wait time. Variation in the wait time depends on two factors: CPU utilization and the number of processors.

TABLE 4.1
Three Queuing Scenarios

Model	RPR	No. of CPUs (P)	CPU Time/ Transaction (S) *	Workload, Transactions/ Hour *	CPU Utilization (U) *	CPU QM	CPU + Wait
A-Load 1	10	1	0.50	3,600	0.50	2.0000	**1.000**
B-Load 1	20	2	0.50	3,600	0.25	1.0667	**0.533**
B-Load 2	20	2	0.50	7,200	0.50	1.3333	**0.667**

You determine CPU utilization (U), or how busy a CPU is, by multiplying transactions per second (also called the arrival rate, or A) by the CPU Time/Transaction value (also called service time, or S) and dividing the result by the number of processors (P):

$$U = \frac{A \times S}{P}$$

If a transaction arrives every second and each transaction takes 0.5 seconds of CPU time, the CPU has a utilization rate of 50 percent.

Utilization rate is related to CPU speed and workload. Table 4.1 shows that if we moved the workload in A-Load 1 to a CPU with twice the capacity but the same speed (B-Load 1), the CPU would be busy only 25 percent of the time. Doubling the workload on the same CPU (B-Load 2) would bring CPU utilization back up to 50 percent.

The relationship between CPU utilization and total CPU response time (CPU + Wait) is represented by the CPU Queuing Multiplier (CPU QM). You estimate the CPU QM value for a single processor using the equation

$$QM = \frac{1}{(1-U)}$$

or, in its more general form,

$$QM = \frac{1}{(1-U^P)}$$

where P is the number of processors. Multiplying the CPU Time/Transaction value (S) by the CPU QM value yields the CPU + Wait time.

Now, let's look at what happens to CPU + Wait time when the workload in A-Load 1 is put on system B-Load 1, which has the same speed but an additional processor. As you would expect, having another processor to service transactions dramatically decreases the CPU QM value and, thus, the total time a transaction spends waiting for and using the CPU (CPU + Wait).

In contrast, here in the real AS/400 world, adding a processor doesn't necessarily reduce the amount of time the CPU spends processing each transaction. Table 4.2 shows the effect on CPU + Wait time of moving a constant workload from one model to another. Although the CPU + Wait time decreases, CPU time/transaction increases. CPU speeds get a little slower as you add processors because additional CPU and hardware control logic is necessary to synchronize the activity of multiple processors. CPU speed (and thus the estimated CPU Time/Transaction) is actually a function of each model's RPR and number of processors. Dividing the RPR by the number of processors yields the relative speed for a particular model. Each processor on a 2051 would have a relative speed of 22.9 and each processor on a 2052 would have a relative speed of 17.75. Therefore, a transaction that takes 0.10 CPU seconds on a 2050 would need 0.11 seconds of CPU on the 2051 and 0.14 CPU seconds on a 2052.

TABLE 4.2

Holding the Workload Constant Across Models

Model	RPR	No. of CPUs (P)	CPU Time/ Transaction (S) *	Workload, Transactions/ Hour *	CPU Utilization (U) *	CPU QM	CPU + Wait
2050	25.7	1	0.10	20,000	0.556	2.2500	**0.225**
2051	45.8	2	0.11	20,000	0.312	1.1000	**0.124**
2052	71.5	4	0.14	20,000	0.200	1.0000	**0.144**

Even though the CPU Time/Transaction in Table 4.2 increases as you add processors, you can see that overall CPU utilization drops sharply. The CPU Time/Transaction also increases in Table 4.3, which doubles the interactive workload for each model upgrade. Still, the overall CPU + Wait performance value remains stable. As seen in Table 4.3, the key advantage of multiple processors is the effect they have on the CPU queuing multiplier and the reduction in the transaction's Wait component. These advantages allow for significant increase in throughput without impact to the individual transaction response time.

Before shopping for an upgrade to your system, make sure you define your performance objectives: faster processing of individual transactions, processing more transactions per unit time, or both. As seen in the above examples, unless you are experiencing long CPU + Wait times, going to a multiple processor may not give you the improvements in response time that you expect.

TABLE 4.3

Doubling the Workload with Each Processor Upgrade

Model	RPR	No. of CPUs (P)	CPU Time/ Transaction (S) *	Workload, Transactions/ Hour *	CPU Utilization (U) *	CPU QM	CPU + Wait
2050	25.7	1	0.10	20,000	0.556	2.2500	**0.225**
2051	45.8	2	0.11	40,000	0.623	1.6300	**0.184**
2052	71.5	4	0.14	80,000	0.799	1.6800	**0.242**

MULTIPLE SYSTEMS

If your business volume is growing faster than your AS/400 capacity, adding processors may not be enough. You may need to consider adding more machines and networking them. IBM has developed a product that makes it possible to process (read and update) the same database files from multiple systems faster than with Distributed Data Management (DDM).

OptiConnect/400 (OC/400), an integrated hardware and software product, moves data between two or more AS/400s much more quickly and efficiently than current DDM functions and hardware. The hardware for OC/400 is an I-listed RPQ (5799-FFR). The software is a special feature for the operating system (5799-FQB). OC/400 lets you use an AS/400 as a file server for other AS/400s attached using a fiber optic bus (its I-listing indicates that special approval from IBM is required to order it).

With just one set of data (on the server system), you can quickly access data from multiple systems while retaining data integrity. You can also offload database processing from the client systems, freeing up CPU cycles for additional work and eliminating the need for extra DASD to hold multiple copies of the data. And, obviously, managing a single set of data is much easier than managing many copies.

But be careful not to make too many assumptions about what OC/400 can do. It is not a shared DASD implementation — nor is it system clustering. It provides a single-system image to applications, but not to operations or system management. OC/400 is simply a faster way to get database data from one system to another.

Speedy Data Access

OC/400 allows you to join up to seven systems across a high-speed, fiber-optic bus running a private communications protocol at 220 Mbps bandwidth (Figure 4.1). The private protocol's only function is to transmit data between the systems, so it doesn't include the overhead normally associated with formal

FIGURE 4.1
The OptiConnect/400 Connection

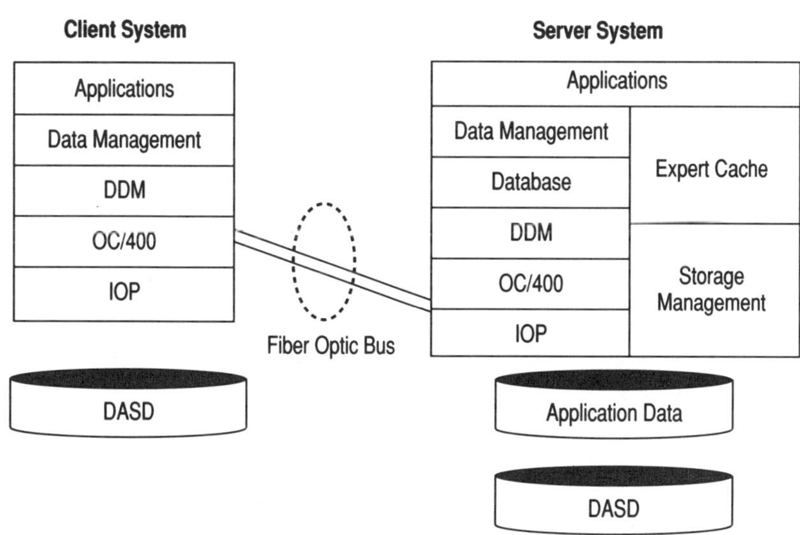

communications protocols. For OC/400, much of the DDM code has been moved into OC/400 hardware to shorten CPU path length and intersystem communications time. In V3R1, OC/400 has also been enhanced to allow Distributed Relational Database access across the OptiConnect link; thus, SQL requests can be made across OptiConnect. V3R1 also makes available ObjectConnect/400 — a PRPQ (5799-FNR) that enables object transfer between systems via a save-restore-like interface from one system to another. ObjectConnect will function over OC/400 as well as a LAN.

With a properly configured serving system (that is, one that's fast enough to keep up with the clients and do its own work, too), OC/400 can probably improve total system throughput. This is especially true in a multisystem environment with heavy interactive database processing. Depending on the speed of the serving system's CPU and its workload, multisystem database access speeds can rival those of single systems. Actual performance depends on a number of factors, including system load and the mix of operations on the file (all reads, all writes, all updates, or some combination of each).

OC/400, however, isn't for everyone. Although using OC/400 with a properly sized server can *probably* improve throughput, server speed is just one part of the OC/400 performance formula. For example, if you have a disk I/O-bound application and a very tight window of time in which to run it, you probably don't want to be accessing data from another system. Doing so would add 2 to 4 ms to the database access time per physical record. Thus, application environments that are heavily oriented to batch processing may not benefit from using OC/400. In addition, when you consolidate your database onto a single system, you may have more activity on the single copy of the file and thus more data contention than you had when a copy of the data resided on each machine.

Because OC/400's benefits are often dependent on the characteristics of the specific application being used, its evaluation is a candidate for benchmarking. The Rochester Benchmark Center has often been used to establish OC/400 expectations for specific environments.

Preserving Data Integrity

OC/400 solves the difficult problem of preserving the data integrity of files that are read and written by applications on multiple systems. One way to address this problem without OC/400 is to replicate the data on each system and then use packages such as Object Management System/400 or Mimix, which use cross-system journaling to propagate changes to the copies.

Figure 4.2 shows an overview of a two-system computing environment in which each system contains a copy of the database. System 1 contains the primary copy of the database; System 2 has the shadow copy. To ensure data consistency in this model, any change to the data on either System 1 or System 2 is

FIGURE 4.2

Database File Access with Cross-System Journaling

System 1

System 2

Applications

Cross-system Journaling, Database, and DDM

Applications

Cross-system Journaling, Database, and DDM

APPC Link

DASD

DASD

Update path from System 1

Direct I/O

Update path from System 2

journaled on System 1, sent via Advanced Program-to-Program Communications (APPC) link to System 2, and finally applied to System 2 using the cross-system journaling functions. All this must happen before an application on System 2 can access the change from its own copy of the data. When systems are very busy, it can take tens of seconds before an application on System 2 can access its own local copy of a file update.

Now, let's look at a multisystem model that uses OC/400 and a separate serving system to provide database access to two client systems (Figure 4.3). Notice that all requests for data access one copy of the database, which is located on the serving system. The server may contain only the database, depending on your configuration, and should include the proper level of database and DASD protection (RAID-5 or mirroring). Not only does this model ensure data integrity, it also eliminates the database processing and the cross-journaling functions from the client systems, thereby freeing up client CPU resources for more work or additional applications.

Of course, not all this saved CPU time is available for more work. In an OC/400 configuration, some of the client CPU time is used to provide the fiber-optic communications interface to the server each time data must be moved in or out of the requesting job's open data path (ODP) buffer (i.e., the database file work area). Just how much CPU this interface requires depends on request frequency, record size, line speed, and ODP buffer size.

FIGURE 4.3
Database File Access with OptiConnect/400

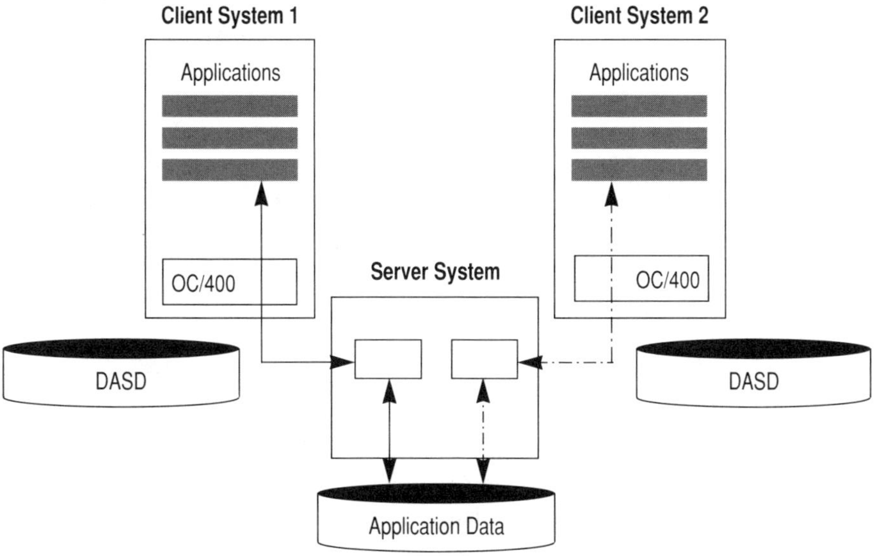

Client System 1
Applications
OC/400
DASD
Client System 2
Applications
OC/400
DASD
Server System
Application Data

Selecting the Server

Now the big question: What AS/400 model should you use as the server in an OC/400 configuration? Again, it depends. OC/400 requires a system with at least five buses, and several AS/400 systems meet this criterion. Which model you choose is governed in part by the number of disk operations per second it must perform for the client systems.

To determine the number of disk operations your server system must perform, let's look at an example. Suppose you have two systems, each performing an average of 500 disk operations per second, excluding the cross-system journaling functions. Your trend data tells you that, on average, the systems are doing 50 percent database operations and 50 percent nondatabase operations. To offload your current database disk I/O to a separate processor that will serve both systems, you need the server to process 500 disk database I/O operations per second.

That capacity is fine for today, but you also need to consider workload growth. If your business is growing at a 30 percent annual rate, it's reasonable to assume the number of disk I/O operations will grow at the same rate. Thus, your server should be able to handle an average of

500 + (30 percent of 500) = 650

disk operations per second. This rate should handle your average processing needs for the next year, but what about peak loads? You should also consider sizing for your busiest times, which would add another 30 percent of the average required capacity, bringing the total to 845 disk operations per second. Table 4.4 shows the number of disk I/Os per second performed by each model and the percentage of CPU used to perform the specified number of disk operations.

Now let's determine how much client CPU time you would save by moving the data from your current system to a server. Table 4.4 shows, by system model, the percentage of CPU time used per disk operation. Looking at this table, you can see that if you reduce the number of disk operations per second on an E70 from 400 per second to 200 per second, the total CPU usage decreases by 20 percent. This 20 percent savings on a 200 operation-per-second decrease indicates that each disk I/O operation uses about 0.1 percent of the E70's CPU, or that the system can do about 10 disk operations per percent of CPU time, which is shown in Table 4.5.

In addition to showing, by system model, the number of disk I/O operations performed per percent of CPU time used, Table 4.5 shows the RPR of each system. If you know how many disk operations per second your particular CPU model is performing (see Chapter 13 for finding this value with the Performance Tools), you can use that number and the RPR for your system to

Table 4.4

Disk Operations per Second and Percent of CPU

	Disk Operations per Second				
	200	400	600	800	1000
AS/400 Model	**Percent of CPU Used**				
D60	33	67			
D70	25	50	74	99	
D80	14	28	43	57	71
E60	28	56	84		
E70	20	40	60	80	
E80	11	23	34	45	57
E90	8	17	25	33	41
E95	7	13	20	27	34
F50	28	57	85		
F60	20	39	59	79	99
F70	14	29	43	57	71
F80	8	16	24	32	40
F90	6	12	18	25	31
F95	5	11	16	21	26
F97	4	9	13	18	22
310-2043	25	50	74	99	
310-2044	14	28	43	57	71
320-2050	12	23	35	47	58
320-2051	7	13	20	26	33
320-2052	4	9	13	18	22

determine the approximate percentage of CPU you would be moving off the system. The formula for calculating this value is

$$\frac{X\,\text{RPR}}{Y\,\text{RPR}} \text{ X } \frac{YN}{XN} = \text{Percent of CPU}$$

X RPR represents your current system's RPR, *XN* is the number of disk operations per second your system is performing, *Y* RPR is the RPR of the server system you're considering, and *YN* is the number of disk operations per second you need it to perform.

Suppose you are considering moving your database I/O from a model E70 (RPR 13.5) performing 200 disk operations per second to an F80 (RPR 33.5) that performs 400 disk operations per second. The equation for determining how much CPU utilization you would be offloading would look like this.

$$\frac{13.5}{33.5} \text{ X } \frac{400}{200} = 80.6 \text{ percent}$$

TABLE 4.5

Disk Operations per Second and RPR

AS/400 Model	Approximate Number of Disk I/O Operations per Percent of CPU Usage	RPR
D60	6.0	8.1
D70	8.1	10.9
D80	14.1	19.0
E60	7.2	9.7
E70	10.0	13.5
E80	17.6	23.8
E90	24.1	32.6
E95	29.8	40.2
F50	7.0	9.5
F60	10.1	13.7
F70	14.0	18.9
F80	24.8	33.5
F90	32.4	43.8
F95	37.8	51.0
F97	45.3	61.2
310-2043	8.1	10.9
310-2044	14.1	19.0
320-2050	17.2	23.2
320-2051	30.6	41.3
320-2052	45.3	61.2

Remember that some of your client CPU time will be needed for intersystem communications; however, no modeling tools have been developed to help you estimate this.

APPLICATION CONSIDERATIONS

Learning why a job or program is using too much CPU time can be one of the most important steps in understanding the cause of poor performance. Some frequent causes of too much use of CPU time are an application's transaction complexity, file open and close operations, job initiation and termination operations, CPU-intensive requests, program optimization, and authority lookup.

Transaction Complexity

The average number of CPU seconds per transaction is a good measure of the relative complexity of an application's transactions. By collecting trace data when using the Performance Monitor, you can use the AS/400 Performance Tools to report the average CPU per transaction (for more information about using Performance Monitor, see Chapter 12). By selecting or omitting specific jobs in the reports, you can collect average CPU per transaction on specific applications.

The job summary part of the PRTTNSRPT (Print Transaction Report) in the Performance Tools gives average CPU per transaction and the maximum CPU per transaction for each job. This information can be a good starting point in finding jobs that are running very complex transactions and using a lot of CPU. You want to make sure that these transactions are running as they should be.

PRTTNSRPT can also detect which programs are using the most CPU time. Although the algorithm that identifies the program using the CPU is not 100 percent accurate, it will generally identify the correct program, or you'll find that the correct program is one that the identified program calls. Combining this information with the detail from the Transition Report will help you learn a lot about what the user is doing in the programs and transactions you're examining.

You can classify transactions as simple, medium, complex, or very complex, depending on the CPU seconds per transaction. These complexity boundaries vary by the CPU model. IBM's Redbook, *AS/400 Performance Management* (GG24-3723), provides a table, "CPU per Transaction Complexity Boundaries," with the information you need.

The complexity guidelines have many uses. For example, you can use them when evaluating a new application. Look for vendors who can give you figures on the complexity of their application's transactions. Such vendors consider application performance an important part of their development process. Similarly, in your own development work, test to find the complexity level of key transactions, and establish goals that they must meet. By doing so, you can head off performance problems and contribute to the total quality of your development effort.

Reducing Transaction Complexity

To focus your performance improvement on the areas of specific applications that will return the greatest benefit, you should identify the programs with the most complex transactions that are run most often. The method outlined below requires running the Performance Monitor with the trace type *ALL option. Once this data has been collected, follow these steps:

1. Use the Print Transaction Report's Summary Report on Interactive Program Statistics to get a ranking of the transaction programs by frequency. (Run PRTTNSRPT with the *SUMMARY option; at the same time specify *FILE to get data for an upcoming query.) An example of the Interactive Program Statistics report is included in Appendix C.

2. Focus on those transaction programs that are the most complex (have the highest CPU per transaction) and have a high frequency. The

transaction programs will stand out in the Interactive Program Statistics report, because they will have the highest cumulative CPU values.

3. Use the query in Appendix C to find the jobs that contain the worst-case transaction programs. In the query, the "Select record tests" entry of TCPU GE 0.5 results in a list of the transactions with CPU use per transaction greater than or equal to 0.5 seconds. You can vary this value depending on the level of transaction complexity you want. (This query is using one of the files created when you specify the *FILE option on the PRTTNSRPT command.)
4. Select some of the jobs from the query output for the transaction programs you're analyzing, and run PRTTNSRPT with the *TNSACT option and a Select Jobs list consisting of the job numbers for the selected jobs. This report will show you the user transaction scenarios that result in these worst-case transactions. An example of this Transaction report is included in Appendix C.
5. Work with the developer most familiar with the specific transaction program to establish potential explanations for the complexity.
6. Use the trace job functions in the Performance Tools (PRTJOBTRC, Print Job Trace) and in the QTPST library (PRTTRCSUM, Print Trace Summary) to confirm the explanation for the transaction complexity.
7. Examine alternatives to the existing program that will reduce the transaction complexity. Be willing to spend added effort when the transaction's logical I/O and/or file open operations are part of the solution, because changes in these areas can return significant savings.
8. Stay focused on transactions with high frequency. Along the way you will see various transactions that are very complex. It is easy to become curious as to why this is the case and be tempted to start more detailed analysis on these other transactions. However, remember that unless the complexity is combined with high frequency you are not likely to get good payback for your efforts.

Reducing Open and Close File Operations

As a job moves among the various programs that provide an application's function, these programs must open and close the database and display files that the job uses. These open and close operations are a frequent contributor to a transaction's increased complexity (CPU usage), but this complexity can be reduced significantly using relatively simple programming techniques. If you anticipate reusing certain files, you can leave those files open on return to a calling program, thereby saving the overhead of opening the files on each call to the program. Also, specifying the SHARE(*YES) option when you create a file (or on an override before opening it the first time) reduces the resources necessary to open the file multiple times. The ideal case is to use both techniques.

Of the two techniques, leaving files open will benefit you most when you repeatedly call programs while providing the application function. On the first call to a program, the system opens the files as usual. The method of exiting the program determines whether you leave it active with its files open. For example, in RPG, doing a RETRN without setting on the LR (Last Record) indicator will keep the program active and its files open. In COBOL, using the EXIT PROGRAM or GOBACK verb will keep the program active (if another COBOL program higher in the job's run unit is active).

The benefit in keeping files open can be significant. However, when using this technique, you need to consider that keeping programs active and files open on exiting a program means that a subsequent call to the program will find field values, indicator values, file buffers, and record positions in the same state they were in when the exit occurred. Thus, your program must ensure that these values and record positions are what you expect or that they are initialized properly. Also, if you're doing output blocking and have not reached the blocking factor, the database does not yet reflect the records in the output buffer. A return without closing the file will not send the records in the buffer to the database. To leave the file open in this case, you have three options: You can specify SEQONLY(*NO) to avoid blocking (which we don't recommend); use FEOD (Force End of Data) in RPG to output the buffered records at the end of a transaction; or use commitment control.

The other technique for reducing complexity is specifying the SHARE(*YES) option when you create a file or on an override command before you open the file. This option allows subsequent opens of a file to share the ODP (Open Data Path) established on the initial file open. An ODP is the internal structure that the operating system uses to link an active program with the file being used. By sharing the ODP among programs in a job, the system saves significant resources over doing a full open, which would establish a totally distinct ODP.

You need to consider the same points when you apply the SHARE(*YES) technique as when you leave files open. The program's level in the invocation stack and the type of open (input, output, update) on the first open determine whether subsequent opens will be shared and the type of open required. You cannot open a file for input and then, at a lower invocation level, for update if you originally opened it SHARE(*YES). Many programmers use a CL program, specifying the OPNDBF (Open Data Base File) command's OPTION(*ALL) parameter, to preopen SHARE(*YES) files at the highest level. With this method, subsequent opens will not have any problem with the type of open.

Note that for a program that uses the file as input only (or output only), this open OPTION(*ALL) precludes sequential-only processing. As a result, this option also takes away the advantages you can gain from blocking. You have to decide case by case which method will give the most benefit.

Record positioning is done via the ODP cursor object. Using a shared ODP you can find that the position of the file cursor has changed on return from a called program. With a single ODP across multiple programs, any one of these programs can reposition the file cursor. Thus, following the return from a call, a program cannot assume anything about cursor position and needs to re-establish the position it needs.

Job Initiation/Termination

Job initiation and termination are complex transactions, but you can easily reduce the number of them. Instead of having users sign off and on during the day, use the DSCJOB (Disconnect Job) command, which does not terminate the job. If the user signs on to the same workstation using the same user profile, the system reconnects the job. This approach requires much less resource and avoids creating and deleting the job structure associated with a job.

The system value QDSCJOBITV (Disconnect Job Interval) specifies how long disconnected jobs remain in disconnected status before the system terminates them. At the end of the QDSCJOBITV time limit, the job is terminated. This value can allow even the last sign-off of the day to be a disconnect.

This approach has other advantages. For example, in a shift-change situation, all the users do not sign off or sign on simultaneously: The system delays sign-off by the interval specified on QDSCJOBITV. Also, at the end of the day, when folks are in a hurry to power down their workstations, sometimes they aren't patient enough to wait for the sign-on screen. Using DSCJOB keeps this terminal power-down from coming in the middle of job termination, thus preventing the system from trying to recover the workstation to display the sign-on screen.

CPU-Intensive Requests

Some applications and system services use a lot of CPU resources. Such services include save/restore, large program compiles, queries, the OPNQRYF (Open Query File) command, and file copy functions. Whenever possible, you should run these services at priorities lower than interactive functions. If they run at priorities equal to or higher than interactive functions, the other interactive jobs already in an activity level have to wait longer before they can run. Run these CPU-intensive functions in batch by specifying the SBMJOB (Submit Job) command. If the frequency of the requests for such functions is very high, you should consider a never-ending server job that takes the requests off a data queue. This approach will eliminate the high numbers of job initiations and terminations caused by the submitted batch job approach. If these functions must run interactively, consider lowering the job's priority before running the particular function.

Program Optimization

The program-optimization compile option can reduce the number of IMPI instructions because it uses register-based operations where possible. Reserve this option for large, high-usage programs, and be sure to test the performance of the program with and without the optimize option. This testing is important because optimization can sometimes result in worse performance, depending on the type of work the program is doing and the structure of the program.

Authority Lookup

Public or owner authority on objects provides the best performance. Use private authority only on objects you want secured. (As a rule, do not use private authority on IBM-supplied objects.) The system stores public and owner authority information in the object and keeps private authority in the user profile object. Using private authority may cause authority lookups, which are system index operations and, as the number of authority lookups increases, can affect CPU performance. From a performance point of view, a good approach to securing objects is to secure the library the object resides in and assign only public authority to the individual objects.

If you use private authority, use a private authority that is greater than public authority for that object. If the private authority is less than public authority, the system takes more CPU to verify adequate authority. When you use private authority, the system must process both the object and the accessing user's profile. If that profile has many private authorities, the processing of the user profile can become excessive.

Group profiles and authorization lists only make maintenance and recordkeeping easier. **They do not improve authority lookup performance**. If an authority list is used to secure an object and private authorities exist for that object, the number of authority lookups could increase as it does when private authority is less than public authority. Group profiles can also cause an increase in authority lookup because the process (job) user profile is examined before the group profile.

The new supplemental group authority and primary group authority features included in V3R1 also have performance implications. Supplemental groups, created with the Create User Profile (CRTUSRPRF) command's SUPGRPPFR parameter, enable a user to be part of more than one group profile. Although this option is an important enhancement, it can **significantly degrade performance if many supplemental group profiles are specified for an object created by the user profile with these supplemental groups**.

Primary group authority identifies the primary group profile and that profile's authority level for an object. This authority information is stored with the object and **can provide a fast path for private authority lookup for group profiles**.

Both the *AS/400 Security Reference - Version 3* (SC41-3302) and the IBM Redbook *An Implementation Guide for AS/400 Security and Auditing: Including C2, Cryptography, Communications, and PC Connectivity* (GG24-4200) provide more details and performance considerations for using supplemental group and primary group profile authorization.

Tools for CPU Analysis

A number of tools are available to help you pinpoint problems in your CPU's performance. The Sampled Address Monitor (SAM), part of the Performance Tools package, identifies which instructions in a program are using the most CPU time. The Trace Job tool, also part of the Performance Tools, analyzes the interactions of both interactive and batch jobs to show how transactions relate. (For more information about using Performance Tools, see Chapters 11 through 14.) In addition to these tools, the Timing and Paging Statistics Tool (TPST), discussed in Appendix B, is a PRPQ (order number 5799-EER) that can give you vital information about your programs. (With V3R6 and later RISC systems, TPST has been made part of the Performance Explorer.)

Sampled Address Monitor

Once you identify the programs with high CPU use, the Performance Tools' Sampled Address Monitor (SAM) commands can identify which program instructions are using the most CPU. (For more information about analyzing performance using Performance Tools, see Chapters 11 through 14.) SAM commands collect and present CPU usage data by individual program instruction. SAM provides data on Integrated Language Environment (ILE) procedures as well as on Original Program Model programs.

SAM Commands

The five commands you use with SAM are listed in Table 4.6.

Table 4.6
SAM Commands

Command	Description
STRSAM	Defines the collection environment
STRSAMCOL	Starts collection
STPSAMCOL	Stops collection
ENDSAM	Ends the definition
PRTSAMDTA	Prints the results

STRSAM identifies the programs you want SAM to gather data on — that is, the SAM collection environment. You can specify one or more programs in the same or different libraries. Because all AS/400 jobs use the same copy of a program, the data SAM collects represents the total use of the program by all callers. It doesn't matter whether the program is active when you start SAM. Once collection begins, SAM samples all instructions in the program except those that fall outside the collection boundary (for more information on the boundary, see the sidebar, "Don't Believe Everything You See," page 68).

STRSAMCOL starts the collection process. You specify a sample time interval, with the default being 1 millisecond (ms). This interval represents how often the CPU will interrupt itself to check whether a program specified on STRSAM is currently using the processor. If you specify a short interval for a heavily used system, the frequent hardware interrupts may affect overall system performance. In such a case, especially in a production environment, you should run the test only for a short time. If you want to run SAM for a longer period of time, use at least a 20 ms interval. The goal is to run SAM long enough to get a balanced statistical sample, which should be 2,000 to 3,000 counts, depending on the size of the program.

STPSAMCOL stops data collection and, if you choose, stores the data in a database file member to be printed by PRTSAMDTA. The ENDSAM command undefines the sampling environment.

To run SAM, you can either use these commands or select the Programmer Utilities option from the Start Performance Tools menu. (For more information about using Performance Tools, see Chapter 11.)

SAM's Window of Opportunity

SAM defines a "window" over the code for each program in the collection environment. Inside the window are "panes" that correspond to a certain number of bytes of executable code, which contain the internal microprogramming interface instructions. SAM calculates the number of panes (up to 4,000) based on program size. The number of bytes each pane represents can vary from 4 to 1,024 or more, depending on the amount of executable code.

When SAM is active, the CPU interrupts itself at the specified interval to determine whether the machine is executing an instruction in a program being tested. If so, SAM increments the corresponding window pane (actually a counter), and the system continues to run. If the machine instruction register isn't in a program being tested, SAM counts the interrupt as being outside the window. If the CPU isn't busy when the interrupt occurs, SAM increments another counter that represents a machine-idle condition.

After you stop data collection and store the data in a database file, you can use PRTSAMDTA to generate a report of CPU usage by instruction. To provide this report, PRTSAMDTA relates the value in each window pane to the

In Depth: SAM Looks at LOKUP

I recently investigated some jobs on an F80 that were using a lot of CPU time. The WRKSYSACT (Work with System Activity) command showed that one job was using up to 40 percent of the CPU resources for seconds at a time. Using the WRKJOB (Work with Job) screen, I viewed the program stack, which showed that one program and RPG instruction (LOKUP) were using the processor for a number of seconds.

Because I had the instruction number I needed, I didn't **have** to run SAM; however, I did for two reasons: First, I wanted to verify what I saw with WRKJOB; second, I wanted to see whether any other instructions were using a lot of CPU time — and some were. Because the LOKUP was taking so much CPU time, the other instructions weren't as apparent on the WRKJOB screen.

How did I cut the appetite of this resource-hogging instruction? I first determined that the program was searching 500 active entries in a 9,999-element array. Shortening the array would have made the LOKUP run faster, but 500 entries is still a lot of searching. Instead, I suggested the company use Jim Sloan's BINSEARCH (Binary Search) routine from the QUSRTOOL library, which comes with the system in V3R1. Beginning with V3R6, all of the TAATOOLs in the QUSRTOOL example library will no longer be shipped with the operating system. Jim Sloan, Inc., c/o Barsa Consulting Group, Inc. (220 Westchester Ave., Port Chester, NY 10573, (914) 939-6100), provides an enhanced version of the TAA Tools for V3R6M0.

A binary search over ordered data has a maximum of nine compares in 512 entries; a linear search has an average of 256 compares (i.e., half the entries). In head-to-head competition, binary search wins hands down.

Consider another situation, in which a LOKUP operation is searching a 500-element array that has only 10 or 20 active entries. In this case, you could improve CPU usage dramatically by filling the array from the back instead of the front and starting the search at the first active entry. ■

Rick Turner

corresponding high-level language (HLL) statement number in the program being tested. If program observability has been removed, PRTSAMDTA can't relate the data to the HLL instruction. In this case, instead of presenting a readable report, PRTSAMDTA will reference Machine Interface instructions, which are almost impossible to relate to their corresponding HLL statements.

Job Trace

The Performance Tools' Job Trace function can be very useful in analyzing what a particular transaction is doing and why it is using so much CPU. Although the operating system provides trace information, the function in the Performance Tools gives you additional reports oriented to performance analysis. Job Trace can help you spot areas where performance improvements can be made by displaying whether a job has full-file opens and closes, uses file creates and deletes, uses shared open data paths (ODPs), or is generating error messages. It's quite versatile because it allows you to investigate individual interactive transactions and shows you what's going on inside a batch job.

With this tool, you may be able to determine which programs have high CPU and disk utilization. You can also observe high fault rates, which suggest that a job has high main storage requirements. Note that because Job Trace adds significantly to the CPU use of the job you're tracing, the trace report shows only an estimate of CPU time. You can use it in comparison from one trace to the next, but don't consider it a true representation of the program's CPU time.

To use the Job Trace function, enter the STRJOBTRC (Start Job Trace) command. No parameters are needed if you're analyzing your own job. If you're going to run for an extended period, allocate more trace records than the default allows. Then enter the command or commands that run the function you want to analyze and enter the ENDJOBTRC (End Job Trace) command. Again, you won't have to change parameters unless you want to specify a different library or member name, specify a report option, or run the command interactively.

Use the PRTJOBTRC command after ENDJOBTRC to generate two summary reports: a Trace Analysis Summary and a Trace Analysis I/O Summary, plus a detail report.

The Trace Analysis Summary report in Figure 4.4 shows the elapsed time of the transaction, both time spent waiting for input and active CPU time. The report also shows a small amount of time used in the Wait state and some time caused by the Trace Job command. You can ignore these figures. Also shown are the physical I/O counts for synchronous database reads (DB READS); non-database reads (NON-DB READS); synchronous writes (WRITES); the number of waits, such as workstation read waits (WAITS); and a detail report line with sequential beginning and ending numbers for the transactions.

From this data, you can answer these questions: Why are the nondatabase I/Os in one transaction so high? What's causing it in all of them? Notice in Figure 4.4 the transaction at Sequence 8243 through 16500, which is boxed in on the report. It had 1042 nondatabase reads that are all synchronous disk operations. This is the kind of transaction you should investigate.

For each interactive transaction, the Trace Analysis I/O Summary report in Figure 4.5 shows

- Transaction elapsed time in seconds (A)
- Sequence numbers (B)
- The name of the first program (the one that performs the transaction I/O) (C)
- The number of issued application program calls (D)

Figure 4.4

Trace Analysis Summary Report

```
PRTJOBTRC  Sample Data           Trace Analysis Summary
  FILE-QAPTTRCJ        LIBRARY-TEST        MBR-ACCTTST1             Job-DSP05.QA.015555
                                           PHYSICAL I/O

            SECONDS  CPU SECONDS  DB READS  NON-DB RDS  WRITES  WAITS  SEQUENCE
  WAIT-ACT    9.069         .106                                              5
  ACTIVE     17.830        3.460   50          312                1        1399

  WAIT-ACT   24.323         .004                                           1404
  ACTIVE      5.754        1.890               144                1        2543

  WAIT-ACT    5.306         .004                                           2548
  ACTIVE     50.373       11.386  127          761        35      1        8238
+------------------------------------------------------------------------------+
  WAIT-ACT   57.924         .004                                           8243
  ACTIVE    163.758      114.993    9         1042         8      1       16500
+------------------------------------------------------------------------------+
  WAIT-ACT   8.199          .004                                          16505
  ACTIVE     9.882         2,563   10          198        11              17789

  AVERAGE   49.519        26.862   39          491        11      1

+-----------------------------------------------------------------

  TOTAL     247.597      134.308  196         2457        54      4
```

- The number of program initiations (E). If the program stays active, you won't have initiations. You want low numbers here.
- The number and type of database I/O operations: get direct (F), get sequential (G), get by key (H), get multiple, put (add) (I), put multiple (J), and update (K). For sequential processing, your design should cause you to have many more get-multiple than get-sequential operations.
- The number of database full opens (L) and closes (M). You want low numbers or zero here.
- The number of database shared opens (N) and closes (O)
- The number of display subfile reads (P) and writes (Q)
- The number of messages generated (R) within the transaction. A high value indicates that you may want to check the trace detail.

This report tells you what the job and application were doing. It also shows program, database, and display activity in the job. Part of the reason for the high disk I/O in some transactions, as shown in Figure 4.4, is the extremely high number of program initialization requests that in turn may have been responsible for the high number of file opens and closes. You begin to wonder if the reason for the high disk I/O in some of the transactions is related to the high number of full database file open and close functions.

FIGURE 4.5

Trace Analysis I/O Summary Report

PRTJO\BTRC Sample Data T r a c e A n a l y s i s I / O S u m m a r y

FILE-QAPTTRCJ LIBRARY-TEST MBR-ACCTTST1 Job - DSP05.QA.015555

		PROGRAM			***********DB I/O***********							FULL		SHARE		FULL SUBFILE		
	(A) SECONDS	(B) SEQNCE	(C) NAME	(D) CALL	(E) INIT	(F) GETDR	(G) GETSQ	(H) GETKY	(I) PUT	(J) PUTM	(K) UDN	(L) OPN	(M) CLS	(N) OPN	(O) CLS	(P) READS	(Q) WRITES	(R) MSGS
WAIT-ACT	9.069	5																
ACTIVE	17.830	1399	A1440328		9		8	55				26	24	25	24	21	20	19
WAIT-ACT	24.323	1404	A14403															
ACTIVE	5.754	2543		24	8		8	54				24	24	24	24	21	20	14
			A14403															
WAIT-ACT	5.306	2548																
ACTIVE	50.373	8238	A1440393		41		65	296		35	10	105	105	115	115	31	80	163
WAIT-ACT	57.924	8243																
ACTIVE	163.758	16500	A14403153		72		97	473	60			68	168	92	192	91	120	147
WAIT-ACT	8.199	16505																
ACTIVE	9.002	17789	A1440312		2		26	134	2			3	2	8	7		20	58
AVERAGE	49.519			62	26		41	202	14			65	65	73	72	33	52	80
TOTAL	247.597			310	132		204	1012	72			326	323	364	362	164	260	401

At this point, you will find the TPST Print Trace Summary (PRTTRCSUM) command useful. This tool uses the outfile from the ENDJOBTRC (End Job Trace) command as its input and provides a summary.

PRTTRCSUM helps you analyze individual job performance, especially for applications converted to the AS/400. When you're examining converted programs, you can see whether the conversion took advantage of OS/400 functions that help improve performance, such as using database file sharing and bypassing program initialization by use of the proper program return logic. In some language environments, such as C/400, you can identify which groups of programs are good candidates for combining (binding) into fewer programs to reduce the number of external calls (calls to separate program objects).

In a compact format, the tool shows which programs are invoking which other programs, the number of calls, and what type of invocation was used (CALL, transfer control, event handler, or others). This information is useful in understanding the implementation of a function and spotting programs that shouldn't be invoked (perhaps because of a bug or design flaw). Most important, it can help you reduce large numbers of calls by restructuring the function (for example, by combining programs that call each other frequently), thereby improving performance.

Data Warehousing on the AS/400

With this new and important technique being used to organize data, the issue of optimizing access methods to your database is more important than ever. The DB2/400 multi-system parallel database option will allow organizations to store up to 16.8 terabytes on database tables spread across multiple systems. Capacity scalability will become virtually unlimited. The normalization and layout of your database has always been important, but with these new options for the AS/400, strategic planning is becoming much more important. ■

Alan Arnold

In Depth: Don't Believe Everything You See

Although TPST (see Appendix B) and SAM can be invaluable for sniffing out poorly performing programs and program instructions, they can be misleading. Knowing what these tools do and do not measure can help you correctly interpret the data they provide. Let's use SAM on COPYTEST, a C program that measures the speed of copying and moving data to and from differently aligned data sources.

COPYTEST (Figure 4.A) moves data among unaligned, aligned, and double-word aligned target fields. An **unaligned** field can start on any boundary (a **boundary**, somewhat simply put, is the address of an operand divided by 1, 4, or 8 that gives no remainder). An **aligned** field starts on a certain, predefined hardware boundary, such as a full word (a 4-byte boundary). The data in a **double-word aligned** field must fit in an 8-byte boundary.

For byte-oriented machines, such as many PCs, the only boundary is 1 byte. On most larger systems, however, the normal target boundary is at least 4 bytes. For double-word operations, such as storing an 8-byte register, the boundary must be 8 bytes. Given these hardware limitations, the performance of an operation such as a multiple-byte move can vary greatly, depending on the alignment of the target and source operands.

Figure 4.B shows COPYTEST's output: how many CPU seconds each function used. Figure 4.C shows the SAM data collected for COPYTEST while it generated the data in Figure 4.B. You would expect some differences between the SAM numbers and the program's numbers because of the variation in sampling versus the absolute values generated by the program's self-timing mechanism. In this example, however, one of the measurements varied much more widely than expected.

continued

In Depth: *continued*

Figure 4.A

C Program COPYTEST

```
#include <string.h>
#include <time.h>
#include <stdlib.h>

void clockon();
void clockoff();
float OLDCPU = 0;

main(argc, argv, envp)
   int argc;
   char *argv[];
   char *envp[];
{
    char IntStr[] = "xxxxxxxxyyyyyyyyzxxxxxxxxyyyyyyyyz", *StrPtr;
    char TrgStr[] = "                                  ";
    char dummy[] = "123";
    char TrgStrUnaligned[] = "                                  ";
    long i,j;
    long loopcount = atol(argv[1]);


  clockon();                             /*start clock            */
  for (j=1;j<=loopcount;j++) {           /*loop control           */
  strcpy(TrgStr,IntStr);     }           /*do the function        */
  clockoff();                            /*stop clock and print it*/
  printf("strcpy(TrgStr,IntStr)\n");     /*tell what function     */

  clockon();
  for (j=1;j<=loopcount;j++) {
  strcpy(TrgStrUnaligned,IntStr); }
  clockoff();
  printf("strcpy(TrgStrUnaligned,IntStr)\n");

  clockon();
  for (i=1; i<=loopcount; i++) {
  memcpy(&TrgStr[0], &IntStr[0], sizeof(IntStr)); }
  clockoff();
  printf("memcpy(&TrgStr[0], &IntStr[0], sizeof(IntStr))\n");

  clockon();
  for (i=1; i<=loopcount; i++) {
  memcpy(&TrgStrUnaligned[0], &IntStr[0], sizeof(IntStr)); }
  clockoff();
  printf("memcpy(&TrgStrUnaligned[0], &IntStr[0], sizeof(IntStr))\n");
```

continued

In Depth: *continued*

Figure 4.A *Continued*

```
 {
 void clockon() {
1  OLDCPU = clock(); }

 void clockoff() {
1 printf("%6.3f CPU seconds for      ,(float)(clock()-OLDCPU)/ 1000);}
```

Figure 4.B

COPYTEST Output

```
 Start of terminal session.      (NOTE:  SAM running)

--   2.483 CPU seconds for

          strcpy(TrgStr,IntStr)

--   2.555 CPU seconds for

          strcpy(TrgStrUnaligned,IntStr)

--   4.497 CPU seconds for

          memcpy(&TrgStr[0], &IntStr[0], sizeof(IntStr))

--   1.921 CPU seconds for

          memcpy(&TrgStrUnaligned[0], &IntStr[0], sizeof(IntStr))

 Press ENTER to end terminal session.
```

Figure 4.D compares the SAM data with the program's internal timing data. Notice that the ratio of the SAM CPU % column to the Pgm CPU % column normally varied between 1.21 and 1.28. However, statement 13 showed a ratio of 0.47. The SAM CPU % reading was much more optimistic than the actual measurement and isn't even relatively accurate for statement 13.

The reason for this discrepancy is related to how a particular system implements its runtime support routines — that is, the system programs that actually perform certain functions in a compiled program. The implementation of runtime support routines is sometimes quite platform dependent. COPYTEST used a runtime support routine for statement 13 — the aligned source and target memcpy instruction.

continued

In Depth: *continued*

FIGURE 4.C

SAM Report on COPYTEST

```
PROGRAM: COPYTEST          LIBRARY: TESTLIB

HLL Range    HLL %      Count      Histogram, scale factor 10

2             0.90        38        ****
3            27.76      1166        ***************************************

7             1.67        70        *******
8            27.95      1174        ***************************************

12            0.81        34        ****
13           18.61       782        *****************************

17            1.62        68        *******
18           20.66       868        *********************************
```

FIGURE 4.D

SAM Data vs. COPYTEST Data

HLL Stmt #	SAM CPU %	Pgm CPU %	SAM Pgm Ratio	Pgm CPU Secs
3	27.76	21.7	1.28	2.483
8	27.95	22.3	1.21	2.555
13	18.61	39.2	0.47	4.497
18	20.66	16.7	1.24	1.921

When we first defined the SAM collection environment for this program, SAM established a window over the program code space. It then sampled all instructions that executed in that code space and ignored any instructions that fell outside that area. Thus, when the program invoked the memcpy runtime support routine, SAM didn't see the support routine's instructions and didn't accumulate performance numbers for them. The program, however, timed the function from start to finish without regard for the location of the instructions.

What kind of data would we receive if we ran TPST for this program? TPST acts similarly to the internal program timer — it starts a clock when the program begins processing and stops it when the program is finished. Thus, TPST would show the full amount of CPU time taken by the program, regardless of where the program instructions were located.

continued

In Depth: *continued*

However, even TPST readings can sometimes mislead you about how the program used its CPU time. The interface to runtime support routines is not a normal external call, so the support routines don't show up in TPST's Cumulative CPU (CCPU) column as externally called programs. Instead, they show up as part of the CPU time used by the main body of the program.

Figure 4.E shows some other functions for which TPST doesn't show calls and SAM doesn't accumulate performance data. Thus, the CPU usage data on a program that used these functions might be misleading. ■

FIGURE 4.E

Some Other Problematic Functions

Main Program	System Routines
substring	RTS
mult x,10000.01	Size Exception Handler
CHKOBJ	Verify Exception Handler

CHAPTER 5

The Disk Component

In most applications, disk activity is a major portion of total response time. In gaining disk service, a job's priority is not a factor, as it is with gaining CPU access. The system grants disk service on a first-come, first-served basis. So, as the number of active jobs increases, waiting for a disk to transfer data can degrade performance.

Several factors related to disk activity influence performance. You can group these factors into six areas for consideration: physical characteristics, system characteristics, protection schemes, workload and cost, database characteristics, and query enhancements.

Physical Characteristics

The physical characteristics of the disk component consist of the disk arm and rotation speed. These characteristics determine how busy the disk arm is and how quick disk access is.

Disk Arm Utilization

One disk utilization guideline is of prime importance for performance: How busy are the disk arms? The key disk measurement for performance is the percent a disk arm is busy, not the space used on the disk, as many people think.

When the average arm utilization is less than 35 percent, your operating environment is stable. Variations and unpredictability in performance will begin occurring when utilization is between 40 and 60 percent. Performance will severely degrade with average arm utilization above 60 percent. (You can monitor this percentage with the WRKDSKSTS (Work with Disk Status) command discussed in Chapter 9 and the Performance Tools discussed in Chapters 11–14.)

Disk Access Time

New disk storage technology continues to be introduced on the AS/400. The performance of these new disk devices is a key system-design point that continues to improve and offers potentially greater total system performance.

System Characteristics

In addition to physical characteristics, you need to consider the disk component's system characteristics. These system characteristics are system paging activity, synchronous and asynchronous disk operations, the amount of data per access arm (or the number of arms accessing the data), and disk cache hits.

System Paging Activity

Paging is the way the system manages the memory resource. As you would expect, the availability of memory resource and the amount of disk I/O taking place are closely related. For details about managing the memory aspect of performance, see Chapter 6.

Synchronous Vs. Asynchronous Disk Operations

The system has two ways of handling disk operations: synchronous and asynchronous disk I/O. The system uses asynchronous disk I/O wherever possible to optimize performance. Let's examine both approaches.

Synchronous I/O

Synchronous disk I/Os occur when the job that issues the I/O request must wait for the operation to finish before continuing processing. A programmer expects synchronous I/O in database operations. For example, in a program that does a database read by key, processing must generally wait until the data is in main memory.

Another important example of synchronous disk I/O is a page fault. A page fault results when a job tries to access something that is not in main memory. The job may be trying to access program instructions, database records, or a long list of other objects it may need to continue processing. The job must wait for the page fault I/O to finish before the job continues. We will consider page faults again in Chapter 6, when we look at the memory component of performance.

Asynchronous I/O

Asynchronous disk I/O refers to operations that don't require the job to wait for the disk operation to finish. OS/400's single-level storage architecture lends itself to the use of asynchronous I/O because the I/O can occur below the Machine Interface (MI). The system uses asynchronous disk I/O wherever possible to optimize performance.

One example of asynchronous I/O occurs when a job updates a database. The record may be updated in main memory, and the job will continue processing. The disk I/O that moves the update to disk can occur later (measured in milliseconds) in a separate, or asynchronous, task below the MI. Another example is a job that is sequentially reading a file. On detecting this sequential processing, the system will often perform asynchronous disk I/O to get additional data into main memory ahead of the program's read request for the data. Because the data is already available in main memory when the job reads it, the performance of the job is significantly improved.

As these examples of asynchronous disk I/O show, OS/400's single-level storage frees the work going on above the MI from having to distinguish between

Disk I/O and Expert Cache

The system optimizes performance by using asynchronous disk I/O wherever possible. Since this optimization takes place below the MI and does not affect the MI interface, the system implementation in this area has evolved from one release to the next and continues to evolve.

The Expert Cache function introduced in V2R3 is a good example of this evolution. Expert Cache monitors the disk I/O activity and the logical reference pattern for each database file accessed within a shared storage pool. Then, Expert Cache dynamically adjusts the size and type of I/Os for these files to maximize use of main storage and minimize the number of disk I/Os. The resulting reduction in disk I/Os, particularly synchronous I/Os, can result in much faster processing. We cover Expert Cache in more detail in Chapter 6. ■

Rick Turner

main memory and disk. Another way to look at this is that user programs and system functions above the MI initiate what they consider disk I/O activity. However, it is the LIC below the MI that decides whether a disk I/O is necessary and whether the disk I/O function will be synchronous or asynchronous.

The Amount of Data per Access Arm

Another system characteristic of the disk component is the amount of data on the disk per access arm. The space used on the disk will influence performance if you run the system at high space utilization. At high space utilization, the disk allocates smaller contiguous areas of disk for data storage. This fragmentation of disk space affects the number of data bytes transferred per disk operation, thus reducing the efficiency of the disk operations. Guidelines for handling this aspect of the disk component are presented in discussions of the WRKSYSSTS command in Chapter 8 and of the WRKDSKSTS command in Chapter 9.

Disk Cache Hits

The final system characteristic we'll consider is disk cache hits. AS/400 cache techniques continue to evolve, providing improved disk I/O performance. Other techniques include the write assist device in the 9337-1XX models and the 1MB nonvolatile write cache in the 9337-2XX models. In Chapter 6, we'll provide details on how to use caching to improve performance.

The newer disk devices associated with the 6502, 6512, and 6530 disk subsystems have improved read-ahead buffers that can provide performance advantages. Read-ahead data from recent I/Os are kept in these buffers. Whether the data needed is already contained in a buffer depends on your data access patterns. If the data is in the buffer, no physical access to the disk is required. Depending on data access patterns, these buffers can significantly improve performance.

PROTECTION SCHEMES

All disk protection schemes influence performance one way or another. The disk protection schemes available are journaling, checksum, mirroring, RAID (Redundant Array of Independent Disks), user Auxiliary Storage Pools (ASPs), and save/restore activity. If you use any of these methods of protection, you need to be aware of their performance implications. If you don't use one of these protection schemes, you may have problems bigger than any performance issue some day (for example, a crashed system). Please investigate these options and implement at least one. For complete descriptions of these schemes, see the IBM *Advanced Backup and Recovery Guide.* Figure 5.1 illustrates the hardware structure for AS/400 disk.

FIGURE 5.1
Hardware Structure for AS/400 Disk

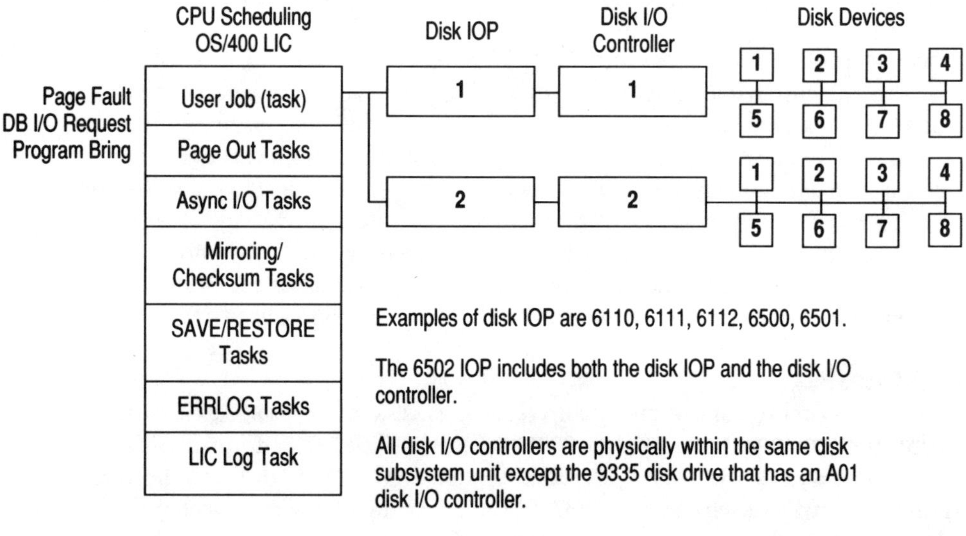

Journaling

Journaling causes synchronous disk I/O. Because synchronous I/O means you can't go on to the next transaction until the current one is finished, the speed of your disk drives is an important performance consideration when you use journaling.

Also, you need to monitor closely the placement of journal receivers to ensure you are not creating a performance bottleneck with actuator contention. If the journal receiver is in the system ASP (Auxiliary Storage Pool), the system will spread the receiver among a number of drives, each of which contains other data. If your system needs to perform a lot of operations to both the journal and non-journal objects on these drives, competition for the arm (or arm contention) will be intense. Arm contention, in turn, increases disk I/O service time. However, if you allocate a separate ASP for the journal receiver, the high disk I/O use will not cause poor performance, because the database journal is the only object in the ASP. The database manages the journal quite well, and having the journal in its own ASP optimizes journal performance.

Checksum

Checksum, the oldest and least expensive of the available protection schemes for the AS/400, affects not only the number of I/Os you generate but also adds substantial overhead to the processor. Checksum uses a parity routine that lets you lose one disk drive in a set without losing any data. Your system can go down, but the recovery is automatic.

When you use checksum, the system requires additional writes and reads to the disk to calculate parity for the checksum sets. The system also uses the CPU to calculate checksum parity, thus causing additional CPU overhead (usually between 5 and 15 percent). When implementing checksum, you must be aware that you will be giving up capacity in your disk units, that you will need extra overhead in the processor (usually between 15 and 20 percent) for running checksum, and that you will have additional I/O. If you decide to use checksum, plan to get a bigger CPU and additional auxiliary storage.

Mirroring

Mirroring is the most comprehensive protection available for the AS/400, but it is also the most expensive because you must buy twice the disk. Mirroring causes two writes instead of one — one write is to the primary drive, and one write is to its mirrored pair. In environments with heavy writes, disk mirroring can slow disk performance (you may see degradation of up to 5 percent). On the other hand, busy systems with more reads than writes can see an improvement in disk performance (at a level of 3 to 5 percent) because the system can pick the quickest path to the data on either set of drives. Most applications do far more reads than writes. Thus, in general, mirroring does not degrade performance, and may even improve it.

Most environments do not show any difference in performance with mirroring. You can mirror your system to the BUS level. This means you duplicate all components related to disk (i.e., BUS, IOP, disk controller, disk unit). One

Disk Protection

Mirroring is a preferred method of protection because it is the only way to protect your AS/400 load source internal disk drives. Because all AS/400 models, except B models, have internal disk units, such protection has been a problem. OS/400 solves this problem because it allows multiple protection schemes within the same ASP. You can mix RAID disk units, which offer much more cost-effective protection than mirroring, with mirrored disk units to protect the internal disk units in the same ASP. ■

Alan Arnold

important note: Even if you mirror your system BUS (BUS 0), if this component fails, the system will stop.

Redundant Array of Independent Disk (RAID)

RAID is the protection scheme of choice for the AS/400 because of its cost effectiveness. RAID is a variation of checksum at the disk subsystem level, with one important difference: If you lose a drive in a RAID 5 disk subsystem, the system will continue to process. The array controller at the disk subsystem level can use parity information to calculate the missing data and pass this information back to the system. Remember that in a checksum environment, you don't have data loss, but the system will go down until you replace the broken disk unit and the system can rebuild the missing data onto the new disk.

The five RAID levels differ in the way an array controller writes data and generates parity information. RAID 1 is similar to mirroring. Technically, to be true RAID 1, the disk mirroring must be at the disk subsystem level. However, on the AS/400, mirroring is optimized to the highest level of hardware protection available, most often giving system-BUS-level protection. Several manufacturers offer RAID 1 disk subsystem protection for the AS/400. The only other RAID protection that is feasible for the AS/400's business transaction environment is RAID 5. The 9337 HA (high availability) is IBM's AS/400 optimized version of RAID 5 disk. Several other manufacturers also have RAID 5 drives for the AS/400.

Because of the advanced caching techniques in RAID subsystems, performance is usually an issue only with very heavy write environments. The write cache algorithm masks the processing overhead caused by calculating parity. The primary advantage of RAID over the AS/400 checksum is that the parity is calculated by the disk subsystem and not the AS/400 CPU.

User Auxiliary Storage Pool (ASP)

User ASPs remove disk arms from general use by the system by dedicating the arms to specific data. This method can significantly change the average arm utilization, both for the system ASP and the user ASP. Monitoring arm utilization becomes even more important when you're managing user ASPs.

Save/Restore Activity

Save/restore can significantly add to the system's physical disk I/O activity. The data you are transferring influences I/O, as does the increased paging caused by the memory reserved during the save/restore process. You need to think through and schedule save/restore carefully.

Note that save/restore runs at a different priority than the job that initiated it. If you specify SAVLIB/RSTOBJ/... in a priority 50 batch job, the functions that perform the operation run at priority 51 (one higher). If the CPU is being used by jobs up to and including priority 50 (the normal batch priority), it's quite possible that the save/restore function will take a very long time to run. In addition, if you're using quarter-inch tape as the input or output medium, it's quite possible that you will encounter device errors from tape problems, and these device errors will slow down the save/restore operations even more. The recommended method is to change the submitting job's priority to 49 or even higher before you start the save/restore operation.

Workload Vs. Cost

You can separate disk I/O into two classifications: physical and logical disk I/O. The system collects data based on these classifications that you can use to show the system's workload and its associated costs in CPU used and physical disk I/O (PDIO) performed. To understand how you can use these classifications to compare workload and cost, let's first look at each classification.

Physical and Logical Disk I/O

A PDIO occurs when the system reads or writes a block of data from or to the disk device. The system performs PDIO below the MI. One form of PDIO is moving data between the disk and the LIC data frames in main memory; another occurs in servicing page faults.

A logical disk I/O (LDIO) occurs when data moves between the application program and the system's LIC data frames via the program's file ODP I/O buffer. The system's I/O management function uses the ODP to link the program's file I/O buffer with the database data frames for the file. Often, data already residing in main memory can satisfy an LDIO. Thus, on average, the system performs many LDIOs before a given physical operation is necessary.

Figure 5.2 helps distinguish between logical and physical I/O on the AS/400. In an LDIO, a job accesses data in memory; the data is transferred between the program's file ODP I/O buffer (part of the job's Process Access Group, or PAG) and database frames that exist in main storage. PDIO, on the other hand, is transfer of data between the database frames that exist in main

FIGURE 5.2
Logical and Physical I/O

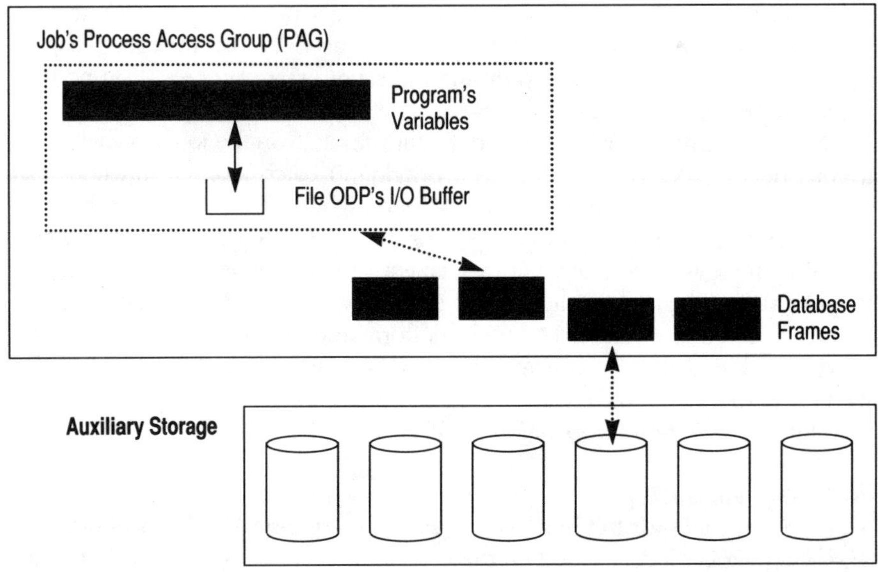

storage and the database as it exists on auxiliary storage (disk). Remember, with the AS/400's single-level storage, once the logical transfer to the database frames has taken place, the data is truly in the database and known to all the jobs in the system.

An important aspect of LDIO is that if the application's blocking and file size remain constant from one run to the next, the LDIO count is the same in each run. In contrast, PDIO will vary between runs because of paging, activity in other jobs, or changes in the size of contiguous blocks of data on the disk.

Using LDIO to Measure Workload Vs. Cost

Because of the uniformity in LDIO counts from run to run, you can use LDIO to measure workload just as you use the number of transactions that an interactive job performs. Because the LDIO count gives you a "batch transaction" that is a meaningful measure of the work the job is doing, this capability is particularly helpful for batch jobs. In addition to these measures of workload, the system also collects the associated costs in the form of CPU used and the PDIO performed.

When you can view all the work on the system as a whole, you can use disk utilization to figure out the physical I/O costs. Figure 5.3 shows the workload (LDIO and transactions) with its associated cost (CPU and disk utilization). We have multiplied the CPU and disk utilizations by 1,000 to put them on a scale comparable with the units we used for workload, which simplifies the graph. The horizontal axis is time (weeks, months, etc.). The graph helps you see the trend in the workload and its related costs over time. This ability is key in determining where you've been, where you are, and where you're going relative to system resources.

You can take this calculation a step further by computing the ratio of the costs to the workload as graphed in Figure 5.4. If the ratio of total cost to total workload goes down, either the system is doing more work or the cost of doing the work is decreasing. An increase in the ratio signals a problem you need to examine. You should expect to see a trend line that shows the ratio remaining constant.

FIGURE 5.3
Workload with Associated Costs

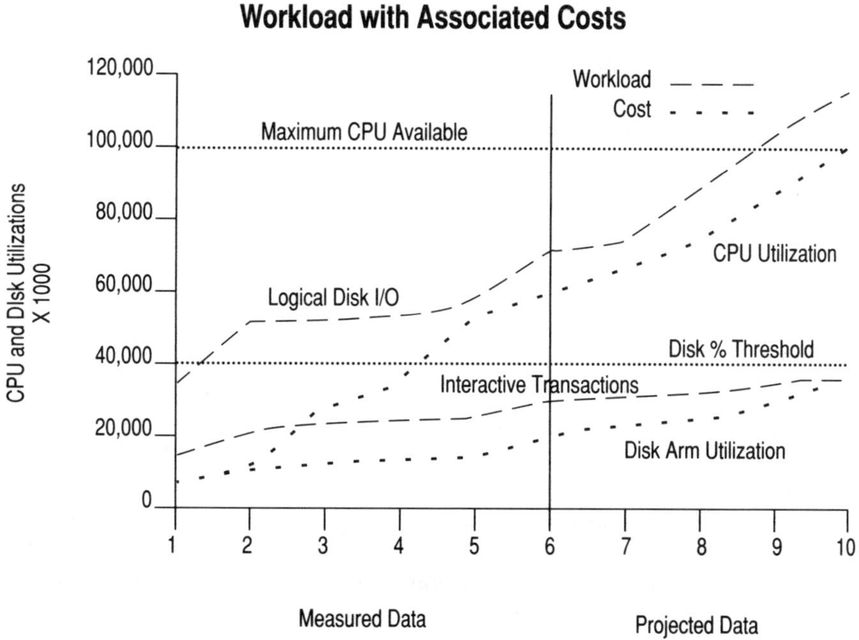

FIGURE 5.4
Ratio of Cost to Workload

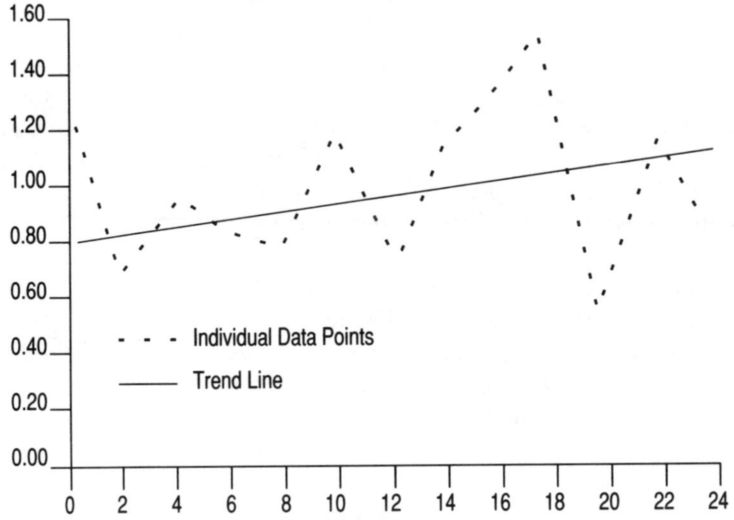

- - - Individual Data Points
——— Trend Line

DATABASE CHARACTERISTICS

Some database files are born at their full size and never change. Others grow throughout their lifetime. Obviously, such file growth devours disk space, but what does it do to processing time? The answer, as is often the case with performance issues, is "it depends."

Using algorithms designed for small files on very large files will slow processing times. And if you periodically read an entire file, processing times will inevitably increase as the file grows, requiring upgrades to improve both CPU and disk speeds. If you process only new records, however, your processing time will correspond only to the number of records added since the last time you processed the file, not to the file's total size. You may often process files in both ways: for example, processing each new order in the customer order file interactively as it occurs and processing the entire file in the weekly order-entry batch job.

However, sometimes floundering performance in the face of growing files has less to do with larger files and more to do with poor coding practices that cause nonlinear performance degradation at increased workload rates. Learning how the ASM (Auxiliary Storage Management) function handles disk space allocation for expanding files and changing some coding procedures can help you control processing time.

How Do Files Grow?

Files grow when you add records — for example, to accommodate more parts, more customers, more locations, or more employees. When you create a file using the CRTPF (Create Physical File) command, you can specify an initial disk space allocation size and a secondary allocation size that defines how much more space to assign to the file if it uses all its initial space. The file creation and extension processes use ASM, one of the system's most basic and most used Licensed Internal Code (LIC) functions. ASM allocates and deallocates disk space for the creation, extension, truncation, and deletion of system objects. To see how ASM processing works, let's look at what happens when, for example, a database function calls ASM to extend a file that's reached its maximum initial size.

ASM maintains information about disk space use through a table called the **Free Space Index** that contains the disk location and size of each piece of available space. For example, if the matrix in Table 5.1 represents units of space on a disk, with "U" meaning "in use" and "A" meaning "available," the Free Space Index might look like Table 5.2.

TABLE 5.1
Location of Space on Disk

	A	B	C	D
1	U	U	A	U
2	A	A	U	A
3	U	A	U	U

TABLE 5.2
Sample Free Space Index

Location	Number of blocks available
C1	2
A2	1
B2	1
D2	2
B3	3

To satisfy the file extension request, ASM accesses the Free Space Index, finds an appropriate amount of space on a disk drive, and allocates it to the file. During ASM's space allocation processing, it removes from the Free Space

Index the record signifying the newly allocated space, thereby ensuring that the same piece of disk can't be used to satisfy some other space request. A delete request, such as DLTF (Delete File), causes ASM to return the space occupied by the deleted file to the Free Space Index.

ASM Overload

ASM's processing is serialized, meaning it processes one disk space request at a time. So when a hundred or more requests per second are arriving at ASM (which is not an uncommon situation), some of them will wait. To ensure you aren't wasting ASM and CPU processing time by repeatedly allocating and deallocating disk space, you need to set reasonable initial and secondary allocation values when you create a database file.

One way to estimate initial file size is to multiply record size by the number of records in the file. If you have a 200-byte customer record and 500 customers, you need a minimum of 100,000 bytes of storage. If your company is estimating 20 percent annual growth in the number of customers, the file at the end of n years should require $200 \times 500 \times 1.20^n$ bytes.

But specifying ample initial and secondary storage when you create a file doesn't mean you won't have any performance problems. Your applications use ASM for much more than just creating and extending database files. In fact, the process of extending a database file's allocated space is usually an infrequent ASM user. Other operations generate many more ASM requests, using precious processing time and making other requests wait. But you can often curb these operations' need for processing time with proper coding procedures.

Coding for Disk Performance

In our discussion of CPU performance issues in Chapter 4, we suggested many ways to improve the performance of your applications, including avoiding full database file opens and closes by keeping the files open, using shared Open Data Paths (ODPs), and using Return instead of setting on LR in RPG for frequently called programs. We recommend these methods because functions such as repetitive full database file opens of the same file increase the use of ASM's space allocation functions, shared ODPs reduce the number of objects allocated, and keeping a program active reduces the number of times program initialization and termination functions must invoke ASM to create and destroy space for program variables.

For example, one full database open allocates five new system objects, and each full close deletes them. It's not unusual to see systems with 15, 20, or more full open/close operations per second. Twenty opens/closes per second require 100 invocations of ASM for the create and delete functions. Add to the mix a bunch of RPG programs returning with LR set on (or Cobol programs using STOP RUN instead of EXIT) and a good measure of file transfers that allocate

Reducing Processing Time

One shop I worked with had an application that took a couple of days to read an entire file. The application programs were extracting the necessary data for all processing in the first pass and then building temporary output files and processing them sequentially in subsequent parallel processing steps. The company modified the programs to perform just one pass over the data and cut a huge chunk out of its file processing time. Other companies have reduced processing time by using various file sorting options. One company's sort took two to four hours, followed by one to two hours of processing -- but it certainly beat the original runtime of three-and-a-half days. ■

Rick Turner

new space for each object being sent or received, and you have a very busy ASM. ASM gets even busier when you add such operations as spool file allocation, Query/400 executions using select/omit logic, and development programmers doing editing and testing. In addition, ASM performs its own tracking functions, logging everything it does so that a system failure won't leave its indexes and other controls in an undetermined state.

But when proper coding procedures still don't seem to help, you need to go back to the application's design. Ensuring that your applications take into account the following issues can improve the performance of your disk component.

Random Processing by Relative Record

On the AS/400, relative-record processing is very efficient. Use it when you have a choice of ways to access data randomly. A word of caution, though — it is an older access method and can cause problems if you try to extend it to new database technologies. For example, the new multi-system database support for the AS/400 does not support relative-record processing.

Sequential-Only Processing

You want to fully exploit opportunities to process records sequentially. The sequential-only processing of a database file can increase asynchronous disk I/O, which, combined with the blocking support available with sequential-only processing, can significantly improve a job's performance.

The parameter SEQONLY(*YES number-of-records) appears on both the OVRDBF (Override with Database File) and the OPNDBF (Open Database File) commands. The number-of-records field specifies the blocking support between the user program and the system's database management support. For the blocking to take effect, you must open the file for sequential input only or sequential output only.

Updating with SEQONLY

Don't rule out the use of SEQONLY on files that you are updating. If the program is reading the file sequentially and updating only some records, consider opening the same file twice: one open for input only and the other open for update. This approach allows blocking and asynchronous disk I/O to occur on the input file. ■

Jim Stewart

Shared Access Paths

Contrary to the belief of many AS/400 programmers, performance gains do not come from minimizing the number of logical files but instead from minimizing the number of unique access paths. The more access paths, the more system resources are necessary to update them when you add or delete records. When you create a logical file, the system checks whether the new file can use an existing access path.

Be aware that select/omit in logical files also interferes with access path sharing. When a logical file selects different records from another logical file, the system creates unique access paths that cannot be shared.

Database Force Ratio

The force write ratio parameter (FRCRATIO) on the Create Physical File command (or the Override Database File command) specifies the number of insert,

Reducing Disk I/O

The top seven ways, in order of importance, to reduce disk I/O and cut your processing time are listed below.

1. Avoid full database file open and close operations by keeping files open.
2. Use Return instead of setting on LR in RPG (or EXIT instead of STOP RUN in Cobol) for frequently called programs.
3. Modify application programs to perform fewer passes over the data.
4. Sort the data before processing.
5. Get rid of deleted records in database files that are processed sequentially.
6. Use shared Open Data Paths.
7. Archive excess data offline or in separate files in other auxiliary storage pools.

Implementing these recommendations will eliminate more than 90 percent of the performance problems most shops face. ■

Rick Turner

delete, or update operations that can occur before these files changes are forced to disk. Low force write ratios interfere with the system's tendency to use asynchronous processing when writing output to database files. Using a force ratio of 1 in a database file causes synchronous output and can seriously degrade performance. Although a low force write ratio can ensure database integrity, journaling is more effective because the system optimizes journaling I/O.

Query Enhancements

Two enhancements for queries were released as part of DB2 for OS/400 announcements for Version 3, Release 1: symmetric multiprocessing (SMP) and multiple key positioning.

SMP provides query performance far beyond that available before V3R1. It consists of query optimization techniques that are leading edge. Combining AS/400 N-way architecture, DB2 for OS/400, and DB2 SMP for OS/400 can give you new levels of scalability, ease-of-use, and price/performance.

Taking advantage of SMP's benefits is simple. The Change Query Attributes (CHGQRYA) Command in V3R1 includes a DEGREE keyword, with parameters of *ANY or *IO. These new options influence the way the system uses the disk and memory components.

The OS/400 database has always been supported by significant parallel processing. Specialized I/O tasks run below the Machine Interface (MI) to asynchronously write changed database pages to auxiliary storage. Asynchronous tasks that bring data into main storage in anticipation of an application's I/O have also evolved over time (Expert Cache is a good example). However, up to this point, most of the parallel processing has been automatic. SMP and the DEGREE parameter give the user some control over the parallel processing used by the DB2/400 query component.

In V3R1, a value of DEGREE(*ANY) on the CHGQRYA command establishes a job attribute that significantly increases parallel I/O processing of the job's query requests. If the job is running in a shared storage pool that has Expert Cache enabled (see the section on Expert Cache in Chapter 6), the DEGREE(*ANY) job attribute will cause asynchronous I/O tasks, running below the MI, to do parallel pre-load of data space records or index reads to get data into main storage to support the job's query request. You could think of this support as a Set Object Access (SETOBJAC) command without the use of a private pool. Underlying controls keep the memory level used by the job to 50 percent of the available memory in the storage pool. Thus, the impact to other jobs running in the pool is kept under control.

This support shows the most benefit when you do not use an index and the query component accesses data with a data space scan. The parallel preload facility can be used with any of the other methods for data access, such as key selection, key positioning and index-from-index methods. The pre-load is started when the query is opened and control is returned to the application while the pre-load is running in parallel. The application continues fetching rows using the other database access methods without knowing that the pre-load is running.

The more main storage that is available, the greater the benefit that pre-loading provides. The pre-load function caches the data retrieved by the multiple input tasks. For large files, the typical extent size is 1 MB; thus, 2 MB of main storage must be available to use two input tasks. Increasing the amount of main storage available allows more parallel input tasks to be used.

You should limit the number of jobs that are running with CHGQRYA DEGREE(*ANY) because the parallel pre-load will aggressively use main storage and disk I/O resources. Any performance benefit would be lost if other jobs are competing to get their data pre-loaded.

DB2 SMP can be ordered as a feature of OS/400 V3R1. The product number is 4733-SP1.

Multiple Key Positioning, another V3R1 extension designed to help query processing, allows you to use multiple keys for positioning in the index. Before V3R1, the key positioning method positioned on only the single left-most key.

With V3R1, key positioning now handles more than one key as long as the keys are contiguous to the left-most key. A starting value is built by concatenating all the selection values and the selection is positioned to the index entry whose left-most keys have that value. You should look at adding indexes with wider key selection to see whether some of your more important queries can be improved. One of the primary benefits of this new feature is that the queries will not only run faster but also use less CPU and have fewer I/Os, which benefits other users competing for these resources.

Multiple key positioning can improve the performance of your queries considerably. Some programmers have termed this support as a wider **frogger.** With it, when you **leap** into the data to get what you want, you can leap farther.

CHAPTER 6

The Memory Component

A transaction requires memory to contain programs and data for the CPU to work with. If both the program and the data are in main memory, a transaction can be completed without delay. A transaction that needs memory for either the program or data will wait while the system allocates memory and brings the objects into memory from disk, thus delaying job processing and degrading performance.

Figuring out how much memory you need so that jobs aren't waiting for data or a program is an imprecise science at best. To manage the memory component of performance, you can adjust two variables: the amount of memory available to jobs and the workload.

PARTITIONING MEMORY

The AS/400 organizes main memory into storage pools. By separating work into different main storage pools, you can help keep different types of work from competing for the same main storage.

When your AS/400 is powered on and goes through the Initial Program Load (IPL) sequence, the Licensed Internal Code (LIC) and OS/400 startup functions allocate the system's memory into two pools: the **machine** pool and the **base** pool. Critical system tasks run in the machine pool; all other memory is allocated to the base pool. You can further split the base pool into as many as 15 additional pools. Many companies segment the base pool into the interactive, batch, and spool pools.

Let's look at the WRKSYSSTS (Work with System Status) display in Figure 6.1. The system pool column on this display shows that the system's main storage is divided into four system storage pools. System pool number 1 is the machine pool (*MACHINE). Active jobs and tasks (such as the workstation I/O managers) that run system functions use this memory. The system value QMCHPOOL controls pool 1's size, and you can adjust it with the CHGSYSVAL (Change System Value) command.

System pool number 2 is the base pool (*BASE). The base pool contains all the storage that is not allocated to other system pools. The system value QBASPOOL controls the base pool's minimum size. As you create main storage pools, they take storage from *BASE until the size of *BASE reaches the value you specified in QBASPOOL.

The other possible system pools, 3 through 16, come into existence only if you start a subsystem that allocates main storage.

FIGURE 6.1
WRKSYSSTS Display

```
                         Work With System Status                          PERF1
                                                          06/16/96     12:00:01

% CPU used ..........:        5.5          Auxiliary Storage:
Elapsed time ........:   00:00:30            System  ASP ..........:    5207 M
Jobs in system  .....:        228            % System ASP Used ....:  81.1072
% Addresses Used:                            Total ................:    5207 M
  Permanent  ........:      5.804            Current unprotect used:     270 M
  Temporary .........:      1.755            Max unprotect  .......:     279 M

System     Pool        Reserved     Max      DB       DB     Non-DB       Non-DB
 Pool    Size (K)     Size (K)   Active   Faults    Pages   Faults        Pages
  1       11200         7394       +++      .0       .0      .0            .0
  2        8000                      7      .0       .0      .0            .0
  3       78964            0        74      .0       .0      .0            .0
  4         140            0         3      .0       .0      .0            .0
                                                                         Bottom

Command
===>_________________________________________________________________
F3=Exit     F10=Restart    F11=Transition Data    F12=Previous    F24=More Keys
F14=Subsystems                F15=Active Jobs               F16=Disk Status
```

Subsystems

Subsystems let you group specific types of work, which is an advantage to the system, because jobs doing the same type of work can share objects that are in memory. For example, users running the same application share program code. Only one copy of a program is necessary in main memory to support all users that are executing the program.

Subsystems can also be divided into up to 10 separate subsystem storage pools. You use the CRTSBSD (Create Subsystem Description) command to define subsystem pools to use when a subsystem becomes active. The Storage Pools parameter on CRTSBSD calls for three values to describe a subsystem pool: the pool identifier (the subsystem pool number, 1 through 10); storage size (in multiples of 1k = 1024 bytes) assigned from *BASE if the pool will be a private pool, or a special value for a system-supplied shared pool; and activity level. Before we consider the difference between private and shared subsystem pools, let's first look at the relationship between system pools and subsystem pools.

The WRKSBS (Work with Subsystems) display in Figure 6.2 shows the relationship between system pools and subsystem pools for the active subsystems. WRKSBS lists the active subsystems in order, with the one started most recently listed first. For a given subsystem, the number under each subsystem pool is the system pool assigned to it. The system pool numbers are assigned based on the order in which you start the subsystems.

For example, in Figure 6.2, QSPL is the second subsystem started. Its subsystem description specified two subsystem pools. The first subsystem pool designates *BASE, so the system assigns system storage pool 2 to it. The second subsystem pool designates storage distinct from *BASE, so system pool 3 comes into existence. The fourth subsystem started, QINTER, also specified two subsystem pools, *BASE and storage that is distinct from both *BASE and system pool 3, so system pool 4 was created. All the other subsystem pools (3 through 10) are blank, indicating that they were not defined on the CRTSBSD command.

As you can see, the system's use of the numbers 1 through 10 to name the **subsystem** pools and its use of the numbers 1 through 16 to designate **system** storage pools can cause major confusion. Be sure to understand the differences between the two as you work with memory partitioning.

Private Vs. Shared Subsystem Pools

When you create a subsystem using the CRTSBSD command, you specify the size of any subsystem storage pools you want to create. If you specify a storage-size number on the Storage Pools parameter, the pool that results when the subsystem becomes active is a private pool that only jobs running in the subsystem

FIGURE 6.2
Work with Subsystems Screen

```
                          Work with Subsystems

Type options, press Enter.
  4=End sybsystem   5=Display subsystem description
  8=Work with subsystem jobs

                    Total     ----------Subsystem Pools------------
Opt  Subsystem   Storage (K)  1   2   3   4   5   6   7   8   9  10
 _    QBATCH            Ø     2   5
 _    QCMN              Ø     2
 _    QCTL              Ø     2
 _    QINTER            Ø     2   4
 _    QSNADS            Ø     2
 _    QSPL              Ø     2   3
 _    QSYSWRK           Ø     2

                                                                Bottom
Parameters or command
===>_____________________________________________________________________
F3=Exit   F5=Refresh   F11=Display system data   F12=Cancel
F14=Work with system status
```

and routed to the pool may use. If you specify storage size by using a special value allowed for the parameter, the resulting pool is a shared pool. The system provides 13 shared storage pools. The special values you can use for the shared pools are: *BASE, *INTERACT, *SPOOL, and *SHRPOOL1 through *SHRPOOL10.

In Figure 6.2, the Total Storage value on the Work with Subsystems display reflects only the private storage assigned to the pool. The Total Storage value is 0 for the QSPL subsystem; therefore, we know that the storage size of subsystem pool number 2 was one of the shared values. To find out which shared pool was designated, use Option 5 on this display.

Shared pools are very useful if you want to separate similar work into different subsystems for scheduling or control purposes, but, because it is similar work, you want to run it in a common pool. An example is a local group of phone order-entry operators and a remote group of operators. For control purposes, you can have two subsystems, say OELCLSBS and OERMTSBS. Because the operators are all using the same application (doing similar work), you can use a shared storage pool (*INTERACT or *SHRPOOL1 - 10) in each subsystem. Use the WRKSHRPOOL (Work with Shared Pools) command to define the size and activity level (Max Active) for the shared pools (Figure 6.3).

FIGURE 6.3

Work with Shared Pools Display

```
                        Work with Shared Pools                  System: PERF1

Main storage size (K) . . :  327680

Type changes (if allowed), press Enter
               Defined    Max   Allocated    Pool
Pool           Size (K)  Active  Size (K)     ID
*MACHINE        50000     +++       50000      1
*BASE          122680      15      122680      2
*INTERACT       50000      10       50000      4
*SPOOL           5000       7        5000      3
*SHRPOOL1        1000       1
*SHRPOOL2          32       1
*SHRPOOL3      100000      12      100000      5
*SHRPOOL4          32       1
*SHRPOOL5       15000       1
*SHRPOOL6           0       0

                                                                More...
Command
===>
F3=Exit   F4=Prompt   F5=Refresh   F9=Retrieve   F11=Display text
F12=Cancel
```

Work Entries and Routing Entries

The complex trail we have been following through system storage pools and subsystem storage pools has yet another turn when we consider work assignments. When a job first becomes active, what determines the subsystem it will run in, and what determines the particular subsystem pool it will execute in? The work entries that you add to a subsystem description control which subsystem a given job will run in.

Work entries describe how jobs gain access to the subsystem for processing. Work can enter a subsystem from five sources: the autostart job entry (ADDAJE), workstation entry (ADDWSE), job queue entry (ADDJOBQE), communications entry (ADDCMNE), and prestart job entry (ADDPJE). In your subsystem description, you specify the work entry for each of these sources using the commands in parentheses.

Routing determines how jobs are processed after they reach the subsystem. Any job will have routing data associated with it. For many jobs, routing data comes from the job description or from the routing data (RTGDTA) parameter on the command that started the job. For a communications job, the routing data can come from information that the program start request receives. You add a routing entry to a subsystem description with the ADDRTGE (Add Routing Entry) command. The system compares the job's routing data against values in the subsystem's routing entries. A match between the job's routing data and the subsystem's routing entry determines, among other things, the pool the job will run in.

We have now followed the trail of a particular job as it ends up in a given system storage pool. Before we leave the topic, note that you specify another important performance-related parameter on the ADDRTGE command: the name of the class object the job uses, which determines its RUNPTY (Run Priority) and its time slice. You issue the CRTCLS (Create Class) command to create a class object. Thus, the same path that determines the system storage pool in which a job runs also determines the job's priority and its time slice.

Monitoring and Limiting Workload

Monitoring your workload's demands on your system's memory is complex. You can't directly measure the amount of memory any given job uses. However, you can estimate memory requirements from controlled tests and you can infer the demand on your system's memory from other measurements.

Estimating Memory Needs

An accurate and relatively easy way to estimate a job's memory needs is to conduct a controlled test in which a repeatable set of transactions are performed by a certain number of jobs in a given amount of memory.

To ensure that the memory storage pool is swept clean of any pages that contain programs or data used by the job, which would skew the results, run the CLRPOOL (Clear Pool) command before each run and before changing pool sizes. CLRPOOL doesn't allow you to clear the interactive pool, but you can circumvent this restriction. Just transfer your job to the base pool using the TFRJOB (Transfer Job) command and then run CLRPOOL, specifying the interactive pool number (found on the WRKSYSSTS display) instead of *INTERACT.

For each run, record the pool size and the performance numbers. To get the most accurate job performance data, you should also run the test with multiple copies of the same job running. You'll likely find that jobs sharing the same data will require less main memory than jobs working on different data, because the shared data will probably already be in main storage for quick access.

Once you've conducted your runs, plot your results to find the minimum pool-size setting you can use and still achieve acceptable performance. As pool size decreases, performance degrades. Your performance metric is an arbitrary value that you must define based on the level of performance that is acceptable in your situation.

Obviously, job performance observed in a controlled test will vary from that of a live production environment. For example, the machine pool's RESERVED size (the amount of memory reserved for the system's dispatching and memory management functions) is determined by a number of factors, including the number of jobs currently running on the system. Each job or LIC task requires 1K of machine pool. This doesn't seem like a lot, but when you have 1,000 interactive jobs all using PC Support, the requirements aren't trivial.

Inferring Memory Demand

When you're ready to try to improve the performance of the memory component, you can infer the effect of memory demand by checking the page faulting rates in the system storage pools. A database (DB) fault occurs when the job references database data or a database index that is not in main memory. A non-database (NDB) fault occurs if a job addresses an object, such as a program, data queue, office document, or user profile, that is not in memory.

The amount of main storage a job uses and the paging it experiences vary over time, depending on the job's size and the demand for memory by other jobs running concurrently in the same storage pool. On systems that are performing well, the page fault rate in each storage pool is usually 10 to 20 NDB faults per second, though on large systems it may go to 100 faults per second in the interactive pool and still run well. Pool 1, the machine pool, is critical to system performance. The NDB fault rate in the machine pool should be between one and three faults per second, or two to five faults per second on a system with remote communications lines. (See IBM's AS/400 *Work Management Guide*, SC41-3306, for current guidelines on pool faulting rates.)

A page fault is a signal that a job needs additional memory. As a result of a page fault, the system reads DB or NDB pages into main memory. If a page is available in the same pool in which the job is running, storage management reads the data into that page. However, if all page frames contain data, the system steals a page from another job to satisfy the current job's needs. When the system steals a page and the data in the page has been changed, the system must write the changed data to disk before reading in the new data. Needless to say, this takes more time than simply writing to an empty page. When it chooses a page to steal, storage management selects the least recently used pages of memory without regard to job priority.

If multiple jobs share insufficient main memory, the result can be increased I/O, along with the CPU needed to perform it. This increase is non-productive and leads to diminished throughput and longer response times. Making more memory available to a set of jobs can help increase the disk and CPU resources available on the system.

The system collects the same performance information during regular intervals for each main storage pool and records this information in database file QAPMPOOL using the STRPFRMON (Start Performance Monitor) command. If you have the Performance Tools Licensed Program Product, you can see this information in three reports: the System Report, which is a summary of the entire collection period; the Component Report, which is a summary by pool for each collection interval; and the Pool Report, which provides detail by interval by pool. For more information about using Performance Tools, see Chapters 11 through 14.

You can take several steps to diminish your workload's contention for memory. Structuring system storage pools so they contain the same type of work is important. If you have enough available memory, you can run each batch job in its own storage pool to eliminate page stealing by other jobs. This approach works well because pages are stolen only from the pool that the job is running in. If the job is stealing pages from itself (especially database pages, as a high database fault rate in the pool suggests), you need to add memory to the pool to reduce the fault rate to a reasonable level.

You should also carefully consider when to use a save/restore command. The memory an active save/restore process uses is not available to other jobs. Also note that a concurrent save/restore in either the batch or the interactive pool will probably increase paging in the pool.

CONTROLLING THE CONTENTS OF MEMORY POOLS

Two features on the AS/400 help you tune the performance of system memory. The SETOBJACC (Set Object Access) command gives you control over what data is in a particular storage pool. The Expert Cache function automatically

In Depth: Page Frames

Main storage consists of a fixed number of bytes of memory partitioned into 512-byte chunks called page frames. The system uses these page frames to transfer data between disk (which is also arranged in page frames) and main storage. To give you an idea of how many page frames you may have to work with, a 4 MB machine contains 8,000 page frames of data.

In the early days of defining the basic hardware architecture of the System/38 and what would become the AS/400, developers defined the entry-level system's storage size as 128 KB. This was a compromise between the 24 KB minimum and 512 KB maximum total storage available on the System/38, which the new system was replacing. Because multiple versions of main storage management weren't feasible, all systems had to use the same page frame size for moving data in and out of main storage. Developers settled on 512 bytes as the most reasonable page-frame value to accommodate a range of main-storage sizes within the System/38 family. In retrospect, developers probably should have chosen a page frame at least four to eight times larger to be able to transfer data faster and with less overhead.

What, exactly, is in a given page frame? The system answers this basic but important question several thousand times each second. The simple answer is that a page frame contains 512 bytes of data, such as part of a database file or program. When a job needs data, the hardware must find that data and make it available via main memory as quickly as possible. If a page frame containing the needed data is already in memory, the job continues processing; otherwise, the hardware alters the job's flow of instructions to have the system's storage management functions move that data from disk to memory in one or more page frames and reestablish normal instruction processing.

So how does the hardware know whether a page frame contains the needed data? Each frame contains either valid or invalid data (i.e., data that is or isn't in main storage, respectively). If the data is valid, it has a virtual address. The application program instruction presents this virtual address to the hardware, which, in turn, uses storage management to determine which page frame contains the needed data. To make the connection between the virtual address and the page frame, the hardware uses a black-box lookup process, with the input being the virtual address and the output being the page frame address.

All this background shows that what the manuals call a "page fault" is really an "address fault" — that is, the data specified by the virtual address isn't in main storage. When such a fault occurs, the hardware invokes storage management to find the needed data on disk and read it into an available page frame. The number of page frames required to satisfy a fault depends primarily on the type of data the job needs. For example, if the job needs program instructions, the system usually brings data into memory in 4K chunks. If the job requires part of a database file, the normal transfer size is 2K chunks, but that number can vary widely depending on whether you specified blocking with the OVRDBF (Override with Database File) command, are using Expert Cache or sorting the data, or are preloading data into a pool with the SETOBJACC (Set Object Access) command. ■

tunes the amount of data read into memory and the length of time it stays there. Let's consider each of these features in detail.

Set Object Access

The SETOBJACC (Set Object Access) command lets you explicitly control what data is in a storage pool and how long it stays there. You **preload** application data into main storage so the system can access that data at the speed of the CPU and main storage, rather than at the much slower pace of the disk.

Be forewarned, though — using this command isn't as easy as flipping a switch. To get the most out of SETOBJACC, you need memory to spare and the time to figure out the right information to preload.

SETOBJACC Benefits

SETOBJACC can dramatically improve the performance of jobs that access a database file randomly (i.e., jobs that do keyed reads). Without preloading, an application that does random processing of a file often reads data synchronously, one record at a time. Because the AS/400's data management functions don't know which record the job wants next, the system can't do asynchronous read-ahead buffering for the job, as it can with sequential access. When the application issues a read request that the data management functions must schedule as a synchronous disk I/O operation, the job must wait until the system has brought the data in from disk.

To get an idea of how long that wait can be, consider a file with 100 MB of data, which uses 200,000 pages in memory. At 0.020 seconds per read, an application would need more than an hour to read just half the pages synchronously. SETOBJACC can preload that data in one-half to one-fifth the time it takes the application program to read it because the loading occurs with multiple overlapped, asynchronous blocked reads.

SETOBJACC is best suited for jobs with large amounts of database disk I/O. In those jobs, random access to physical and logical files causes much longer runtime than does sequential access to the same data. One type of database file processing that's a good candidate for preloading is one with high synchronous read activity (lots of random keyed reads). Sequentially processed and output-only files probably are not good candidates — they usually don't cause jobs to wait as much for disk I/O and don't require as much memory as randomly processed input files.

When to Use SETOBJACC

It isn't easy to identify which files might gain the most from preloading with SETOBJACC, because you can't get a count of the physical disk I/O by file. Your best option for assessing file activity is to get a count of logical disk I/O by file within a job, which represents processing in the system's database that relates to the job's file-processing activity. It doesn't directly represent any physical disk I/O operations, but it might give you a lead on files that might have high disk activity.

You get this value by running the Performance Tools DSPACCGRP (Display Access Group) command over the jobs you're interested in, directing the output to an outfile, and then using the ANZACCGRP (Analyze Access Group) command's File Report to see which files have the most logical-file I/O activity. (For more information about working with Performance Tools, see Chapters 11 through 14.) You can also observe a job's logical I/O operations by file via the WRKJOB (Work with Job) command's option 14, Display Open Files, which shows open files by name and by the number of I/O operations. (Remember that with DSPACCGRP and WRKJOB, you're getting only a snapshot of system performance.)

In addition, if the job is processing logical files, there's no indication in the job as to which underlying physical file(s) are being processed. SETOBJACC can preload the logical files, but you'll probably get better performance if you also use it to identify and preload the associated physical files.

Once you know which files you're going to preload, you need to determine whether these files, or a subset of them, will fit into a main storage pool. If the pool can hold all of a database file's data, all read accesses to the file occur without a disk read, doing away with a good deal of the disk input-processing time for that file. If all the files won't fit into memory simultaneously, you must determine whether the work requires that all files be in memory at the same time or whether they can be loaded separately. Even if your files are too large to load in their entirety, you might still see some improvement by preloading the database file indexes.

To determine file size, apply the DSPFD (Display File Description) command to the database files you want to preload. Multiply the number of records (including the number of deleted records) by the record size. The SETOBJACC loaded file size will be about 20 KB to 30 KB larger, to provide room for operating system overhead. If a file has many deleted records and you're not using the Reuse Deleted Records option on the database file, you should reduce the file's memory requirement beforehand by eliminating the deleted records.

To determine a **program**'s main storage requirement, use SETOBJACC's completion message, CPC1141, rather than the DSPOBJD (Display Object Description) command, which shows program elements such as debug tables and MI program templates that don't pertain to executable instructions. Message CPC1141 tells you the amount of memory used to load the executable instructions and other parts of the program needed for execution. It also tells you the unused space in the pool before loading the object. Compare the amount of space the object requires to the amount of available pool space to be sure there's adequate space.

If an object doesn't fit into the pool, part of it will be overlaid when SETOBJACC is run (SETOBJACC assumes that the entire pool is available), in which case you may not get the expected performance results. Because object loading uses asynchronous, block-transferred disk operations and SETOBJACC issues simultaneous asynchronous reads for an object's data, the loading process doesn't preserve the data sequence. As a result, there's no guarantee that the latter part of the object will overlay the first part.

SETOBJACC lets you specify whether to load data into a specific pool (private or shared) or the pool in which your job is running. If you specified a pool other than the job's pool and the object was only partially loaded, faults that occur on the object create database page faults and subsequent disk I/O operation in the job's storage pool. Page faults can also occur when you process added records. After SETOBJACC has loaded (or even partially loaded) a file, all of that file's loaded pages are in the specified storage pool, even if they were already in memory and in different pools before you issued SETOBJACC. In other words, SETOBJACC consolidates file pages already in memory into the destination pool specified on the command.

SETOBJACC doesn't make the data permanently resident in memory, so if you use the current job's pool, the system can steal the data to satisfy a page fault or perform other processing that requires storage pool memory.

On the other hand, if you use a dedicated shared pool, make sure IBM's automatic storage pool tuner isn't active by setting system value QPFRADJ to zero. You want to turn off the tuner because there will be no paging activity in the pool, and the IBM tuner reduces pool size dramatically when there's no paging activity. Reducing the pool size will cause the pages containing the preloaded data to end up in other pools and probably get stolen to satisfy paging requirements in those pools. To guarantee that the data stays in memory, you should use a separate, private pool.

You might want to load data into the job's pool rather than a separate pool when you're running multiple batch jobs simultaneously and there aren't enough pools for all jobs to use. You could still take advantage of preloading by running each batch job in its own pool and telling SETOBJACC to load data into the job's pool. How you configure your pool setup depends on the amount of time that a number of different batch jobs are running together, the size of the files you want to preload, and the amount of available memory.

Everybody Out of the Pool

You empty the pool you use for preloading on two occasions, and each time requires a different technique. When you first allocate the pool, you should use the CLRPOOL (Clear Pool) command. To remove preloaded files from the pool, you use SETOBJACC's *PURGE option after allocation.

CLRPOOL gets rid of **everything** in the pool and is not interruptible. Once it starts, you can't cancel it; it runs until the pool is empty. CLRPOOL writes all changed pages in a pool to disk and indicates that all pages in the pool are empty. The first time you run the command, it may run for a long time if there are lots of changed pages in the pool. If you've set up a separate pool for data and that pool exists at IPL time, the best time to clear it is immediately after IPL, when the pool contains the fewest changed pages.

When you're finished with the preloaded files, you then purge objects explicitly using SETOBJACC. SETOBJACC passes a list of object addresses to the AS/400's storage management, which can efficiently locate the objects' pages and asynchronously block writes to disk. The *PURGE option removes objects entirely from main storage.

*PURGE can be helpful for batch work in which multiple steps use the same file — you can use SETOBJACC to preserve the file in main storage across job steps. You should occasionally review the batch job logs to be sure pre-loaded objects continue to fit in the pool. *PURGE also comes in handy when you don't use a separate pool and a job step uses several files, one or more of which are going to be used in the subsequent job step — use *PURGE for the files that aren't used in the next step.

Reading, Writing, and Runtime

Once you've preloaded a file using SETOBJACC, there will be few if any physical database reads. Database writes, however, will still be handled the same way — usually asynchronously to the user's job by system output tasks. Because the system processes database reads much faster once a file is preloaded, programs that also do updates, adds, or deletes may do database writes more frequently, causing occasional overrun of the system output tasks. If an overrun occurs, there will be a small amount of physical disk I/O that the job must wait for. However, if all the data fits into the storage pool, the job will probably be much faster with preloading than without it.

Don't forget to measure performance before and after using SETOBJACC to evaluate the effect of preloading in **your** processing environment. And always keep track of objects loaded and purged. If you don't track and manage pool contents properly, you won't get all the performance improvements you're looking for.

Expert Cache

Another way to manage the memory component is with Expert Cache. A **cache** — a temporary data repository — makes frequently used data more rapidly accessible to the component that needs it. Expert Cache takes advantage of OS/400's single-level storage architecture by using main storage as a

In Depth: Cache Flow

Expert Cache tunes itself according to the demand for data and the way data is loaded into main storage. It monitors applications as they access objects, analyzes and categorizes how each job accesses the data — randomly, which means small transfer sizes, or sequentially, which means large — and then varies the amount of data transferred accordingly.

Expert Cache classifies object access behavior as follows:

- Access is random (i.e., unpredictable); a disk operation occurs for almost every record a job accesses.
- Access is somewhat predictable (in IBM parlance, it has some "locality of reference"); several records are accessed per disk operation.
- Access is localized and predictable within a limited range inside the object (high locality of reference); the job processes one segment immediately after processing its neighbor (sequential processing). Also, large portions of the object are in main storage.

Once it classifies the object access behavior, Expert Cache acts on the object by varying the transfer size and by ensuring that highly used database data stays in memory longer. When a job can effectively use more than one page (512 bytes) of data, Expert Cache uses **data blocking**. That is, it brings from disk into main storage a large block of data, most or all of which it expects the job to use, to enable the most efficient use of data and memory. Depending on the amount of data the job uses, Expert Cache varies the blocking factor up to 128 KB for database and 32 KB for nondatabase objects.

Many jobs access data that's both logically and physically adjacent in the same object. When Expert Cache detects this sequential processing, it does an **anticipatory read** — that is, it starts another read before the job asks for the data so that the data is in memory by the time the job is ready for it. ■

dynamic cache for database files and other objects being accessed within a shared storage pool.

How Expert Cache Works

Jobs go through phases — for example, first accessing data and building output records and then sorting the output and printing a report. Each phase has characteristic patterns of CPU utilization and disk access. Under normal storage management, a job's request for data causes the system to transfer a fixed amount into memory. Expert Cache changes the way the AS/400 manages data transfer by automatically changing the amount of data read from DASD into memory and varying the length of time changed database data stays in memory. These dynamic adjustments optimize main storage utilization and minimize the volume of DASD I/O per object (such as a database file) into the job's main storage pool.

Expert Cache differs from traditional DASD caches in several ways. A DASD cache reads *x* number of disk sectors of data, starting with the sector requested by the read operation, without analyzing how much data should be brought in. Expert Cache, on the other hand, determines how much data to read into the job's main storage pool.

Also, the size of the buffers in the DASD and its controller limits the amount of storage available for DASD caching. But with Expert Cache, much of main storage is available as a cache. Main storage holds programs, data, and control information in a number of pools, and data can take up most of a pool — whatever programs aren't using. Expert Cache optimizes main storage's room for data by bringing large or small blocks of data into a pool based on the application's access patterns.

Expert Cache may also vary the length of time the data is in main storage, thus helping safeguard data integrity. It periodically "sweeps" pages changed by an application out of main storage sooner than the system otherwise would have written them out. By moving the changed pages to disk more frequently, Expert Cache functions like journaling, ensuring that if the system crashes, the information on disk is up-to-date.

You activate Expert Cache by changing the setting of the CHGSHRPOOL (Change Shared Storage Pool) command's Paging Option parameter to *CALC. (For more information about CHGSHRPOOL, see the command's help text or the *Control Language Reference Manual*, SC21-9776.) Expert Cache works only with shared pools. Control is at the individual storage pool level, not the object level, so adjustments to object transfer sizes depend on what the jobs running in a pool are doing with the object. If jobs in various pools are using the same object, Expert Cache could determine a different transfer size for the object in each pool.

Assume, for example, that Expert Cache is active, you're running interactive jobs in one pool and batch jobs in another, and the jobs are accessing the same database file. It's quite likely that the amount of data read into the batch pool per disk I/O operation will be much higher than the amount read into the interactive pool. The file has different data transfer attributes for each of the two pools, just as if the jobs had the file blocking parameters set differently.

If the interactive jobs do fairly normal processing, they access only one or two random records for each transaction and the transfer size is relatively small. For batch jobs reading the same file in file sequence, the data transfer sizes are much larger. In either pool, if the file processing characteristics change, Expert Cache changes with them.

Taking Advantage of Expert Cache

Expert Cache can produce a large improvement in runtime, depending on how an application accesses the data and especially on the amount of memory available. Expert Cache is good for jobs that spend most of their time waiting for disk I/O and is especially good for applications with lots of update or add activity. Expert Cache will benefit you if disk I/O is affecting job performance or the application's data reference pattern is sequential; however, it won't provide much benefit if main storage or CPU is over committed. Expert Cache's ability to help is closely tied to data access patterns and data organization on disk. It's very helpful if you organize your data along the most-used keys and keep your disks fairly clean (removing deleted records and reducing file fragmentation). Of course, file cleanup also helps performance without Expert Cache.

The amount of improvement you get from using Expert Cache depends on the characteristics of the job. A typical reduction for the elapsed time of a batch job ranges from 5 to 50 percent. The key factor is the pool's main storage size. You can continually improve the performance of most jobs by increasing the pool size until the CPU resource constrains the job.

Improved performance will show up in your system data. Not only will there be fewer disk I/O operations per job (because of the larger block sizes), but also each job will use less CPU time (because each disk I/O operation requires some CPU processing). On the other hand, CPU utilization — the amount of CPU resources used over a given period of time — might increase, but don't worry. If that happens, you're seeing a phenomenon known as **workload compression**, whereby the system does the same amount of work and uses the same amount of resources in a shorter period of time. When Expert Cache reduces your runtime, jobs use somewhat less CPU time in less real time than before. The only potential drawback is that you might not have the excess CPU capacity you used to have during peak load times.

You'll probably want to run Expert Cache in all your shared pools. When you first try it, though, turn it on one pool at a time, let it run for a day or two, and vary the pool's size. Then, evaluate the results. Expert Cache doesn't always help. If you're already getting good blocking via the OVRDBF (Override with Database Files) command's SEQONLY parameter, or if you're getting lousy performance because of wildly random data access patterns, and Expert Cache doesn't help, then turn it off. It'll just burn some CPU time you might be able to use in the application.

CHAPTER 7

The Object-Contention and Error-Handling Components

Every second it's processing a job, your system resolves conflicts over objects and corrects errors. These two components can have an enormous impact on your system's performance. This chapter considers each of these performance components in detail.

THE OBJECT-CONTENTION COMPONENT

AS/400 objects include files, records, and message queues. Object contention occurs when two jobs require control of the same object to proceed with processing. You may have experienced object contention as a kid: If somebody else had a toy and you wanted it, the game stopped while you argued.

The object-contention component of performance is a natural result of multiprocessing. We expect frequent conflicts over a variety of objects during normal system operation. Contention is the way the system ensures the integrity of objects that many jobs or tasks need simultaneously.

Seizes Vs. Locks

When Licensed Internal Code (LIC), which runs below the Machine Interface (MI), protects an object from use by others, that protection is called a **seize**. Seize conflicts can occur on objects that you might never expect, such as libraries, device descriptions, and user profiles. Even internal objects that are not defined above the MI can be involved in seize conflicts.

Above the MI, on the level of OS/400 or application code, protection of an object is called a **lock**. Examples include getting a database record for update, explicitly locking a data area using the ALCOBJ (Allocate Object) command, and putting a message queue into *BREAK mode.

When it's involved in a seize conflict, a job retains its activity level. Because a seize occurs at a low level in the machine, a seize usually lasts a very short time. In contrast, lock conflicts can cause a waiting job to lose its activity level. Application programs can explicitly request a lock, and the system will hold a lock as long as the current program needs it. Thus, the job requesting a lock that it cannot get will go to a long wait and give up its activity level. (For a detailed discussion of activity levels, see Chapter 3.)

Lock waits can also time out, which is manifested as an error message. You should take the time to include message-handling logic in your programs. We will consider error handling in detail on page 108.

Object Contention Terminology

Some terminology needs clarification. AS/400 MI (the Machine Interface) represents a boundary between OS/400 and the base machine. The base machine includes the AS/400 LIC and the hardware, plus external I/O interface devices.

A terminology change occurs as you cross the MI boundary. For example, we call a unit of work running above MI in support of the operating system or a user application a job (or, sometimes, a process). Below the MI, a unit of work is a task. These are not the only examples of terminology shift. Above MI, the system locks objects a job needs. Below the MI, the system seizes objects a task needs.

This terminology shift, while confusing at first, does distinguish which specific environment you're discussing. It also communicates the machine level at which the particular topic is operating. ■

Rick Turner

A seize request is unconditional: once the LIC operation requests control of an object, it cannot withdraw the request. Therefore, a seize, unlike a lock, doesn't have an adjustable wait time. Most seize waits last only a few milliseconds; however, some may last longer, causing noticeable processing delays.

Lock requests can be initiated by OS/400 or application programs and are conditional; that is, they have an adjustable wait time. Conflicts result from explicit lock requests using the ALCOBJ (Allocate Object) command, database record locks, and other locks performed on behalf of a job by system functions — for example, job termination and print spool operations. Because a job leaves the activity level during a lock wait, the wait can be responsible for additional delays beyond the time-out itself. For instance, storage management can steal some of the waiting job's pages, such as database records. When the job reenters the activity level, its stolen pages must be brought in from disk, which requires additional CPU and disk I/O time.

Monitoring Object Contention

The performance goal, of course, is to reduce delayed response time that results from object contention. To help you reach this goal, you should monitor the number and duration of the conflicts that are occurring. You can use the TRACE parameter of the STRPFRMON (Start Performance Monitor) command to collect trace data in the QAPMDMPT database file. (For more information about using the Performance Monitor, see Chapters 10 and 12.) You can then print reports using the Performance Tools PRTLCKRPT (Print Lock Report) or PRTTNSRPT (Print Transaction Report) commands. (For more information about using the Performance Tools, see Chapters 11 through 14.)

When you analyze the object-contention component of performance, keep in mind that jobs experiencing long delays are the effect and not the cause. The jobs with a long response time because of object conflicts are usually the victims of other jobs that are holding an object too long. Job priority or I/O problems are often related to excessive seize/lock time.

Priority Adjust

During some seize/lock conflicts, the AS/400 uses an internal priority-adjust algorithm to reduce job wait time. When a conflict occurs, this priority-adjust function checks whether the requesting job has a higher priority than the holding job. If so, the system temporarily promotes the holding job to the priority of the requesting job until the seize/lock is released.

The effect of this adjustment is to give the lower-priority job enough CPU time to finish its processing and release the seize/lock as quickly as possible. Once the system releases the seize or lock, OS/400 resets the job's priority to its original value.

Although you have no external control over this function, you need to know what is occurring. This knowledge may explain observations that seem to contradict normal job priority handling.

Minimizing Object Contention

Lock and seize conflicts are more likely to occur when many users are doing the same thing at the same time, such as opening files or signing off. You can control the circumstances causing object lock contention by specifying whether an object can be shared and by providing a maximum time-out value.

You determine whether an object can be shared by specifying the appropriate lock-state value in the OBJ parameter of the ALCOBJ command. You supply the length of the maximum time-out in the WAITRCD parameter of the create, change, or override command for a database file. The default is 30 seconds. If you don't specify a WAITRCD value, you can specify a maximum wait time in the DFTWAIT parameter of the CHGJOB (Change Job) command. The system

Application Considerations for Growing Numbers of Users

I ran across an application that used a single user profile. This single user profile owned all objects the application created. Whenever the application created or deleted an object, the user profile needed updating.

With few users, this setup presents no problem. However, as more users come onto the system, the application seize contention on the user profile increases. With many users, the wait resulting from this contention becomes significant. ■

Jim Stewart

allows a maximum wait time of 32,767 seconds in WAITCRD and a maximum of 9,999,999 seconds in DFTWAIT.

The Error-Handling Component

Errors occur at all levels of the system — in LIC, OS/400, and applications. These errors, and the way your system responds to them, can impair performance. Error handling is not a component of performance in the same sense as the other components we have discussed. In fact, error handling is a critical aspect of performance in each of those components. Nevertheless, we want to consider error handling separately to emphasize its potential for resource consumption, added response time, and reduced throughput.

Errors occurring at all system levels can affect performance. Errors within the job include program errors, time-outs, and unhandled device error conditions. External errors include communications line and device error recovery and logging. Improperly handled errors are expensive. The easiest place to handle errors is in your applications. If an application does not handle an error, the system may detect it and terminate the job, or the job may loop or hang until you cancel it.

How to Detect Errors

You can find information about errors in a variety of places. Data about external device errors is written to the system error logs. The system history log, the system operator's message queue, and individual job logs are good sources for detecting errors.

An increase in processing by the ERRLOG and VLOG tasks can signal LIC errors. The WRKSYSACT (Work With System Activity) command in the Performance Tools provides a very fast, efficient way to view the currently active OS/400 jobs and LIC tasks. (For more information about using WRKSYSACT, see Chapter 11.) If you have used the Performance Monitor to capture trace data over the slowdown period, adding the *HV value to the OPTIONS parameter on the PRTTNSRPT (Print Transaction Report) command will give you a list of the LIC tasks in the Job Summary Report. (For more information about working with the Performance Monitor, see Chapter 10.) With this report, you can also examine the ERRLOG and VLOG total CPU and disk I/O activity.

The communications link between the application and the display device is particularly prone to errors. A line failure can cause many jobs to attempt to recover from the error simultaneously. If you do not handle these errors properly, the impact on the system can be severe.

Influencing Performance of the Error-Handling Component

To avoid inconveniencing your users, you should use the MONMSG (Monitor Message) command to handle error messages in your applications. You can use

New Applications

Error-handling is a key area to explore when you are evaluating a new third-party application. If the application does not have this type of recovery support, it signals a lack of quality that may help you choose among several applications. At the very least, such a lack should make you do some other error-recovery testing of the application to see just what you are getting. ■

Jim Stewart

prompts to instruct users to take a certain action (for example, retrying the operation) when a lock wait time-out occurs. You will be rewarded for the extra work with reduced CPU and disk I/O processing times.

To handle communications link errors, have the application detect the major/minor return code that signals the error and set the job to specify a DEVRCYACN (Device Recovery Action) attribute of *DSCMSG (Disconnect Message). When the application detects the error, the job will be disconnected (or suspended). When the users can sign on to the device again with the same user profile, they will be reconnected to the suspended job. A second major/minor return code tells the program that the screen contents have been destroyed and that the program should restart the transaction where the error occurred. You can use the system value QDSCJOBITV (Disconnect Job Interval) to end the disconnected jobs after the period you specified on QDSCJOBITV has expired.

What if your application is ignoring major/minor return codes? To help reduce impact on the CPU from these applications' attempts at recovery, you can specify the following DEVRCYACN job attributes, which will provide a next-best level of recovery action:

- DSCENDRQS, Disconnect and end the request
- ENDJOB, End the job
- ENDJOBNOLIST, End the job and do not generate a job log.

When you terminate the job (*ENDJOB or *ENDJOBNOLIST), the system reduces the job priority and changes the time slice to 100 milliseconds. These changes reduce the impact of many jobs terminating at the same time. You can use the system value QDEVRCYACN to establish the Device Recovery Action for all workstation and PC Support Workstation Function jobs on the system.

CHAPTER 8

Performance Tuning Without Tools: the WRKSYSSTS Command

This chapter is the first in a section that gives you ways to tune your AS/400 using just the base operating system: commands, reports, and interactive status screens. You can do a nice job of performance tuning without using Performance Tools or **any** tools other than these few functions. If you have worked on an AS/400 for a while, chances are good that you have seen one of these command's interactive status screens, even if you did not know how to read it. You can also write your own commands and reports through Query, SQL, DFU, or any other file utility.

The three status commands available to every AS/400 user are WRKSYSSTS (Work with System Status), WRKACTJOB (Work with Active Jobs), and WRKDSKSTS (Work with Disk Status). The Work with System Status command does just what its name implies: It lets you look at the status of your system's resources. Work with Active Jobs shows you the active jobs on the system. Work with Disk Status lets you monitor your system's disk drive activity. If you look at the information displayed on all these command screens, you can get a good indication of what is happening to your system's resources at a given time.

Usually, you use these commands to monitor performance in short time periods — five to fifteen minutes. This section will examine each screen in detail and help you identify exactly what to look for. For example, many AS/400 users know that the WRKACTJOB command shows which users are signed on to the system and who is using the most system resources. But this command's screen shows much more, and Chapter 9 will give you those details.

Although the interactive status commands are excellent for identifying how your system is performing during a short period, they are not good at giving you the big picture of overall system performance. To monitor performance over long periods, you can use other OS/400 functions, including job accounting and the Performance Monitor.

Without performance tools, you have several options for capturing and analyzing data on the AS/400. You just need to understand what these options are, how to use them, when to use which option, and most important, what to do with the information once you collect it.

THE WORK WITH SYSTEM STATUS COMMAND

The WRKSYSSTS (Work with System Status) command helps identify how you are using AS/400 system resources and, probably more important, how efficiently you are using them. From this command's main screen, you can monitor storage pool statistics or change the amount of memory allocated to the various storage pools. You may also change the activity levels within each storage pool, except the machine pool. Other information on this command's display is data that gives statistics on job state transitions.

You can also use this command to display the total number of jobs currently in the system, the total capacity of the system ASP, the percentage of the system ASP currently in use, and the percentage of permanent and temporary machine address used. In this chapter, we will discuss each of these values in detail.

How to Use WRKSYSSTS

To run this command, type WRKSYSSTS at any command line. You can specify several parameters, and you view these parameters by pressing F4 with the command. Figure 8.1 shows the prompted command.

The definition for each parameter of WRKSYSSTS appears in Table 8.1.

When you type the command, the screen in Figure 8.2 appears. It shows statistical information collected over a time period you specify. The Reset parameter (the F10 key) can be used to restart the collection of system status statistics.

FIGURE 8.1

Work with System Status Command Prompt

```
                     Work with System Status (WRKSYSSTS)

Type choices, press Enter.
Output  ..........................  *         *, *PRINT
Reset status statistics ..........  *NO       *NO, *YES
Assistance Level  ................  *PRV      *PRV, *USRPRF, *BASIC...

F3=Exit F4=Prompt    F5=Refresh    F10=Additional parameters  F12=Cancel
F13=How to use this display        F24=More key
```

TABLE 8.1

Parameters for the Work with System Status Command

Parameter	Options	Definition
Output	*	Displays the output to the interactive user or prints it with the job's spooled output for batch jobs
	*PRINT	Prints the output with the job's spooled output
Reset	*NO	Does not reset the system status statistics
	*YES	Resets the system status statistics; this is the same as pressing F10 while using the command
Assistance Level	*PRV	Presents the previously used assistance level
	*USRPRF	Uses the assistance level set in the user profile
	*BASIC	Uses the OA (Operational Assistant) interface
	*INTERMED	Presents the system user interface
	*ADVANCED	Presents the system user interface expert mode (no command keys are displayed in this mode)

CPU, Time, Job, and Address Data

In Figure 8.2, the **% CPU used** field shows the extent to which your system is employing the processing power available to it. If you are running a multi-processor machine, this number is the average use of all the processors. Four plus signs (++++) here indicate that your system is using 100 percent of its processor capability.

Systems often run at a high CPU utilization rate, and if your system is performing batch work during the evaluation period, don't be surprised to see 100 percent usage. The AS/400's CPU allocation implementation architecture ensures that all CPU cycles left over from interactive and other high-priority work are used for lower-priority batch work. On the other hand, if you aren't running low-priority batch work and your CPU utilization is consistently at 100 percent, you may have a problem.

Guidelines for interactive (or high) priority workload are shown in Table 8.2. When your CPU utilization exceeds these guidelines, interactive response time becomes inconsistent. To maintain stable interactive response time, you want the processor utilization to be below 70 percent for a single-processor AS/400 running interactive and other high-priority work. The figure for multiprocessor systems ranges from 75 percent to 81 percent.

The **Elapsed time** field in Figure 8.2 shows the period during which the WRKSYSSTS command gathered the information displayed on the screen. The format is hours:minutes:seconds, so Figure 8.2 shows a period of 30 seconds. Because most numbers on this screen are averages of the data gathered over that period, the length of the evaluation period is important. An elapsed time

FIGURE 8.2
Work with System Status Screen

```
                          Work with System Status                    PERF1
                                                   06/16/96       12:00:01
% CPU used .........:           5.5        Auxiliary Storage:
Elapsed time .......:      00:00:30        System  ASP ..........:     5207 M
Jobs in system  ....:           228        % System ASP Used ....:    81.1072
% Addresses Used:                          Total ................:     5207 M
  Permanent  .......:         5.804        Current unprotect used:      270 M
  Temporary  .......:         1.755        Max unprotect  .......:      279 M

System      Pool         Reserved        Max      DB      DB     Non-DB      Non-DB
  Pool    Size (K)       Size (K)     Active  Faults   Pages     Faults       Pages
     1      11200          7394          +++      .0       0         .0          .0
     2       8000                          7      .0      .0         .0          .0
     3      78964             0           74      .0      .0         .0          .0
     4        140             0            3      .0      .0         .0          .0

                                                                          Bottom
Command
===>
F3=Exit     F10=Restart     F11=Transition Data     F12=Previous    F24=More Keys
F14=Subsystems              F15=Active Jobs         F16=Disk Status
```

of 4.5 hours is probably too long to give you a good indication of how your system is currently running: Perhaps activity was very high for the first two hours and low for the last two and a half. A short period (e.g., 30 seconds) may misrepresent the system's status if you had, say, a CPU spike. A useful elapsed time is between 5 and 15 minutes. During busy periods, a shorter elapsed time will do; during slow ones, a longer elapsed time is better.

TABLE 8.2
Guidelines for Interactive Priority Workload

Number of Processors	High-Priority CPU Utilization Guideline
1	70%
2	75%
3	79%
4	81%

The **Elapsed time** field tells you how long ago you issued the command. You can get a new sample in one of two ways. First, you can reset the clock by pressing F10 or by setting the reset option to *YES when you start the command. Second, you can press F5 to calculate a new average that combines the previous data with the data collected since the last time you pressed F10 or issued the WRKSYSSTS command with the reset option of *YES. In other words, if you press F5 two minutes after recording an elapsed time of 5 minutes and 30 seconds, the new elapsed time will be 7 minutes and 30 seconds.

You don't have to watch the system collect data. When you press F3 to exit the screen, the command stays active in the program stack, and the statistics are updated the next time you invoke the command. This option is particularly useful if you want a longer elapsed time but have other work to do while the data is being collected.

Jobs in system, the third field of Figure 8.2, counts all active jobs, jobs on job queues, and jobs that have finished running but still have output in output queues. Commands such as WRKACTJOB, WRKJOBQ (Work with Job Queue), and WRKOUTQ (Work with Output Queue) can help you break down this total.

You need to monitor this field for an abnormally high number of jobs, which could decrease performance. The definition of "abnormal" depends on your system environment. The best way to become familiar with your users' jobs is to track the average number of jobs over a couple of weeks. If the number is usually around 150 and one day you see 450, you will want to investigate why.

Unless you have new programs or procedures that would account for such an increase, the logical area to investigate is spooled files. System-generated job logs or program-generated reports with spooled files in output queues use a lot of resources because the system must keep track of those jobs. You should print or delete all unnecessary spooled files every day. Also, you can use a parameter in the job description to suppress generation of spooled job logs for jobs that complete normally. Use the OA (Operational Assistant) to automatically delete system spooled files, such as job logs and dumps, at preset intervals.

In Figure 8.2, notice the two fields under **% Addresses Used**. These subfields represent the percentage of permanent and temporary addresses in use; that is, the percentage of the AS/400's maximum number of possible addresses. Permanent addresses are allocated to objects such as database files and programs, which stay in the system until someone with the required authority deletes them. The system allocates temporary addresses to objects such as open data paths and compiler work areas, which the system automatically deletes when it is finished with them.

Watch for increases in these numbers; as with jobs, you need to be familiar with the normal number of addresses in use. If the numbers are higher than normal, you may have to IPL your system to reclaim the temporary addresses. You should investigate any unusual increases. For example, if the number grows by 5 percent per day, you must IPL your system before 20 days, or it will stop when the temporary address count reaches 100 percent. At that point, you will be **forced** to IPL.

A rapid increase in temporary address use implies a corresponding increase in creation and destruction of objects, which points to an application design problem. If you are experiencing problems with temporary address usage, you may need to involve IBM support or a very good systems analyst to find out what is causing the problem. Although the AS/400 rarely runs out of permanent addresses, temporary addresses are another story.

Storage Data

The upper right quadrant of the WRKSYSSTS screen in Figure 8.2 shows data about **Auxiliary Storage** (i.e., disk space). Many AS/400s have only one auxiliary storage pool (ASP), called ASP 1 or the System ASP; the **System ASP** field on the display shows its status. The **Total** field shows all the auxiliary storage on the system; that is, ASPs 1 through 16. For example, if you have two ASPs that contain 5 GB and 4 GB, respectively, this field displays 9,000 MB.

The **% System ASP Used** field in Figure 8.2 gives you the percentage of ASP 1 in use. If you have multiple ASPs, you can figure out how full the other ASPs' pools are by using either the WRKDSKSTS (Work with Disk Status) command (see Chapter 9) or the AS/400 Performance Tools (see Chapters 11–14). IBM's optional WRKASP (Work with Auxiliary Storage Pools) command, available from the AS/400 Support Family Project Office, is inexpensive and helpful. This command will display each ASP on the system and show you the percent used and other useful ASP information.

The **Current unprotected used** field displays the amount of temporary object and machine data in unprotected storage when checksum protection is in effect. The **Max unprotect** field displays the largest amount of storage used for unprotected data at any time since the last IPL. These two fields help you determine the amount of unprotected storage you need if you decide to use checksum protection. You can find more detailed information about checksum calculations in IBM's *Advanced Backup and Recovery Guide* (SC41-3305).

For analyzing performance, the only auxiliary storage field that matters is **% System ASP Used**. For optimal disk performance, you should not use more than 80 to 90 percent of the system ASP. For any given system, however, performance varies according to disk activity, system activity, and program and file structure. Your system may slow down at 75 percent, or you may still get good performance at 95 percent.

Why does a system perform better when you use less disk space? As disks fill, the AS/400 must work harder to find available space. However, because of the way the system allocates disk space, sometimes the system performs well with full disks, too. All disk space is allocated in **extents** whose size is a power of 2 number of sectors; extents can be up to 64 sectors (32 KB). Each sector is 512 bytes long. All available free space is recorded in the free space directory. When space is needed, such as to create or extend a database file, the system goes to this directory, finds the space, updates the directory to reflect the removal of some space, and gives a pointer to that space back to the requesting function (in this case, the database). In the same fashion, when an object is deleted, the space it occupied is returned to the free space directory.

When a system is first used, most of the available space is represented by large sections of free space, many of them 32 KB in length. As space is allocated to objects, the amount of available space goes down. If most of the available disk space is filled up when a system is first used, it is quite possible (especially for database files) that the disk space is allocated in single contiguous 32 KB extents. In this case, up to 32 KB of database data can be read or written in a single disk operation. Therefore, even when the percentage of disk space used is high, the system can run very efficiently because it can transfer 32 KB of data per disk operation.

When objects smaller than 32 KB are created and destroyed, the original 32 KB extents of available space can become fragmented. For example, if you create a data area (DTAARA), its base size is 2 KB. If the system allocated the 2 KB from a 32 KB extent, the system is left with 30 KB available in that area. Because space is allocated in a power of 2 number of sectors, the remaining 30 KB is allocated in extents of 16 KB, 8 KB, 4 KB, and 2 KB. In time, although enough disk space may still be left to allocate 32 KB, those 32 KB may no longer be contiguous — the data could be allocated in 32 1-KB segments scattered over multiple disks. In that case, a 32 KB disk I/O transfer operation would result in 32 separate disk operations. It's a good practice to track the amount of work a system is doing and compare it to the number of disk operations needed to do that work (i.e., the cost).

To reduce the amount of disk fragmentation, try the following steps.

- Identify and delete old or obsolete objects.
- Purge any old or obsolete data from your files.
- Identify the most frequently used files that have grown recently or steadily. Look especially for records with deleted records.
- Copy these suspect files to remove deleted records, and repackage the disk allocations. Consider REUSEDLT(*YES) for the new version of the files. The Reuse Deleted Records (REUSEDLT) command, specified on the Create or Change Physical File command, determines whether the space used by deleted records is reclaimed by future requests to insert records.

These efforts should significantly reduce disk fragmentation. If they don't, the last and most expensive options are to

- Save the system *NONSYS, scratch the non-system libraries, and reload them. The *NONSYS value can be specified on the Save Library command for the library parameter. When it is used, all user-created libraries, QGPL and QUSRSYS libraries, and licensed program libraries (such as QRPG and QIDU) are saved.

- Save the system, reinitialize all the disks, and reload the system.

System Storage Pool Use

The bottom half of the WRKSYSSTS screen in Figure 8.2 displays information about your system storage pools. Most AS/400s have at least four such pools, each identified by a number and a description. The maximum number of storage pools is 16. All system memory is divided among the available pools, which makes the system storage pools an excellent way to isolate different types of work — system, interactive, batch, communications, and spooled — and thus to get optimum performance for each. (For more information about storage pools, see Chapter 6.)

System pool 1 is the machine pool, and system pool 2 is the base pool. The machine pool is for highly shared machine and operating system programs and pageable and non-pageable main storage. The base pool is the shared system pool, in which many operating system functions and some system jobs run. It contains all main storage not allocated to the other pools. When you add memory to your system, that memory goes into system pool 2. In Figure 8.2, 8 MB (or 8,000 KB) are allocated to the base pool. If you added 24 MB to the system and performed an IPL, the value for system pool 2 would be 32,000.

The other storage pools are displayed in numeric order. The WRKSYSSTS screen in Figure 8.2 shows four system storage pools (the default setup). To see each one's associated description, press function key F11, which brings up the screen in Figure 8.3.

The WRKSYSSTS command makes it easy to add and subtract memory from the pools. Memory added to a pool always comes out of the base pool, and memory subtracted from a pool always returns to the base pool. For example, if you type 18,000 over the 11,200 value for system pool 1 in Figure 8.3 and press Enter, the system moves 6,800 KB from the base pool to the machine pool. System pools 1 and 2 are both very important for system performance, so you need to monitor the number of faults carefully. Did we say faults. . . ?

Faults: Database and Non-Database

You want to keep page faults to a minimum because each fault increases disk I/O, which could dramatically decrease system performance. On an AS/400, two types of faults (database and non-database) can occur in a storage pool. A non-database fault, which involves objects such as programs, configuration objects, and internal objects, can affect performance as much as a database fault. For more information about database and non-database faults, see Chapter 5.

FIGURE 8.3

Work with System Status Screen with Pool Descriptions

```
                              Work With System Status                    PERF1
                                                        06/16/96     12:05:11
% CPU used ......:         5.5          Auxiliary Storage:
Elapsed time ....:    00:08:45            System ASP ...........:       5207 M
Jobs in system  .:         228            % System ASP Used.....:    81.1072
% Addresses Used.:                        Total ................:       5207 M
  Permanent  ....:       5.804            Current unprotect used:        270 M
  Temporary  ....:       1.755            Max unprotect  .......:        279 M

System      Pool      Reserved      Max
  Pool    Size (K)    Size (K)    Active     Pool       Subsystem     Library
    1      11200         7394       +++    *Machine
    2       8000                      7    *Base
    3      78964            0        74    *Interact
    4        140            0         3    *Spool

                                                                       Bottom

Command
===>
F3=Exit       F11=Paging Option    F12=Previous     F21=Expand Views
F15=Active Jobs                                     F16=Disk Status
```

Guidelines for non-database faults in the machine pool are shown in Table 8.3. These guidelines are based on the IBM *AS/400 Work Management Guide*. The acceptable number of faults depends on the amount of memory available. The number of faults shown on the display is the average of the number of faults per second that occur during the elapsed time. Figure 8.4 shows that the machine pool has 11.2 MB of storage, so more than five faults in this pool would signal a problem. Data faults that involve file data, indexes over data, and journal objects may not affect performance as much as machine pool faults.

TABLE 8.3

Guidelines for Non-Database Faults in the Machine Pool

Good	Acceptable	Poor
<2	2-5	>5

FIGURE 8.4

Work with System Status Screen Showing Faulting Information

```
                          Work With System Status                        PERF1
                                                      06/16/96        12:00:01
% CPU used .......:        5.5                Auxiliary Storage:
Elapsed time .....:   00:00:30                System  ASP ..........:   5207 M
Jobs in system  ..:        228                System ASP Used ......:  81.1072
% Addresses Used..:                           Total    .............:   5207 M
  Permanent  .....:      5.804                Current unprotect used:    270 M
  Temporary  .....:      1.755                Max unprotect  .......:    279 M

System     Pool       Reserved      Max      DB       DB       Non-DB     Non-DB
  Pool   Size (K)     Size (K)    Active   Faults    Pages     Faults      Pages
    1      11200        7394        +++       .0       .0         .0         .0
    2       8000                      7       .0       .0         .0         .0
    3      78964           0         74       .0       .0         .0         .0
    4        140           0          3       .0       .0         .0         .0





                                                                      Bottom

Command
===>
F3=Exit   F10=Restart     F11=Transition Data    F12=Previous   F24=More Keys
F14=Subsystems            F15=Active Jobs        F16=Disk Status
```

For best performance, try to keep the total of all database and non-database faults within the guidelines in Tables 8.3, 8.4, and 8.5.

If your total faults fall into the poor range, check whether you have some storage pools with few or no faults. If so, you should move memory from these pools to the ones with the highest levels of faulting — being careful, of

TABLE 8.4

Guidelines for Sum of Database and Non-Database Faults per Second in All Pools

AS/400 Model	Good	Acceptable	Poor
D02-F02, C04-E04, C06-D06, B10-D10, B20-C20	<15	15–25	>25
F04, E06, E10, D20, C25, B30, B35-D35, B40, B45	<25	25–40	>40
F06, F10, E20-F20, D25-F25, E35-F35, D45-F45, B50-F50, B60-E60, B70	<30	35–60	>60
F60, D70-F70, D80-E80	<80	80–130	>130
F80, E90, E95	<180	180–300	>300
F90, F95, F97	<250	250–440	>440

TABLE 8.5

Guidelines for Sum of Database and Non-Database Faults per Second in Each Pool

AS/400 Model	Good	Acceptable	Poor
D02-F02, C04-E04, C06-D06, B10-D10, B20-C20	<10	10–15	>15
F04, E06, E10, D20, C25, B30, B35-D35, B40, B45	<15	15–25	>25
F06, F10, E20-F20, D25-F25, E35-F35, D45-F45, B50-F50, B60-E60, B70	<20	25–50	>50
F60, D70-F70, D80-E80	<50	50–100	>100
F80, E90, E95	<100	100–200	>200
F90, F95, F97	<150	150–350	>350

course, not to create a problem in the pool from which you're taking memory. At times like these, system tuning becomes an art: You're trying to find the right amount of memory for each pool that will yield optimum performance and minimum faults.

QPFRADJ is a system value that can be set to control automating tuning on the system (for more information, see IBM's *AS/400 Work Management Guide*, SC41-3306). Auto tuners, such as QPFRADJ or some commercially available auto tuners, move memory between the storage pools for you automatically, usually based on the workload in the pools. If the faulting level doesn't go down, you may need to add memory to your system. You can reduce the demand on your memory resource somewhat by tuning applications or changing the way you process files. Although the last thing anyone wants to do is purposely decrease the amount of work on the system, you may have to look at rescheduling or reducing work.

System Workload

An easy way to reduce the system's workload is to reduce the activity level. To assess the activity level, press F11 to reveal the transition data, as shown in Figure 8.5. (You can also press F21 and select the *ADVANCED assistance level option to display fault and transition data simultaneously.) For more information about activity levels and job states, see Chapter 3.

The Max Active column in Figure 8.5 shows the activity level — the number of jobs that can be active in a given pool at one time. You can change that number simply by typing over the existing number, except for system pool 1, which you can't change here. The Max Active number for batch pools needs to account for each batch job allowed. The number for communications pools needs to support the number of communications jobs running. The number for spooled pools needs to reflect the number of printers (one active job for each printer).

FIGURE 8.5
Work with System Status Screen Showing Transition Data

```
                           Work with System Status                    PERF1
                                                      06/16/96     12:00:11
% CPU used ......:          5.5             Auxiliary Storage:
Elapsed time ....:     00:05:30             System ASP............:   5207 M
Jobs in system  .:          228             % System ASP Used ....: 81.1072
% Addresses Used.:                          Total     ............:   5207 M
  Permanent  ....:        5.804             Current unprotect used:    270 M
  Temporary  ....:        1.755             Max unprotect  .......:    279 M

System      Pool     Reserved       Max      Active-       Wait-       Active-
  Pool    Size (K)   Size (K)     Active      Wait          Inel         Inel
     1     11200       7394         +++          .0           .0           .0
     2      8000                      7          .0           .0           .0
     3     78964          0          74        35.9           .0           .0
     4       140          0           3          .0           .0           .0

                                                                        Bottom
Command
===>
F3=Exit   F10=Restart    F11=Transition Data   F12=Previous   F24=More Keys
F14=Subsystems           F15=Active Jobs       F16=Disk Status
```

Be aware that if you accept the default pool configuration, the console, batch, communications, and programming jobs will all run together in the base pool, and performance can suffer as a result. It is to your advantage to separate similar types of work into their own system storage pools.

Paging Option

If you press F11 (Paging Option), the WRKSYSSTS command screen with paging information will appear, as in Figure 8.6. IBM added this screen to the command as part of the new Expert Cache function. You use this new paging option for each storage pool to tell the system whether to use Expert Cache to dynamically adjust the paging characteristics of the storage pool for optimum performance. The paging option values are as follows.

- *FIXED: The system does not dynamically adjust the paging characteristics of the storage pool; it uses system default values.
- *CALC: The system dynamically adjusts the paging characteristics of the storage pool for optimum performance.
- *USRDFN: The system does not dynamically adjust the paging characteristics of the storage pool.

FIGURE 8.6

Work with System Status Screen Showing Paging Options

```
                          Work with System Status                      PERF1
                                                    06/16/96     12:05:11
 % CPU used    . . . :            5.5        Auxiliary Storage:
 Elapsed time  . . :         00:08:45        System ASP     . . . . . . . :    5207 M
 Jobs in system   :              228        % System ASP Used . . . . . :   81.1072
 % Addresses Used:                           Total         . . . . . . . . . . . . :    5207 M
    Permanent   . . :          5.804         Current unprotect used. :     270 M
    Temporary   . . :          1.755         Max unprotect     . . . . . . :     279 M

 System        Pool        Reserved       Max        Paging
   Pool      Size (K)      Size (K)     Active       Option
     1         11200          7394        +++        *Fixed
     2          8000                        7        *Fixed
     3         78964             0         15        *Fixed
     4           140             0          3        *Fixed

                                                                         Bottom
 Command
 ===>
 F3=Exit         F4=Prompt          F5=Refresh       F9=Retrieve          F10=Restart
 F11=Display Paging Data            F12=Cancel       F24=More Keys
```

You define the value through the QUSCHGPA API. The API to change pool-tuning information is QWCCHGTN, which tells the system whether to dynamically tune private storage pools. (To find these APIs, check IBM's *AS/400 System API Reference*, SC41-3801.) You can change the paging information by typing one of these values into the Paging Option field. The default value is *FIXED. You change the paging option for shared pools by issuing the WRK-SHRPOOL (Work with Shared Pool) command.

As you can tell, you can monitor and change a lot of system information with the WRKSYSSTS command. This command is one of the most useful on the system. A word of warning, however: because it lets users change pool sizes and activity levels, you need to restrict who has the authority to use it. Users who don't need WRKSYSSTS can use DSPSYSSTS (Display System Status), which shows the same information as WRKSYSSTS but doesn't permit input. Or you could revoke object authority on the WRKSYSSTS command.

CHAPTER 9

More Performance Tuning: The Work with Active Jobs Command and the Work with Disk Status Command

In Chapter 8, we introduced you to performance tuning without special tools by discussing the Work with System Status command. In this chapter, we will consider two more commands that also provide you with valuable performance tuning information: the Work with Active Jobs command and the Work with Disk Status command.

THE WORK WITH ACTIVE JOBS COMMAND

Most people who have ever worked on an AS/400 have used the WRKACTJOB (Work with Active Jobs) command — one of its most common uses is to cancel a job. However, WRKACTJOB is also useful for performance tuning because it displays performance and status information for all the jobs that are active on the system.

On rare occasions, a job does not appear on the Work with Active Jobs display. If you use the WRKSBMJOB (Work with Submitted Jobs) command and then immediately enter the WRKACTJOB command, the job you just submitted may not be listed with the other active jobs on the screen. This delay happens on very busy systems when the system cannot update the status indicators quickly. Normally, the time that a job is in this state is very short, but sometimes this problem can occur.

When using the WRKACTJOB command to track down a performance problem, most people just look for the job that is hogging the biggest percentage of the CPU. However, this command can do more than give you this information; you may also carry out several other tasks. For example, you can change a job's attributes, hold a job, release a job, display a job's attributes and program information, display messages, work with a job's generated spool files, and disconnect a job.

How to Use the WRKACTJOB Command

To run this command, simply type WRKACTJOB and press the Enter key at any command line. The command has several parameters, for which you can get a prompt by pressing F4 after entering the command. Figure 9.1 shows the prompted command. The parameters are listed in Table 9.1. If you are using the WRKACTJOB command to find jobs that use more than their share of the CPU,

FIGURE 9.1
Work with Active Jobs Command Parameters

```
                    Work with Active Jobs (WRKACTJOB)

Type choices, press Enter.
Output  . . . . . . . . . . . . . . .   *      *, *PRINT
Reset status statistics . . . . . .   *NO   *NO, *YES
Subsystem . . . . . . . . . . . . .   *ALL Name, *ALL
CPU percent limit . . . . . . . . .   *NONE.1-99.9, *NONE
Response time limit . . . . . . . .   *NONE.1-999.9 seconds, *NONE
Sequence  . . . . . . . . . . . . .   *SBS  *SBS, *AUXIO, *CPU...


F3=Exit  F4=Prompt  F5=Refresh  F10=Additional parameters  F12=Cancel
F13=How to use this display     F24=More keys
```

you can set the CPU % Limit parameter to find jobs using more than that percentage of the CPU.

When you enter the WRKACTJOB command with its default parameters, the screen in Figure 9.2 appears. The first field is **CPU %**. This percentage represents the average processor utilization during the elapsed time. The value in the **CPU %** field is the ratio of the amount of processing time to the total elapsed time. This value includes processing time for system overhead, excluded jobs, and jobs that have ended during the measurement time. This field is zero when the elapsed time is zero. If the system has multiple processors, this field contains the average processing unit time of all the processors.

Suppose this field has a very high value, but none of the jobs listed on the display are using a lot of CPU and the total of all jobs' CPU use is much less than this field's value. The system is using the CPU for something; you should investigate why and for what. You may have a system problem that requires a PTF or IBM's assistance. The WRKSYSACT (Work with System Activity) command that comes with the Performance Tools is the only way to measure what the system tasks and jobs are doing interactively. We cover this command in Chapter 11.

As it does in the WRKSYSSTS displays, the **Elapsed Time** field shows the period during which the WRKACTJOB command gathered the information that

TABLE 9.1

Parameters for the Work with Active Jobs Command

Parameter	Options	Definition
Output	*	The output is displayed to the interactive user or printed with the job's spooled output for batch jobs.
	*PRINT	The output is printed with the job's spooled output.
Reset	*NO	The job statistics are not reset.
	*YES	The job statistics are reset. This is the same as pressing F10 while using the command.
Subsystem	*ALL or NAME	Specifies the name of the subsystems or all subsystems whose active jobs are displayed. You can enter multiple values for this parameter. For example, if you want to see only subsystems QINTER and QBATCH, they are the two subsystems you enter on these lines.
CPU % Limit	*NONE 0.1 to 99.9	This command will display only jobs that are equal to or exceed this value, which is the percent of CPU processing a job uses.
Response Time Limit	*NONE 0.1 to 99.9	Specifies the minimum response time before a job is included on the display.
Sequence	Option Order	Specifies the order in which the display sorts the data. The following options are allowed: subsystem, aux I/O, CPU, CPU Percent, function, operator interactions, job, pool, priority, response time, status, type, user.

is on the screen. This period appears in the format of hours:minutes:seconds, so Figure 9.2 shows a period of 7 minutes and 28 seconds. For more information about the **Elapsed Time** field, see page 113.

The **Active Jobs** field is a count of the number of user and system jobs that are active and have not ended during the elapsed time. Jobs that ended during the elapsed time are not included in this count.

Using the WRKACTJOB Command for Performance Analysis and Tuning

The options underneath the top line of the display allow you to control your jobs. The WRKACTJOB command displays job information by subsystems beneath the list of options. The list of jobs within subsystems is in alphabetical order by job name. The job names are indented under the subsystem monitor job they are associated with. System jobs are also displayed; they are alphabetized by job name and presented following the subsystem monitors and jobs within the subsystems. A plus sign (+) next to the job name identifies group jobs.

To control your jobs, enter a number in the **Option** field and press Enter. For example, in Figure 9.2, if you want to hold job DSP10, type a 3 in the Option column next to DSP10 and press Enter. Depending on how busy your

FIGURE 9.2
Work with Active Jobs Screen

```
                        Work with Active Jobs                    PERF1
                                                   06/16/96   12:10:01
CPU %:  65.4   Elapsed Time:  00:07:28   Active Jobs:    115

Type Options, Press Enter
  2=Change   3=Hold   4=End   5=Work With   6=Release   8=Spooled Files
  9=Exclude  10=Program Stack 11=Locks

Opt  Subsystem/Job  User      Type  CPU%  Function          Status
___    QCTL         QSYS      SBS     .0                    DEQW
___     DSP01       QSECOFR   INT   24.9  CMD-WRKACTJOB     RUN
___    QINTER       QSYS      SBS     .5                    DEQW
___     DSP56       ARNOLD    INT     .8  PGM-AR100         DSPW
___     DSP14       TURNER    INT    1.6  PGM-AR100         DSPW
___     DSP35       STEWART   INT     .3  CMD-DSPLIB        DSPW
___     DSP10       JONES     INT   11.9  PGM-AP101         DSPW

                                                          More...
Command
===>___________________________________________________________
F3=Exit    F5=Refresh    F10=Restart Statistics   F11=Display Elapsed Data
F12=Cancel               F24=More Keys
```

system is and what the job that you want to hold is doing, the **Status** field changes immediately, in a few seconds, or possibly in a few minutes to HLD.

The **User** field identifies the user who submitted the job and the user profile under which the job is running. If you are in a System/36 environment that uses multiple requester terminal jobs (MRTs), be aware that the name of the user who initially started the MRT will appear here.

The **Type** field shows the type of active job that is running. For example, if you are running an interactive job, the type is INT. All subsystem monitor jobs are SBS types. Table 9.2 shows the 12 valid job types.

The next field is **CPU %** for the job. This field is different from the previously described CPU percentage, because this field shows the percent of processing unit time that **this particular job** used over the elapsed time. Watch this field closely to identify jobs that use a large portion of the processor.

The WRKACTJOB command gives you several options that provide more clues about what a job is doing. If a job is showing a high CPU percent utilization, you can gain more information about the job using Option 5, Work with Job. Option 10 of the Work with Job option shows the job log; from the log, you see whether any messages are being generated. Option 11 displays the program stack, which gives you the name of the program(s) involved. Option 14 shows the open files and database or logical display I/O counts related to

TABLE 9.2
Valid Job Types

Job Type	Description
ASJ	Autostart job
BCH	Batch job
BCI	Batch immediate job
EVK	Job started by a procedure start request
INT	Interactive job
MRT	Multiple requester terminal job
PJ	Prestart job
PDJ	Print driver job
RDR	Reader job
SBS	Subsystem monitor
SYS	System job
WTR	Writer job

the job that is causing the problem. If your exploration of these other options tells you the job shouldn't be doing what it is doing, you can hold or cancel it back at the main WRKACTJOB display.

Returning to the example in Figure 9.2, the **Function** field shows the high-level function the job is performing. This field is blank if the program did not perform a logged function. The prefix of this field indicates what kind of function the job performs; the suffix names the specific function or job. For example, in Figure 9.2, CMD-WRKACTJOB tells you that a command is running, and the name of the command is Work with Active Jobs.

The **Status** field gives the status of the running job. This screen displays only one status per job. A blank status field indicates that a job is in transition. More than forty different status codes are possible. In Figure 9.2, the WRKACTJOB command's status is RUN.

You can view another set of information, Elapsed Data, from this command by pressing the F11 key. The **Pool** field tells you which jobs are running in which pool. For example, if you have set up your system with separate pools for different types of work, and a user is running an interactive job in Pool 2 when your usual interactive pool is Pool 3, you have a problem. You need to find out why this job is going to the wrong pool. The most obvious reasons are that the job description is wrong or a user transferred the job. This field is a really easy way to identify how your jobs are running. Are they running where you expect them to be running? If not, you need to adjust your system.

The **Priority** field is also very important because it shows at which priority your jobs are running. As with pools, you usually group jobs of similar types to run at the same priority. You can monitor this grouping here. If a job's priority is different from what it should be, you need to investigate. If someone changed the priority, did that change create a performance problem because this job is now getting too much processor and not allowing the other jobs enough access?

Limiting Access to WRKACTJOB

Don't let the WRKACTJOB command become a performance problem itself. Yes, using the command can cause a performance problem if you give too many users access to it — with "too many users" defined as more than one. When you issue this command, it goes out to every job structure on the system, sees what all the jobs are doing out there, and brings back that information. Performing all these tasks uses a lot of CPU and disk. In Figure 9.2, the job identified in the **Function** field as Work with Active Jobs is using 24.9 percent of the CPU. On medium-sized and small AS/400s, it is not uncommon to see this command use this much system resource to run.

We recommend that you revoke object authority for this command for everyone except people who are knowledgeable about and responsible for performance. Then, grant authority to this command only to the people who absolutely need it.

The Work with Disk Status Command

The WRKDSKSTS (Work with Disk Status) command helps you identify how your disk resources are being used. From this command's main screen, you can monitor your disk (auxiliary storage) space utilization, percent busy, read/write ratios, and the type of auxiliary storage protection. Because disk is a key component of performance, and one of the slowest components, it is important to optimize it.

One of the AS/400's nicest features is its storage management capability. When you create an object, you don't have to manage its disk placement — the system takes care of that chore automatically. You just have to make sure you have enough disk space. And because the system typically scatters fragments of a single object across several disks (rather than having one object occupy one contiguous block), the system employs several disk heads to retrieve an object. This approach can reduce disk head contention and improve performance. The WRKDSKSTS command can help you determine whether you have the disk space to implement this approach.

Using WRKDSKSTS

To run this command, type WRKDSKSTS and press the Enter key at any command line. You can view the command's parameters by pressing F4 with the command at any command line. Figure 9.3 shows the prompted command.

Because this command has several parameters, you may not be familiar with them all. Table 9.3 shows the definition of each parameter of WRKDSKSTS.

FIGURE 9.3
Work with Disk Status Command Parameters

```
                         Work with Disk Status (WRKDSKSTS)

Type choices, press Enter.

  Output  ..........................  *           *, *PRINT
  Reset status statistics ......      *NO         *NO, *YES
  Assistance Level  ...........       *PRV        *PRV, *USRPRF, *BASIC...

F3=Exit F4=Prompt    F5=Refresh    F10=Additional parameters  F12=CanceL
F13=How to use this display     F24=More key
```

TABLE 9.3
Parameters for the Work with System Status Command

Parameter	Options	Definition
Output	*	Displays the output to the interactive user or prints it with the job's spooled output for batch jobs
	*PRINT	Prints the output with the job's spooled output
Reset	*NO	Does not reset the system status statistics
	*YES	Resets the system status statistics; this is the same as pressing F10 while using the command
Assistance Level	*PRV	Presents the previously used assistance level
	*USRPRF	Uses the assistance level set in the user profile
	*BASIC	Uses the OA (Operational Assistant) interface
	*INTERMED	Presents the system user interface
	*ADVANCED	Presents the system user interface expert mode (no command keys are displayed in this mode)

After you enter the required parameters or just type WRKDSKSTS, the screen in Figure 9.4 appears. Let's discuss the performance-related fields on this screen.

FIGURE 9.4
Work with Disk Status Screen

```
                          Work with Disk Status                       PERF1
                                                          06/16/94    12:10:01
  Elapsed Time:   00:09:01

               Size     %      I/O   Request   Read  Write    Read  Write   %
 Unit   Type    (M)    Used    RQS   Size (K)   RQS    RQS     (K)    (K)  Busy
   1    2800    300    59.7    1.6     1.1       .2    1.3     1.8     .9    5
   1    2800    300    59.7    1.7     1.2       .4    1.3     2.1    1.0    5
   2    2800    300    56.4    2.4     2.6      1.2    1.1     4.1    1.0    8
   2    2800    300    56.4    2.2     2.5      1.1    1.0     3.8    1.1    7
   3    9335    427    55.9    3.0     3.0       .6    1.3     4.8    1.0    9
   3    9335    427    55.9    2.7     1.9       .4    1.3     2.6    1.0   10

                                                                       More...
 Command
 ===>
 F3=Exit          F5=Refresh          F12=Cancel          F24=More Keys
```

Performance-Related Fields on the WRKDSKSTS Screen

The **Elapsed Time** field shows the period during which the WRKDSKSTS command gathered the information. The format is hours:minutes:seconds, so Figure 9.4 shows a period of nine minutes and one second. Because most numbers on this screen are averages of the data gathered over that period, the length of the evaluation period is important. For more information about the **Elapsed Time** field, see page 113.

The number in the **Unit** field specifies the disk unit. This figure does not represent the number of actuators a disk drive has — a number that significantly affects the figure in the **Size** field. For example, a 9335 disk drive has two actuators. The **Size** field in Figure 9.4 for the 9335 disk drive shows that **each** drive unit has 427 MB of storage, so the **total** storage on the 9335 disk drive is 854 MB. Most new drives (9336 and newer) have only one actuator per drive, so remembering this relationship between actuators and storage will not be an issue with these drives.

TABLE 9.4
Disk Drive Performance Guidelines

Disk Drive Description	Guideline for Disk Utilization
9332	40%
9335 A01 (disk controller)	20%
9335 B01	40%
9336	50%
9337	50%
all internal disk drives	50%

The **Type** field displays the type of disk drive installed, which must be a valid disk model as IBM defines the term. If you are using third-party disk, remember that all other companies that manufacture disks for your system must emulate a valid IBM disk model.

The **% Used** field shows how full your disk drives are. Usually, all drives within the same ASP should be about the same percent full.

The primary use for the WRKDSKSTS command is to monitor how full the disk drives are. If you are using multiple ASPs, this command allows you to monitor the utilization of user ASPs 2 through 16. Remember that all AS/400s have a system ASP, ASP 1, and you have the option of setting up user ASPs, which are ASPs 2 through 16. (If you have only one ASP and are looking only for utilization information, the WRKSYSSTS command can also give you the percent full information. For more information about the WRKSYSSTS command, see Chapter 8.) The general performance guideline we suggest is to keep your disk drives at less than 80 percent utilization. However, this guideline varies from system to system.

The **% Busy** field shows how hard your drives are working. All disk drives have guidelines for each particular model type. For performance reasons, you need to monitor the guidelines for your model and type closely. Table 9.4 shows the guidelines for several AS/400 disk drives.

The **% Busy** field on the WRKDSKSTS command should not be used to plan capacity or predict performance, because it is only an estimate of how busy the drive is and can be off significantly in either direction. On the other hand, the output of the PRTSYSRPT report's disk section is quite accurate because the Performance Monitor collects the disk busy values from the disk devices. The PRTSYSRPT report is part of the Performance Tools; for more information about this report, see Chapter 13.

Are there exceptions to these guidelines? You bet. For example, it is not uncommon to have a value in the **% Busy** field as high as 90 percent for a journal receiver in a dedicated ASP without a decrease in overall system performance. The reason is that the writes to the journal receiver are happening sequentially, so the actuator and disk arm do not have to reposition themselves between write operations.

Be careful when setting up ASPs. They are a nice feature and help protect you in case of a disk drive failure. However, the number one performance problem with ASPs is not having enough actuators in the ASP to support the workload. This lack will create a bottleneck. You can easily monitor whether you have enough actuators by checking the WRKDSKSTS command's **% Busy** field. Be careful not to put all your most active data files in a separate ASP without the correct number of actuators. Careful planning is important with ASPs. Understanding the characteristics of the data and programs you place in a user ASP will help you avoid problems.

CHAPTER 10

Using Job Accounting and the Performance Monitor

In this chapter, we will consider two powerful ways to collect performance-related information: the job accounting feature and the Performance Monitor. You should consider the Performance Monitor the primary tool for collecting your performance data. These components can provide you with reams of data from which you can select the information that is most important to your particular system and performance problems.

JOB ACCOUNTING FOR PERFORMANCE

IBM originally designed the AS/400 job accounting feature as an easy way to capture data about system use and charge users for the resources they were using. However, job accounting can also capture performance-related data. Job accounting is an integrated part of OS/400 on every AS/400 and can be a nice alternative to purchasing the Performance Tools. Job accounting data includes such useful information as the jobs running on your system and resources those jobs are using, including processor time, printers, display stations, and database and communications functions. One particularly handy feature of job accounting is that its system overhead is very low, especially compared to the Performance Monitor. Here, we will cover how to use job accounting to capture and report performance-related information.

Information Captured Using Job Accounting

When you're working with job accounting, a basic understanding of journals and how to use them is helpful. You will need to perform journal management operations such as saving, changing, and deleting journal receivers. Detailed information about how to use job accounting is in the IBM *AS/400 Backup and Recovery Guide* (SC41-3304).

You keep job accounting statistics by using the journal entries in the system accounting journal, QSYS/QACGJRN. To use the job accounting information, you must use the DSPJRN (Display Journal) command to extract the data from the QACGJRN journal and write it into a database file. At that point, you may write a query or application program to analyze the job accounting data you have captured. The process is shown in Figure 10.1.

IBM split the job accounting feature into two main parts: resource accounting (JB journal entry) and printer file accounting (DP and/or SP journal entry). Although you can capture either or both types of data, we will focus on

FIGURE 10.1
Steps from Job Runs to Queries

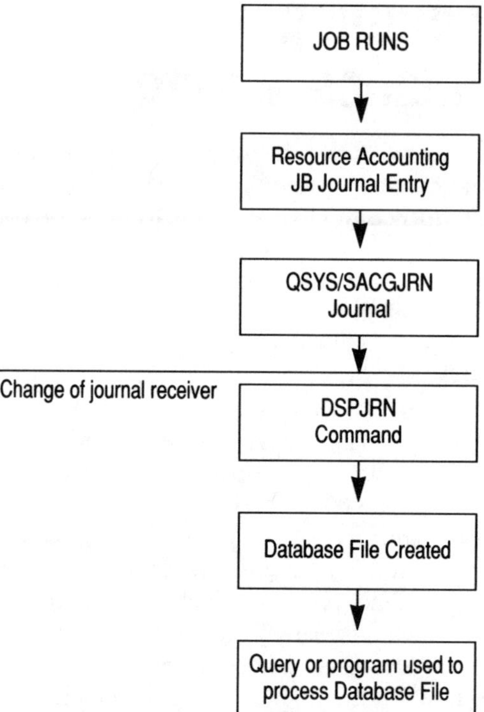

resource accounting data because it is the most useful for performance tuning. For further information about printer file entries, see the IBM *AS/400 Backup and Recovery Guide* or *Work Management Guide* (SC41-3306).

You will find resource accounting data summarized in the JB journal entry at the completion of a job. In addition, the system creates a JB journal entry each time a CHGACGCDE (Change Accounting Code) command occurs. The JB journal entry includes the following information:

- Fully qualified job name
- Accounting code for the accounting segment just ended
- Processing unit time
- Number of routing steps
- Date and time the job entered the system
- Date and time the job started

- Total transaction time (which includes service time)
- Ineligible time and active time
- Number of transactions for all interactive jobs
- Auxiliary I/O operations
- Job type
- Job completion code
- Printing statistics
- Number of database file reads and writes

How to Start Job Accounting

Starting job accounting is a simple process. The following steps will help you use job accounting to track resources on your system.

1. Create a journal receiver in a library of your choice by using the CRTJRNRCV (Create Journal Receiver) command.

   ```
   CRTJRNRCV       JRNRCV(USERLIB/ACGJRN01)
   ```

   Your journal receiver name should end with a sequence number that you can increment each time you switch journal receivers. Such naming lets you use the JRNRCV(*GEN) option with the CHGJRN (Change Journal) command. We recommend a sequence number that has at least two digits — maybe three, depending on how often you will be changing your journal receivers. For example, we used ACGJRN01 as our journal receiver name. The next time we issue the CHGJRN command with the JRNRCV(*GEN) parameter, the journal receiver name will become ACGJRN02.

2. Use the CRTJRN (Create Journal) command to create the journal QSYS/QACGJRN. You must use the name QSYS/QACGJRN, and you must have authority to add objects to the library QSYS. You need to specify the name of the journal receiver you created in the previous step.

3. The final step in using job accounting is to change the system value QACGLVL so that the system starts writing journal entries. Use the CHGSYSVAL (Change System Value) or WRKSYSVAL (Work with System Values) command to change this value (which is set to *NONE as the default) to *JOB, as shown below.

   ```
   CHSYSVAL       VALUE(*JOB)
   ```

   The *JOB entry produces a JB journal entry for each accounting segment of a job. Note that the system requires that you create the QSYS/QACGJRN journal before you can change this system value.

It is important to remember that the system summarizes the resources used and writes the JB journal entry to the QACGJRN journal when the job has completed or when you use the CHGACGCDE command to change the accounting code during the job. If you change the accounting code while the job is still on the job queue, the system also writes a JB entry, even though the job has not used any system resources yet. For example, if you change the accounting code three times during one job, at the end of the job you will see four entries: one for each accounting code change, and one for the end of the job.

The fields used when job accounting writes a journal entry in QSYS/QACGJRN are listed in Table 10.1 and in the reference file QSYS/QAJBACG.

Processing Job Accounting Information

After you have collected job accounting information, you must convert this information from a journal receiver to a database file for processing. You can use the OUTFILE parameter on the DSPJRN (Display Journal) command to write the job accounting journal entries into a database file. The OUTFILE parameter lets you name a file or member. If the member exists, the system clears it before writing the records. If the member does not exist, the system simply adds it. If the file does not exist, OS/400 creates a file, using the record format QJORDJE. This format defines the standard heading fields for each journal entry, but the job accounting data is a single large field. You can use the following example if you have a physical file for the JB information and use the same names for members.

```
DSPJRN  JRN(QACGJRN) JRNCDE(A) ENTTYP(JB) OUTPUT(*NONE) +
        OUTFILE(LIBNAME/QAJBACG)
```

So that you don't have to process the resource accounting data as a single large field, the field reference file QSYS/JB contains record format QSPJAJBE for JB entries. You can also process the JB entries by using one of the supplied field reference files (QSYS/QAJBACG) to create an externally described file. You can then process this file using a query utility or a high-level language program. You can also use the QAJBACG record format to define a DDS (Data Definition Specification) physical file:

```
A    R QWTJAJBE       FORMAT (QSYS/QAJBACG)
```

You can then use the CRTPF (Create Physical File) command against this DDS to create the physical file. Once you have created the physical file, you can process this information with either a query or a high-level program.

The Performance Monitor

Every AS/400 has the Performance Monitor and its STRPFRMON (Start Performance Monitor) command as part of the operating system. The Performance Monitor lets you capture data at regular intervals; you can then use

TABLE 10.1

JB Accounting Journal Entry Information

Field Name	Description	Field Attributes
JAJOB	Job name	Char (10)
JAUSER	Job user	Char (10)
JANBR	Job number	Char (15)
JACDE	Accounting code	Zoned (6,0)
JACPU	Processing unit time used (msec)	Packed decimal (11,0)
JARTGS	Number of routing steps	Packed decimal (5,0)
JAEDTE	Job entry date MMDDYY	Char (6)
JAETIM	Job entry time HHMMSS	Char (6)
JASDTE	Job start date MMDDYY	Char (6)
JASTIM	Job start time HHMMSS	Char (6)
JATRNT	Total transaction time (sec)	Packed decimal (11,0)
JATRNS	Number of transactions	Packed decimal (11,0)
JAAUX	Aux I/O operations and database operations	Packed decimal (11,0)
JATYPE	Job type	Char (1)
JACDE	Completion code	Packed decimal (11,0)
JALINE	Number of printed lines	Packed decimal (11,0)
JAPAGE	Number of printed pages	Packed decimal (11,0)
JAPRTF	Number of print files	Packed decimal (11,0)
JADBPT	Number of database logical write operations	Packed decimal (11,0)
JADBGT	Number of database logical read operations	Packed decimal (11,0)
JADBUP	Number of database logical updates, deletes	Packed decimal (11,0)
JACMPT	Number of communications write operations	Packed decimal (11,0)
JACMGT	Number of communications read operations	Packed decimal (11,0)
JAACT	Time job was active (msec)	Packed decimal (11,0)
JASPN	Time job was suspended (msec)	Packed decimal (11,0)

the Performance Tools, queries, or your own programs to analyze this data. For more information about using the Performance Monitor with Performance Tools, see Chapter 12.

STRPFRMON usually runs in the QCTL subsystem and uses about 3 percent of the CPU. The percentage of CPU it uses depends on how you set up the Performance Monitor's parameters, the number of jobs in the system, and the number of active communications lines on the system.

What STRPFRMON Collects

The STRPFRMON command is the backbone of performance tuning. With the data it collects, you can examine the percent of CPU utilized, disk I/Os per second, transaction data, faults per second, percent of your disk that's busy, and percent of disk space utilized. Although the Performance Tools provide an easy way to view the mountain of performance data collected, they are not necessary to use the Performance Monitor.

With the Performance Monitor's trace option, you can collect additional performance data for jobs, programs, and transactions. With this data, you can create top-10 lists, including jobs with the most transactions and jobs with the largest average response time, average CPU/transaction, synchronous disk I/O, asynchronous disk I/O, seize conflicts, record lock conflicts, active-to-wait occurrences, and wait-to-ineligible occurrences.

Trace data is very useful when you are trying to find the cause of a performance problem. Although you do not want to collect trace data for trend analysis in normal operation, it is a good idea to collect some trace data just before any major change to the system, such as a new release or application update. If a problem results from the change, comparing the trace data reports will often pinpoint the problem's cause.

Before we get into the STRPFRMON command's parameters, we want to warn you to be careful of some potential problems we have seen when trying to start the Performance Monitor command. First, check whether your QCTL subsystem (or whichever subsystem you run the command in) has an available job activity slot. If the Performance Monitor job is still waiting in a job queue after you issue the STRPFRMON command, increase the Max Active parameter value on the subsystem description with the CHGSBSD (Change Subsystem Description) command.

Second, check whether the performance files are the same release as the Performance Monitor command.

Third, check whether you have installed all of the current PTFs. This check is especially important after a new release of the operating system.

Collecting Data with STRPFRMON

As with most AS/400 commands, you have some options when you start the Performance Monitor command. You may type STRPFRMON at any command line and press F4 to prompt the command. You can also use the job scheduling function of the Operational Assistant to schedule the monitor on a regular basis.

Another way to collect performance data consistently is with the ADDPFRCOL (Add Performance Collection) command. With this command, you can select specific days of the week on which the Performance Monitor will automatically collect data. To use this command, type ADDPFRCOL and press F4 to fill in the parameters. The options for ADDPFRCOL's Collection

Days parameter are *MON, *TUE, *WED, *THU, *FRI, *SAT, *SUN, and *ALL. You may use the CHGPFRCOL (Change Performance Collection) command to change any existing collections. Use RMVPFRCOL (Remove Performance Collection) to delete performance collections that you have defined.

STRPFRMON Parameters

When you type STRPFRMON and press CMD-4 to prompt, the Start Performance Monitor command screen will appear, as in Figure 10.2.

On this screen, you may specify a unique member name at the **Member** parameter. The default is *GEN (Generation), which gives you a unique name based on the year, the Gregorian date, and the time the sample started. An example of a *GEN name is Q932940733, which means that the sample was taken in (19)93, on the 294th day of the year (10/21), and the sample started at 7:33 A.M. If the *GEN name is hard for you to work with, you could use a name such as TU0602AM, which you can immediately identify as a sample you took on Tuesday, June 2, in the morning. The naming is up to you — either way will work.

If the member you specify doesn't exist, the monitor adds the member to each of the many underlying performance database files, which takes some time. The performance database files that the Performance Monitor creates are listed in Table 10.2.

FIGURE 10.2

Start Performance Monitor Command Screen

```
                    Start Performance Monitor (STRPFRMON)

Type Choices, Press Enter.

Member  ....................  *GEN        Name, *GEN
Library  ..................  QPFRDATA    Name
Text 'Description'  .......  *Same
Time Interval (In Minutes)  15          5, 10, 15, 20, 25, 30, 35, ...
Stops Data Collection  ....  *ELAPSED    *ELAPSED, *TIME, *NOMAX
Days From Current Day  ....  0           0-9
Hour  .....................  2           0-999
Minutes  ..................  0           0-99
Data Type  ................  *ALL        *ALL, *SYS
Trace Type  ...............  *NONE       *NONE, *ALL
Dump the Trace  ...........  *YES        *YES, *NO
Job Trace Interval  .......  .5          .5 - 9.9 Seconds
Job Types  ................  *DFT        *NONE, *DFT, *ASJ, *BCH...
                                                   + For More Values

                                                   More...

F3=Exit   F4=Prompt   F5=Refresh   F10=Additional Parameters   F12=Cancel
F13=How to Use This Display        F24=More Keys
```

TABLE 10.2

Performance Monitor Files

File Name	File Description
QAPMASYN	ASYNC performance data
QAPMBSC	BISYNC performance data
QAPMBUS	BUS counter performance data
QAPMCIOP	Communications IOP performance data
QAPMCONF	System configuration information data
QAPMDDI	Distributed Data Interface (DDI) data
QAPMDIOP	Storage device controller performance data
QAPMDISK	Disk drive performance data
QAPMECL	Token Ring performance data
QAPMETH	Ethernet performance data
QAPMFRLY	Frame relay data
QAPMHDLC	High-level data link performance data
QAPMJOBS	Job-related performance data
QAPMLIOP	Local workstation controller performance data
QAPMMIOP	Multifunction controller performance data
QAPMPOOL	Storage pool performance data
QAPMRESP	Local workstation response-time performance data
QAPMSCOL	Performance Monitor collection data
QAPMSYS	General system performance data
QAPMX25	X.25 performance data

Because the Performance Monitor creates so many files, adding a member to each file uses a lot of system resources. Some installations avoid this overhead by setting up standard member names and periodically collecting data into those members (for example, MON_AM, MON_PM, WED_AM, or FRI_PM).

The QPFRDATA library is the default for the **Library** parameter. You need to verify that this library exists on your system. The first time you run the monitor, it checks the library specified in this parameter. If the performance files exist, the system adds a member to the files with the name you specified in the member parameter. If the performance files don't exist in the library you specify, the Performance Monitor creates the files and then adds the first member to each file.

Next, you need to enter a **Text 'Description'**.

In the **Time Interval** parameter, you specify how frequently you want to collect the performance data. For example, if you specify 15, as in Figure 10.2, and run the monitor for two hours, you get eight sets of performance data summary records — one every 15 minutes. Be careful with the averages that result from long sample periods. It is best to collect data for intervals of no more than 30 minutes. When you are looking for a particular problem, shorter intervals, probably 5 minutes, are better, because they help you see problems that can sometimes remain hidden in samples with long intervals. Most performance analysis work requires short intervals.

You set the **Data Type** parameter to *ALL to include communications performance data. We recommend that you always collect this data.

The **Trace Type** parameter turns trace data collection on or off. Trace data is useful when you are trying to look at specific problems with applications. The trace collection overhead is minimal. However, the trace option will add considerable overhead to the performance collection process when the system dumps the trace data, so be careful when using it.

The default for the **Dump the Trace** parameter is *YES, which means that the system dumps the trace data from an internal system area to a database file at the end of the collection periods. You should consider setting this parameter to *NO, which stops the trace from dumping, because the performance impact of the trace dump can be large. You should allow it only when you have minimum activity on your system. If you specify *NO, you can still run the DMPTRC (Dump Trace) command later.

Deferring the trace dump in this way is very useful when you want to catch an intermittent performance problem. You can start the tools and specify *NO for the dump trace option. Then, if the system does not experience the problem in the collection period, you can restart the Performance Monitor, specifying the same collection member. In this way, you avoid the overhead of dumping the trace data and the overhead of creating additional members in the database files. When you finally capture a period that contains the intermittent problem, you use the DMPTRC command to retain the trace data that reflects the problem.

We have discussed only the key parameters of the STRPFRMON command. Try experimenting with the various parameters until you get the exact data you need. Once you discover the right mix of parameters, stick with them and be consistent so that you have appropriate data for your long-term trend analysis.

After you have entered the required parameters, press Enter to run the Performance Monitor.

Processing the Performance Monitor Files

You can use the performance data files by writing programs or queries to access them. You can determine the layouts for these files by running the DSPFFD (Display File Field Description) command. They are also listed in the *AS/400 Work Management Guide* (SC41-3306). Because multiple members are in data files, make sure you are using the correct member. Remember, we recommend that you use member names that are meaningful so that you can easily pick the correct member to process.

These files are a good source of performance data. For example, if you want to find out your system's average response time, you can use the QAPMJOBS (Job Data) file. First, select all interactive jobs (Job Type Field, JBTYPE, with a value I). Then place Total Response Time (JBRSP) and Total Number of Transactions (JBNTR) into two work fields: Total Responses and Total Number of Transactions. After you have read all records, divide the Total Responses by the Total Number of Transactions to get the average response time for all your interactive jobs.

The QAPMJOBS file is a particularly useful performance data file because it contains information such as the user, number of transactions processed, type of job, and CPU time used. However, QAPMJOBS is just one example, and you should be creative in your use of the performance data available in the other performance files, as well.

CHAPTER 11

Performance Tools: Overview and Group One, Status Displays

As you can see from the previous section, you can do a great deal of performance tuning without any tools. However, tools can add to your capabilities. Several sets of tools are available to help you investigate your system's performance. This section will examine these optional performance tools, and, more important, how you can use them to enhance your system's performance.

We will focus on the performance tools available from IBM, but many new and exciting tools are available from third-party vendors (see Appendix E). Because writing about third-party performance tools could be construed as an endorsement of these products and because there are too many tools to review, we'll cover only IBM-supplied tools.

AS/400 Performance Tools: Overview

The most obvious and widely known set of AS/400 performance tools is a collection IBM calls the AS/400 Performance Tools. This tool set is an optional program product, which means you must purchase it separately. This product includes reports, interactive commands, and several other functions.

Most AS/400 users purchase the Performance Tools for the reports. The reports organize Performance Monitor information in a more logical and useful format. Some people argue that the reports show too much information, and they may be right. However, the information the performance reports provide can be very useful — if you know where to look. In this section, we will show you exactly where to look and what to look for in the reports.

Another popular part of the Performance Tools is the Advisor. The Advisor examines the Performance Monitor data and recommends ways to improve your system's performance. We will look at the pros and cons of using the Advisor.

You may not think you are ready for the Performance Tools because you don't have anybody on staff who can take the time to figure out what information is in the reports. For people in your situation, IBM offers a subset version of the Performance Tools, the IBM Performance Tools Subset/400 (product number 5798-RYP). This entry-level subset of the Performance Tools costs about half the price of the regular Performance Tools. IBM designed this product for customers who do not require all the reports in the regular Performance Tools.

Why Use the Performance Tools?

Why should you use the Performance Tools instead of or in addition to the commands and techniques we covered in the previous section? One important difference between the Tools and the interactive commands is the elapsed time factor. Remember that when you use commands such as WRKSYSSTS and WRKACTJOB, you look at short time periods. For example, we suggested you use an elapsed period of between 5 and 10 minutes to get a good measurement of your system's performance. However, to get an accurate measurement of your system's performance over a longer time, you need to use the Work with System Activity (WRKSYSACT) command in the AS/400 Performance Tools. The Performance Tools are also versatile — for example, the In-Depth Perspective at the end of this chapter discusses a special case in which the WRKSYSACT command was used for very short time periods.

As you recall, to know whether your system's performance is abnormal, you have to understand what normal performance levels are. The hard-copy information the tools supply helps you document trends on your system. For example, say you are using the performance reports to track your transactions per hour (TPH) and you print reports every day. You know that your system averages 21,000 TPH, so you can quickly recognize that something needs investigation if you suddenly see 35,000 TPH. The point is that if you are not documenting your performance trends, it is hard — if not impossible — to know what is abnormal in your system's environment. The Performance Tools are excellent for trend analysis.

Who Should Use the Performance Tools?

We believe that the Performance Tools convey useful information for everyone. However, to understand some of this information, you probably need some systems experience. That experience may be as an operator, a programmer, a technical manager, or an experienced end user.

The original Performance Tools were designed to help IBM Rochester's technical support people understand performance issues on the System/38. Once S/38 users found out about these tools, they started asking IBM to make the tools available to users. The AS/400 Performance Tools are similar to the S/38 Performance Tools because IBM carried forward the best parts of the S/38 Performance Tools to the AS/400 and then improved on them.

Few people, except systems engineers and heavyweight systems people, used the S/38 Performance Tools. On the AS/400, all types of users work with the Performance Tools. Several factors explain this heavy use, but mainly, it is because many people need to get optimum performance from their AS/400.

This section explains how to use the Performance Tools and interpret the results you get when you use the Tools' reports. When you finish this section, you will be able to find useful information with the Performance Tools, no matter what your background or experience level.

How to Find the Performance Tools

You can purchase the Performance Tools (licensed program product number 5738-PT1) from IBM or wherever you purchase your system software. Library QPFR contains the Performance Tools programs. QPFRDATA is the default library for performance data, but performance data may be kept in any library.

To check whether you have the Performance Tools installed on your system, use the GO LICPGM (Go Licensed Program) command, and press Enter. The licensed programs screen will appear. Option 10 on this screen lets you display the licensed program products on your system. If you see the AS/400 Performance Tools listed, you have installed the Performance Tools. While you are on this screen, verify that the Performance Tools' version is the same as the operating system's: Look at the version number to the right of the program product description. If the versions do not match, the Performance Tools will not run (and will create a pretty nasty system dump if you try to run them).

The default output queue for all your performance reports is QPFROUTQ in library QPFR. The job description is QPFRJOBD. This default job description is adequate to run all the Performance Tools.

If you are working with multiple AS/400s, you may not want to purchase the Performance Tools for each system in your network. You can transfer the performance data files generated on one system to other systems. So, if you back up library QPFRDATA and move it to a system where the Performance Tools are installed, you may run the Performance Tools against the data from the other system. Be sure to restore the library with another library name so that you do not overlay your original QPFRDATA library.

One last note about moving files between systems: Be sure to convert the performance files to the same OS/400 version as the tools. A conversion utility (CVTPFRDTA) comes with the tools. Also, note that you may convert the performance data files only upward. For example, if your remote systems are running under V2R3 and your host system with the Performance Tools is running under V3R1, you can run the conversion utility to make the files compatible with the tools. On the other hand, if your tools are at V2R3 and your files are at V3R1, you cannot convert the data files.

To get to the main Performance Tools menu, use the STRPFRT (Start Performance Tools) or GO PERFORM command. Either command will take you to the main Performance Tools menu, which you can see in Figure 11.1. Both commands will modify the library list so that your work environment is ready to run the tools.

FIGURE 11.1
Performance Tools Option

```
PERFORM                    AS/400 Performance Tools
                                                          System:   PERF1
 Select one of the following:

1. Select type of status
2. Collect performance data
3. Print performance reports
4. Capacity planning/modeling
5. Programmer performance utilities
6. Configure and manage tools
7. Display performance data
8. System activity
9. Performance graphics
10. Advisor

70. Related commands




Selection or command
===>>_____________________________________________________
 F3=Exit   F4=Prompt   F9=Retrieve   F12=Cancel   F13=User support
 F16=System main menu
```

The Performance Tools Options

We divide the functions of the Performance Tools into four different groups: status displays, Performance Monitor data, Performance Tools utilities, and miscellaneous functions. We will explain how to use the Performance Tools by looking at each of these four groups.

If you look at the AS/400 Performance Tools main menu in Figure 11.1, you can see 10 options. Using our four groups, we have organized these options as follows.

- Status Displays
    - Option 1: Select type of status
    - Option 8: System activity
- Performance Monitor Data
    - Option 2: Collect performance data
    - Option 3: Print performance reports
    - Option 4: Capacity planning/modeling — BEST/1
    - Option 7: Display performance data
    - Option 9: Performance graphics
    - Option 10: Advisor

- Performance Tools Utilities
  - Option 5: Programmer performance utilities
- Miscellaneous Functions
  - Option 6: Configure and manage tools

Let's now look at each of these four groups in detail. In this chapter, we will examine Group One, the Status Displays. In Chapter 12, you will learn about the options associated with the Performance Monitor. The details of the Performance Tools' System Report and Component Report are considered in Chapter 13. And finally, Chapter 14 covers Group Three, Performance Tools Utilities, and Group Four, Miscellaneous Functions.

Group One: Status Displays

We group the commands you can reach through Option 1 (Select type of status) or 8 (System activity) on the Performance Tools menu shown in Figure 11.1 as status displays. These commands are mainly for interactive use, although you may use them to generate print files.

Option 1: Select Type of Status

All the commands accessible through Option 1 (Select type of status) are available without the Performance Tools. Through Option 1, you can access the performance status commands, including WRKSYSSTS, WRKACTJOB, and WRKDSKSTS. For more information about using these commands, see Chapters 8 and 9. This option also includes several other status commands, such as WRKSBMJOB (Work with Submitted Jobs), WRKSBS (Work with Subsystem), and WRKCURJOB (Work with Current Job), that provide helpful information for performance programming. However, because our focus is on mastering system performance, we will not address these commands in detail.

Option 8: System Activity

The System Activity menu gives you two options: the WRKSYSACT command itself, and an option that allows you to print a WRKSYSACT report.

The WRKSYSACT command is a veritable Swiss Army knife that provides lots of information about lots of situations. An interactive command, WRKSYSACT is available to only one user at a time. Compared to the WRKACTJOB and WRKSYSSTS commands, the WRKSYSACT command runs very quickly and efficiently and gives detailed information such as the OS/400 jobs and LIC tasks that are active — information that is not available through other interactive commands. Thus, WRKSYSACT is one of the most powerful and helpful commands for performance analysis work.

Note that this command shows jobs that are using CPU or performing disk I/O operations only during the measured interval. This interval can be from 1 second to 15 minutes long. In addition, WRKSYSACT has a unique feature that lets you automatically update your screen at an interval of your choice. (We will discuss this feature in detail later.) With multiple processor systems, the display shows utilization of each processor.

To run WRKSYSACT, select Option 8, System Activity, on the main Performance Tools menu, and then select Option 1 (Work with system activity) and press Enter. You will see the command prompt screen illustrated in Figure 11.2.

FIGURE 11.2
WRKSYSACT Command Prompt Screen

```
                  Work with System Activity (WRKSYSACT)

 Type choices, press Enter.

 Output .................... *          *, *FILE, *BOTH
 Interval length ........... 5          1 - 900 seconds
 Sequence .................. *CPU       *CPU, *IO
 Type of information ....... *ALL       *ALL, *JOBS, *TASKS
 Member .................... QAITMON    Name
 Library ................... QPFRDATA   Name





                                                                Bottom




 F3=Exit  F4=Prompt  F5=Refresh  F12=Cancel  F13=How to use this display
 F24=More keys
```

From this screen, you specify how you want the command to run. The parameters for the WRKSYSACT command are listed in Table 11.1. To run this command, you can use the default parameters or change them and press Enter. The screen in Figure 11.3 will appear.

Working with the WRKSYSACT Command

One of this command's most useful functions is to identify the jobs and tasks that are running at any given time. The WRKSYSACT command gives you better information than the WRKACTJOB command. Although the WRKACTJOB command displays the total amount of CPU in use at any time, its **CPU %** field does

Table 11.1

WRKSYSACT Parameters

Parameter	Options	Definition
	*	The output is displayed to the interactive user
Output	*FILE	The output is sent to a file. You are prompted for a file name.
	*BOTH	The output is displayed and sent to a file
Interval length	1 - 900 sec.	How often the automatic refresh should occur
Sequence	*CPU	Lists information by highest CPU usage
	*IO	Lists information by highest I/O generation
Type of	*ALL	Lists all jobs and tasks being run
information	*JOB	Lists only jobs being run
	*TASK	Lists only tasks being run
Member	QAITMON	The default member (this parameter is only displayed when you specify *File or *Both in Output)
Library	QPFRDATA	The library for the performance file member

Figure 11.3

Parameters for WRKSYSACT

```
                        Work with System Activity

 Automatic refresh in seconds  . . . . . . . .  5

 Elapsed time . . . . :    00:00:02

 CPU 1 util . . :    24.6                      CPU 2 util . . :    22.1

 Type options, press Enter.
 1=Monitor job   5=Work with job
                                                    Total    Total
     Job or                                  CPU     Sync    Async      PAG     EAO
 Opt  Task       User      Number     Pty    Util     I/O      I/O     Fault    Excp
  _   AWC        ARNOLD    046039      1      8.4      11       0        0        0
  _   RCCINT                           0       .1       0       0        0        0
  _   DSP02      TURNER    046000     20     29.5     135      16        0        0
  _   QSYSARB    QSYS      009928      0       .2      12       0        0        0




                                                                        Bottom

 F3=Exit   F10=Update list   F11=View 2   F12=Cancel   F19=Automatic refresh
 F24=More keys
```

not add up to the total of all displayed jobs' CPU utilization because the system tasks are not displayed. They count toward the total in the Total CPU field, but their detail does not appear. In contrast, WRKSYSACT displays the CPU and I/O detail of all jobs and tasks.

Obviously, it is important to identify system tasks that are using a large amount of CPU. Abnormally high CPU usage can indicate a problem with the system and the need for a PTF or a review of your system by IBM support. On the other hand, such a situation can also mean a program is consistently and repeatedly calling a system function.

What is a large amount of CPU? The specific value depends on what you are running at a particular time. To recognize when system tasks are using an abnormally large number of CPU cycles, you need to become familiar with your system's environment.

If you want to know more about system tasks, you can check the listings provided by IBM that give definitions of what each system task is and does. One task to watch for is ERRLOG. If WRKSYSACT often shows this task active, the system is reporting an excessive number of error conditions. You can view entries in the system error log using Option 2 from the STRSST (Start Service Tools) or PRTERRLOG (Printer Error Log) command. Some errors will be self-explanatory, and others will require service assistance.

When you issue the WRKSYSACT command to see what jobs use the largest amount of the CPU and generate the most disk I/O, you should consider using a helpful feature of WRKSYSACT, the automatic refresh mode option. By pressing F19, you can put the command into an automatic refresh mode, which updates the command at the interval you set. The default update interval is five seconds, which is short enough for most situations.

When you use the WRKSYSACT command with the automatic refresh mode, you can watch your monitor display the top CPU and disk I/O users at your set interval. If you consistently see the same jobs or system tasks at the top or near the top of the stack and they are using a large percentage of the CPU, you should investigate.

Another nice feature of the WRKSYSACT command is the *FILE option on the OUTPUT parameter. Although Option 2 on the System Activity menu allows you to print a WRKSYSACT report, the information on this report is not as helpful as the data you get by using the *FILE output parameter.

The MEMBER parameter specifies the name of the member to which the data will be sent; the default member is QAITMON. The collected performance data is in the file QAITMON, which is by default in the QPFRDATA library. You may specify another library by changing the command's LIBRARY parameter. You have one record for each active job or task in an interval. Be careful when your system is busy and you're using small intervals, because you will generate many records in a short period.

Table 11.2 describes the content of each record in QAITMON. You may write your own programs against this data to get some very useful performance information.

TABLE 11.2
The Records in QUAITMON

Field Name	Attributes	Description
LVLID	CHAR(7)	The level of the module that collected this data and the level of this file in the form VVRRRFF, where VV = version, RRR = release number, and FF = file level.
DTETIM	CHAR(13)	The date (CMMDDYY) and time (HHMMSS) data was collected.
ITVTIM	PACKED(11,0)	The time between data collections, where one unit equals 4,096 microseconds.
CPUTOT	PACKED(11,0)	The total processing unit time all tasks and jobs use during the interval, where one unit equals 4,096 microseconds. For multiple-processor systems, this is the average use by all processors.
NAME	CHAR(10)	The job or task name for this entry.
JOBUSR	CHAR(10)	The user profile associated with a job.
JOBNBR	CHAR(6)	The number assigned to the job.
PTY	CHAR(3)	The priority of the job or task when the data was collected.
CPUDLT	PACKED(11,0)	The processing unit time this task or job uses during the interval, where one unit equals 4,096 microseconds. For multiple-processor systems, this value is the average use by all processors.
IOTOT	PACKED(11,0)	The total physical I/O operations (synchronous and asynchronous) this job or task performed.
SDBR	PACKED(11,0)	The number of synchronous database reads.
SNDBR	PACKED(11,0)	The number of synchronous non-database reads.
SDBW	PACKED(11,0)	The number of synchronous database writes.
SNDBW	PACKED(11,0)	The number of synchronous non-database writes.
ADBR	PACKED(11,0)	The number of asynchronous database reads.
ANDBR	PACKED(11,0)	The number of asynchronous non-database reads.
ADBW	PACKED(11,0)	The number of asynchronous database writes.
ANDBW	PACKED(11,0)	The number of asynchronous non-database writes.
PAGFLT	PACKED(11,0)	The number of process access group faults.
EAOCNT	PACKED(11,0)	The number of effective address overflow exceptions.
JTFLAG	CHAR(1)	A flag indicating whether this record represents a job or task, where '00'X = Job and '80'X = Task.
RSRV1	CHAR(4)	Reserved for future use by IBM.
PERMW	PACKED(11,0)	The number of writes that were for permanent objects.

continued

TABLE 11.2 CONTINUED

Field Name	Attributes	Description
IOPND	PACKED(11,0)	The number of I/O pending page faults.
SYMSYNC	PACKED(11,0)	The number of waits for asynchronous I/O operations to complete.
OVRTOT	PACKED(11,0)	The total number of binary, decimal, and floating-point overflow exceptions.
CPU1	PACKED(11,0)	For multiple-processor systems, the time jobs and tasks used in processor one during the interval. One unit of time equals 4,096 microseconds.
CPU2	PACKED(11,0)	For multiple-processor systems, the time jobs and tasks used in processor two during the interval. One unit of time equals 4,096 microseconds.
CPUCNT	PACKED(3,0)	The number of active processors in the system during data collection.
CPU3	PACKED(11,0)	For multiple-processor systems, the time jobs and tasks used in processor three during the interval. One unit of time equals 4,096 microseconds.
CPU4	PACKED(11,0)	For multiple-processor systems, the time jobs and tasks used in processor four during the interval. One unit of time equals 4,096 microseconds.

Third-Party Performance Tools

I have seen many third-party tools over the years that augment the capabilities of the IBM AS/400 performance tools. The one area in which I have the most requests for help is the ability to monitor performance in a real-time mode, either on a single or on a multiple set of AS/400s. The third-party vendors listed in Appendix G have different capabilities in this area. Because of many of the new technologies emerging in the area of third-party performance tools, I recommend that a review of third-party tools be included in your organization's performance management program. ■

Alan Arnold

In Depth: Examining Priorities

WRKSYSACT Versus the Performance Monitor

Has your system's response time ever increased dramatically from one day to the next for no apparent reason? The people affected tell you they didn't change anything, but suddenly the system is running much more slowly.

Company X ran into this problem. The company's normal daily runtime environment consists of three types of work running concurrently: interactive work at priority 20, remote communications at priority 25, and batch jobs at priority 50. The problem was that the communications jobs — remote sites dialing in to do interactive work — weren't getting done. Response times were erratic, and communications time-outs and error recovery frequently interrupted the work. As a result, the system would drop the communications device, forcing the remote users to redial the system to pick up where they left off.

The AS/400 Performance Tools' System Report, which we will discuss in detail in Chapter 13, revealed some significant information. Table 11A shows a condensed version of that information — the CPU% value for priority 20 includes the data from all priorities and job types at and above priority 20.

TABLE 11.A

Condensed System Report

Priority	Job Type	CPU%	Cumulative CPU%
20	INT	60	60
25	INT	5	65
50	BATCH	35	100

Surprisingly, the priority 50 jobs were getting a much higher percentage of the CPU time than were the priority 25 jobs, from which you might infer that the priority 25 jobs were running just fine. After all, CPU cycles are supposed to trickle down from higher to lower priority. Yet the priority 25 work wasn't getting done. Either those jobs were running poorly, or they weren't getting enough CPU time.

Using the WRKSYSACT Command

It was unlikely that the AS/400 wasn't honoring CPU priority, but obviously something unexpected was going on. The System Report had provided a bird's-eye view, but it hadn't answered the question of why the priority 25 jobs were faring so poorly. The System Report's job-level data summarizes CPU usage by the **assigned** job run priority (set in the RUNPTY parameter of the CHGJOB (Change Job) command). But jobs don't always spend their whole lifetime at their assigned priorities, because the system sometimes temporarily promotes a job to a higher priority. What the

continued

In Depth: *continued*

System Report doesn't show is how much time a job spends at its assigned priority versus how much time (if any) it spends in a promoted state.

The WRKSYSACT command offers a different look at system use. The WRKSYSACT command shows the jobs, their current priority, and the extent to which they're using the CPU. In addition, it can look at intervals of time as small as 5 seconds (as compared with the 5-minute minimum of the Performance Monitor, which collects the data for the System Report).

The target of investigation was the priority 50 jobs. The WRKSYSACT command's OUTPUT parameter created a database file (QAITMON), which produced a machine-readable audit trail of job activity. Next, the outfile data became input to a query to select, sort, summarize, and report the data. Because we knew what jobs were running, the queries selected and sorted by the batch job names and then did a secondary sort and break by job priority. That output was used to produce, by job, a summary of the number of records at different priorities.

The Real Priorities

The query output (Table 11B) shows that three jobs with an assigned priority of 50 actually were spending more than 90 percent of their runtime at a priority of 20. The priority 50 jobs were using 35 percent of the CPU, so more than 90 percent of that 35 percent (31 percent of the CPU) was used to run these low-priority jobs at priority 20.

TABLE 11.B

Query Report on Priority 50 Jobs

Job	Number of priority 50 records	Number of priority 20 records	Percent of priority 20 records
1	11	126	91.97
2	8	105	92.92
3	14	146	91.25

Therefore, the real priority 20 CPU usage in this case was more than 96 percent: 65 percent from the jobs assigned priority 20 and more than 31 percent from the promoted priority 50 jobs. But because this situation occurred on a relatively fast AS/400 with a small interactive CPU/transaction rate, CPU queuing didn't have a significant impact on the interactive transaction response time. Because the promoted priority 50 jobs used most of the CPU that the interactive jobs didn't use, less than 5 percent of the engine remained for the priority 25 communications work.

This disparity meant that the priority 25 jobs generally were at the far end of the CPU queue when they were trying to respond. The resulting delay caused numerous line errors that had to be

continued

In Depth: *continued*

processed, which put even more of a demand (including high-priority system jobs) on the CPU, which caused even less of the CPU to be available for the communications jobs — a vicious circle.

Why were the priority 50 jobs being promoted? They were accessing production database files using numerous ad hoc queries (i.e., there were no preexisting indexes over the database files) with select/omit criteria. A part of running such queries requires building a logical file over the physical file. Building logical files is a lengthy and CPU-intensive task, and seize conflicts can occur when other jobs need to change a file over which the system is building an index. (These conflicts last until the build is completed.) Which job wins such a conflict? The job that currently holds the file, of course.

Ironically, this inefficiency can happen because the AS/400 is designed to keep things running smoothly. One part of that design is the job priority a user sets to indicate a performance objective. But when a low-priority job holds a resource (in this case, a database file) that a higher-priority job needs, the system's response is to get the lower-priority job out of the way as soon as possible so that the higher-priority job can continue. At Company X, therefore, the AS/400's reaction to the seize conflict was to promote the priority 50 job (the holder) temporarily to priority 20 (the priority of the requester) until it could release the resource. Even with the promotion, however, the build took a long time.

Quick and Other Fixes

Company X was following IBM's recommendation: Run your queries in batch mode at low priority so they don't interfere with high-priority interactive work. Unfortunately, in this situation the recommended setup couldn't avoid the problem.

A quick fix is to raise the priority of the priority 25 communications jobs. These jobs require little CPU time; but when they need it, they need it immediately. If they don't get the CPU soon enough, the resulting communications time-outs instigate the error recovery process and sever the communications link. Changing the priority of these jobs to 19 lets them get the CPU when they need it.

The interactive users won't notice any difference. After changing the priority from 25 to 19, the cumulative usage of the CPU for priority 20 and above is still in the range of 90 percent to 95 percent; that is, it's already so high that the additional CPU queuing effect caused by the change is minimal.

A longer-term fix is to have the ad hoc queries use a copy of the production files rather than the "live" version. This arrangement ensures that priority 50 work stays at priority 50. Even so, the communications jobs should be at priority 19. Putting those jobs at that priority makes for a more stable, consistent service time for running low-speed devices (such as communications lines, as well as printers and tape drives) that need a tiny amount of CPU time, and it avoids errors such as time-outs and device overrun/underrun and the associated error recovery processing. If these types of jobs starve for the CPU, the inevitable result is more error recovery and its associated CPU usage whenever higher-priority work hits peak load at the same time the devices need to be serviced.

continued

In Depth: *continued*

Another option (which wasn't available in this situation) is to use fewer ad hoc queries. After analyzing the queries being done by the batch jobs, logical files could have been built and maintained for the most common of them. This option reduces promotion but doesn't eliminate it.

The art of analyzing system performance often lies in knowing which tool to use for the problem at hand. Be cautious when modeling data from a combined batch and interactive environment. As the AS/400 grows in speed and capacity, the workloads and mixes are much more complex than they used to be. You may have to do additional analysis to understand what's really happening. ■

CHAPTER 12

Group Two: Performance Monitor Data

The Performance Monitor data commands cover all Performance Tools options that relate to the Performance Monitor and the files that this tool generates. On the Performance Tools menu (Figure 12.1), these options are

- Option 2: Collect performance data
- Option 3: Print performance reports
- Option 4: Capacity planning/modeling
- Option 7: Display performance data
- Option 9: Performance graphics
- Option 10: Advisor

We will not rewrite the AS/400 Performance Tools user guide here, but we will explain the Performance Monitor information so that the Performance Tools

FIGURE 12.1
AS/400 Performance Tools Menu

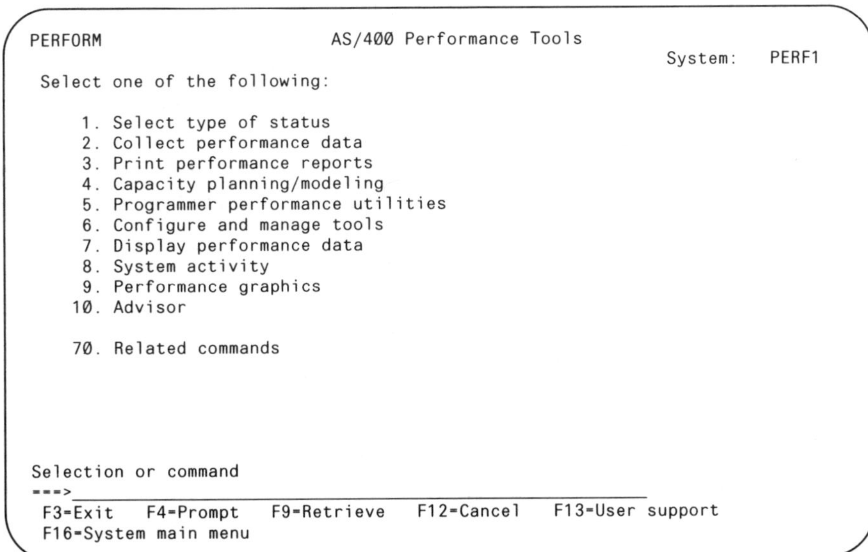

```
PERFORM                     AS/400 Performance Tools
                                                             System:   PERF1
 Select one of the following:

     1. Select type of status
     2. Collect performance data
     3. Print performance reports
     4. Capacity planning/modeling
     5. Programmer performance utilities
     6. Configure and manage tools
     7. Display performance data
     8. System activity
     9. Performance graphics
    10. Advisor

    70. Related commands

Selection or command
===>
 F3=Exit   F4=Prompt   F9=Retrieve   F12=Cancel   F13=User support
 F16=System main menu
```

are a little easier to use. Our goal is for you to understand how to use the tools, learn what information you can find by using the tools, and see what to do with the information once you find it.

Option 2: Collect Performance Data

Option 2 gives you access to the STRPFRMON (Start Performance Monitor) command, which collects the performance data against which you will run the Performance Tools. With this data, you can examine a system overview that tells the percent of CPU utilized, disk I/O per second, transaction data, and faults per second. You also get a disk summary that includes I/O requests per second, percent busy, and percent of space utilized. In addition, you can run three more summaries: a pool summary (pages and page faults per second, interactive transactions per hour, and wait counts), a line summary (communications utilization, workstation controller utilization), and a job summary (average response time, average CPU per transaction, average disk I/O per transaction, percent CPU utilization, total I/O, and read and write requests).

As we've mentioned, every AS/400 has the STRPFRMON command, and it usually runs in the QCTL subsystem using a small percentage of the CPU. The percentage of the CPU depends on how you set up the Performance Monitor command parameters, the number of jobs in the system, and the number of active communications lines on the system. On average, the Performance Monitor usually uses less than 3 percent of the CPU.

With the Performance Monitor's trace option, you can collect additional performance data for jobs, programs, and transactions. This data lets you report top-10 lists of jobs with the most transactions or the longest average response time, average CPU/transactions, synchronous disk I/O, asynchronous disk I/O, seize conflicts, record lock conflicts, active-to-wait occurrences, and wait-to-ineligible occurrences. The trace option also collects transition detail within a transaction, including extremely detailed information about selected transactions.

Trace data gathers information at the individual transaction level and lets you categorize the transactions. It is very useful when you are trying to find the cause of a performance problem. In normal operation, for trend analysis purposes, you do not want to collect trace data. However, it is a good idea to collect some trace periods just before any major change to the system, such as a new release or application update. If a problem results from the change, comparing the trace data reports from before and after the change will often pinpoint the problem's cause.

Before we get into the STRPFRMON command's parameters, we want to warn you about some problems we have seen when trying to start the Performance Monitor command. First, check whether your QCTL subsystem (or whichever subsystem you run the command in) has an available job activity slot. If the Performance Monitor job is still waiting in a job queue after you issue the

STRPFRMON command, increase the Max Active parameter value on the subsystem description via the CHGSBSD (Change Subsystem Description) command.

Second, check whether the performance files are the same release as the Performance Monitor command. Run the convert utility, which is Option 5, Programmer performance utilities, on the Performance Tools menu. (For more information about the Programmer performance utilities option, see Chapter 14.) Also verify that the Performance Tools are the same release as the operating system. If the Performance Tools are not current, you should not run the convert utility because it will convert the files to a version that is incompatible with the Performance Monitor command.

Third, check whether your PTFs are current. This check is especially important after a new release of the operating system. Remember, STRPFRMON and the Performance Tools are in separate program products. Because STRPFRMON is part of the operating system, you should check operating PTFs; you need to check for additional PTFs because they may affect the Performance Tools. If you haven't used your Performance Tools since you installed your system a few years back, you should definitely ensure that your PTFs are up-to-date.

Collecting Performance Samples

As with most AS/400 commands, you have options when you use the Performance Monitor command to collect performance data. You can select Option 2 from the Performance Tools menu and press Enter, or you can use the job scheduling function of the Operational Assistant to schedule the Performance Monitor regularly.

Another way to collect performance data consistently is with the ADDPFRCOL (Add Performance Collection) command. With automatic performance collection, you can select specific days of the week on which the Performance Monitor will automatically collect data. You may type the ADDPFRCOL command and press F4 to prompt it and fill in the parameters, or you may choose Option 2 on the main Performance Tools menu and then Option 3 to access the Work with Performance Collection menu.

The ADDPFRCOL displays are similar to those of the STRPFRMON command. With ADDPFRCOL's **Collection Days** parameter, you can establish a regular schedule for collecting performance data automatically. The options for this parameter are *MON, *TUE, *WED, *THU, *FRI, *SAT, *SUN, and *ALL. You may use the CHGPFRCOL (Change Performance Collection) command to change any existing collections and the RMVPFRCOL (Remove Performance Collection) command to delete performance collections that you have defined. (For information about files the Performance Monitor generates or about running the Performance Monitor without the Performance Tools, see Chapter 10.)

When you start the Performance Monitor by selecting Option 2 from the Performance Tools menu and pressing Enter, the screen in Figure 12.2 appears.

FIGURE 12.2
Collect Performance Data Screen

```
                        Collect Performance Data                       PERF1
                                                          06/26/96  17:07:04
Performance monitor status:
  Status . . . . . . . . . :     Not running




Select one of the following:

     1. Start collecting data
     2. Stop collecting data
     3. Work with performance collection








Selection or command
===>____________________________________________________________
F3=Exit    F4=Prompt    F5=Refresh    F9=Retrieve    F12=Cancel
```

This is the Collect Performance Data screen. When the Performance Monitor is running, the top of this screen displays status information, including the person who started the Performance Monitor, the date and time it was started, and the date and time it will end. If the Monitor is running and you want to stop it, select Option 2 and press Enter.

STRPFRMON Parameters

Next select Option 1, Start Collecting Data, and press Enter. The screen in Figure 12.3 appears.

On the Start Collecting Data screen, you have several options. Option 1 will start the STRPFRMON command with the defaults. The defaults will run the command for two hours, taking performance interval snapshots every fifteen minutes. Option 2, Collect data with menus, will step you through a series of menus to help you fill out the parameters necessary to run the Performance Monitor command. This option is not a bad way of learning to use the monitor the first few times you attempt to run it. The third option, Collect data with command, is the easiest and most straightforward approach to running the Performance Monitor. When you select Option 3 and press Enter, the Start Performance Monitor Command screen will appear, as in Figure 12.4.

FIGURE 12.3
Start Collecting Data Screen

```
                    Start Collecting Data

Select one of the following:

     1. Collect data with defaults
     2. Collect data with menus
     3. Collect data with command

Selection
     3

F3=Exit   F12=Cancel
```

FIGURE 12.4
Start Performance Monitor Command Screen (Screen 1)

```
                  Start Performance Monitor (STRPFRMON)

Type Choices, Press Enter.

Member  ...................  *GEN       Name, *GEN
Library  ..................  QPFRDATA   Name
Text 'Description'  .......  *Same
Time Interval (In Minutes)   15         5, 10, 15, 20, 25, 30, 35, ...
Stops Data Collection  ....  *ELAPSED   *ELAPSED, *TIME, *NOMAX
Days From Current Day  ....  0          0-9
Hour  .....................  2          0-999
Minutes  ..................  0          0-99
Data Type  ................  *ALL       *ALL, *SYS
Trace Type  ...............  *NONE      *NONE, *ALL
Dump the Trace  ...........  *YES       *YES, *NO
Job Trace Interval  .......  .5         .5 - 9.9 Seconds
Job Types  ................  *DFT       *NONE, *DFT, *ASJ, *BCH...
                                                  + For More Values

                                                 More...

F3=Exit   F4=Prompt   F5=Refresh   F10=Additional Parameters   F12=Cancel
F13=How to Use This Display        F24=More Keys
```

On this screen, you may specify a unique member name at the Member parameter. The default is *GEN (Generation), which gives you a unique name based on the year, the Gregorian date, and the time the sample started. An example of a *GEN name is Q932940733, which is a sample taken in 1993, on the 294th day of the year (10/21), starting at 7:33 A.M. If the *GEN name is hard for you to work with, you could use a name such as TU0602AM, which you can immediately identify as a sample you took on Tuesday, June 2, in the morning.

If the member you specify doesn't exist, the monitor adds the member to each of the many underlying performance database files, which takes a while. Some companies avoid this overhead by setting up standard member names and always collecting data into those members (for example, MON_AM, MON_PM, WED_AM, or FRI_PM).

The QPFRDATA library is the default for the **Library** parameter. You need to verify that this library exists on your system. If you have the Performance Tools, it will be there unless someone deleted it. The first time you run the monitor, it checks the library that you specify in this parameter. If the performance files exist, the system adds a member to the files with the name you specified in the member parameter. If the performance files don't exist in the library you specify, the Performance Monitor creates the files and then adds the first member to each file.

Next, you may want to enter a **Text 'Description'**. You will see this description any time you are working with a list of the members associated with the different data samples collected using the Performance Monitor in the Performance Tools. You can use it to give you an expanded description of when and why you collected this data. This description will help you most often when you are going to print performance reports, because it will be displayed to help you identify which sample you want to work with.

Time Interval specifies how frequently you want to collect the performance data. For example, if you specify 15, as in Figure 12.4, and run the monitor for two hours, you get eight sets of performance data summary records. Every 15 minutes, the system dumps the collected performance data into a summary record in the performance data files. For longer periods, you can use a larger interval, from 30 minutes up to an hour.

You need to be careful with the averages that result from long sample periods. It is best not to sample at intervals of longer than 30 minutes. Also, when you are looking for a particular problem, it is to your advantage to use smaller intervals of about 5 minutes. Small intervals help you see problems that can sometimes remain hidden in samples with big intervals. Most performance analysis work requires small intervals.

You set the **Data Type** parameter to *ALL if you want to include communications performance data. We recommend that you always collect this data, in case you need it sometime.

The **Trace Type** parameter turns trace data collection on or off. Trace data is necessary for some performance reports. You must collect trace data if you want to print the transaction, lock, or batch job trace reports. Trace data is useful when you are trying to look at specific problems with applications.

The trace collection overhead is minimal. However, the trace option will add considerable overhead to the performance collection process when the system dumps the trace data, so be careful when using it.

The **Dump the Trace** parameter is related to the Trace Type parameter. The default is *YES, which means that the system dumps the trace data from an internal system area to a database file at the end of the collection period. When you collect trace data, you should consider setting this parameter to *NO. This setting stops the trace from dumping. The performance impact of the trace dump can be large, so allow it only when you have minimal activity on your system. If you defer the dump, you can run the DMPTRC (Dump Trace) command later.

Deferring the trace dump is very useful when you want to catch an intermittent performance problem. You can start the tools and specify *NO for the dump trace option. Then, if the system does not experience the problem in the collection period, you can restart the Performance Monitor, specifying the same collection member. In this way, you avoid the overhead of dumping the trace data and the overhead of creating additional members in the database files. When you finally capture a period that contains the intermittent problem, you use the DMPTRC command to retain the trace data that reflects the problem.

The **Exit Program** parameter, which you can see in Figure 12.5, will let you automatically run any program you choose when the performance monitor stops. The program can run one or all of the performance reports for you automatically each time the Performance Monitor ends. This is a nice enhancement to the Performance Monitor.

We have discussed only the key parameters of the STRPFRMON command. We have left out many more, including a third screen. The definitions of these additional parameters are in IBM's *AS/400 Performance Tools Guide*. Try experimenting with the various parameters until you get the exact data you need. Once you discover the right mix of parameters, be consistent. This consistency is important for long-term trend analysis.

Once you have entered the required parameters, press Enter to start the Performance Monitor.

Option 3: Print Performance Reports

The performance reports let you look at the performance of major components of the AS/400. Some information is redundant, duplicating information you can see through interactive commands, such as WRKSYSSTS. On the other hand, you can get quite a bit of information about the system (e.g., IOP utilization,

FIGURE 12.5

Performance Monitor Command, Continued

```
Type Choices, Press Enter.

Local Response Time:
 Boundary 1  ............... *SYS              Number, *SYS
 Boundary 2  ...............                   Number
 Boundary 3  ...............                   Number
 Boundary 4  ...............                   Number
Remote Response Time:
 Boundary 1  ............... *NONE             Number, *SYS, *NONE
 Boundary 2  ...............                   Number
 Boundary 3  ...............                   Number
 Boundary 4  ...............                   Number
Job Queue  ................. QCTL              Name
 Library  .................. *LIBL             Name, *LIBL, *CURLIB
Message Queue  ............. *NONE             Name, *NONE
 Library  ..................                   Name, *LIBL, *CURLIB
Exit Program  .............. *NONE             Name, *NONE
 Library  ..................                   Name, *LIBL, *CURLIB



                                                              Bottom

F3=Exit   F4=Prompt   F5=Refresh   F10=Additional Parameters   F12=Cancel
F13=How to Use This Display        F24=More Keys
```

communications utilization, transactions per hour) only through the performance reports.

Many people try to use the performance reports and give up because of the massive amount of information these reports produce. The reports can be overwhelming the first few times you try to read them. We will show you how to run the performance reports and how to find the significant data for your performance management. We don't mean to say that some of the information in these reports is not useful — all of it has a use under certain circumstances.

Running the Reports

To run the performance reports, select Option 3, Print performance reports, from the Performance Tools menu, which you can see in Figure 12.6. This option will display the Print Performance Report screen, which is shown in Figure 12.7. Let's examine this display.

The default **Library** field is QPFRDATA. You should see performance members listed below the available reports. If you placed your performance data in a different library when you ran the Performance Monitor, you won't see members — you need to change the **Library** field to the name of the library you used and press Enter. If the display still doesn't list any performance members, verify that you put the correct library name in the **Library** field.

FIGURE 12.6
AS/400 Performance Tools Menu

```
PERFORM                    AS/400 Performance Tools
                                                           System:   PERF1
 Select one of the following:

      1. Select type of status
      2. Collect performance data
      3. Print performance reports
      4. Capacity planning/modeling
      5. Programmer performance utilities
      6. Configure and manage tools
      7. Display performance data
      8. System activity
      9. Performance graphics
     10. Advisor

     70. Related commands




 Selection or command
 ===>3
 F3=Exit   F4=Prompt   F9=Retrieve   F12=Cancel   F13=User support
 F16=System main menu
```

FIGURE 12.7
Print Performance Report Screen

```
                              Print Performance Report

 Library . . . . . .   QPFRDATA

 Type option, press Enter.
   1=System report  2=Component report  3=Transaction report  4=Lock report
   5=Job report  6=Pool report  7=Resource report  8=Batch job trace report

 Option   Member     Description                              Date      Time
   1      TU0602AM   Sample during high Activity           06/02/96  08:30:00
   _      TU0602PM   Sample during high Activity           06/02/96  13:28:34
   _      WE0603AM   Sample during high Activity           06/03/96  08:30:00
   _      WE0603PM   Sample during high Activity           06/03/96  13:30:00
   _      Q942940733 Sample during high Activity           10/21/96  07:33:12





                                                                       Bottom

 F3=Exit   F5=Refresh   F11=Work with your spooled output files   F12=Cancel
 F24=More keys
```

You can run the reports listed above the members from this screen. Table 12.1 is an overview of each option and its equivalent CL commands. This table also briefly describes the kind of information each report provides and how you can use that information. Also, remember from our discussion of the STRPFRMON command that you can collect trace data. Some reports (e.g., those you get from Options 3 and 4) require trace data to run. If you try to run one of these reports and the performance data sample does not contain trace data, you will get the message, "Trace data required to run this report."

TABLE 12.1
Performance Tools Reports Overview

Report Option	Report Command	What Is Shown	Where the Information Is Used	Trace Data Required?
1	PRTSYSRPT	• System workload	• Workload projection	No
2	PRTCPTRPT	• Resource use • Communications • System and user jobs	• Hardware growth • Configuration processing trends	No
3	PRTTNSRPT	• Workload and utilization of CPU • Disk • Main storage • Transaction workload • Object contention	• Workload projection • Pool configuration • Application design • File contention • Program use	Yes
4	PRTLCKRPT	• File, record, or object contention by time • Holding/requesting job/object name	• Problem determination • Reduction or elimination of object contention	Yes
	PRTACTRPT	• Job/Task CPU • Disk exception	• Problem determination	Yes
	PRTTRCRPT	• Job class time-slice end • Trace data	• Problem determination • Batch job progress	Yes
5	PRTJOBRPT	• Jobs by interval	• Job data	No
6	PRTPOLRPT	• Pools by interval	• Pool data	No
7	PRTTRSCRPT	• Resources by interval	• System resource use	No

To run the performance reports, place the number of the report you want to run next to the performance sample you want to analyze and press Enter. For example, if you want to run the system report for the first sample, TU0602AM, place a 1 next to the sample name, as illustrated in Figure 12.7, and press Enter. You may choose only one option at a time.

All the performance reports follow the same process with a few variations. We'll take you through a complex scenario to show you how the reports work. Once you understand this process, you can run any of the performance reports.

With all these different reports, you must fill out some parameters on secondary screens. Let's continue our previous example of running the system report. After you place a 1 next to the sample you want to process and press Enter, the Select Categories for Report screen appears, as shown in Figure 12.8.

At this screen, you may narrow the scope of the report you are about to run. You can type a 1 next to each category you want to select to narrow your report scope. We recommend selecting all the categories the first time you run these reports; once you're familiar with the reports and your system, you can use different categories to narrow the amount of data you get. We emphasize that you need to be consistent for long-term trend analysis. Don't include certain categories of data sometimes and exclude those categories other times unless you do so for a specific reason.

FIGURE 12.8
Select Categories for Report

```
                     Select Categories for Report

Member . . . . . . . . . . . . :    TU0602AM

Type options, press Enter.  Press F6 to print entire report.
  1=Select

Option     Category
  _        Time interval
  _        Job
  _        User ID
  _        Subsystem
  _        Pool
  _        Communications line
  _        Control unit
  _        Functional area

                                                             Bottom


F3=Exit   F6=Print entire report   F12=Cancel
```

The **Time interval** category is one of the most useful. When you select this category, you can review the performance samples by each interval collected, as Figure 12.9 shows. In Figure 12.9, the Performance Monitor started at 7:34 a.m. The next interval began at 07:49, so you can tell that the monitor ran in 15-minute intervals. The last interval began at 09:18, which means that it completed at 9:33; therefore, the Performance Monitor ran for 2 hours and generated eight samples.

This option is useful for picking out the samples with high CPU use or high response times. Place a 1 next to each interval you want to include in the system report and press Enter. Figure 12.9 shows a 1 next to the third interval, which shows a total processor use of 99 percent. For larger samples, it is helpful to sort the data by transaction count or response time using the function keys listed at the bottom of the screen.

When you select other categories for your system reports — the **Job**, **User ID**, **Subsystem**, **Pool**, **Communications line**, or **Control unit** categories — you see a screen of blank fields, into which you key the name of an item in that category. For example, if you want to include job AR0001R, you type a 1 next to the **Job** category in Figure 12.8, and press Enter. Then you type the name of the job into the blank **Job** field and press Enter. This parameter can be helpful if you are trying to find out the performance impact of a particular job or group of jobs.

FIGURE 12.9
Select Time Intervals on Performance Reports

```
                             Select Time Intervals

 Library . . . .    QPFRDATA               Performance Data . . . . . TU0602AM

 Type option, press Enter.
   1=Select                        CPU           High         Pool
                 Transaction   -Utilization-   --Util--   -Fault/Sec-
Opt  Date    Time Count   Resp  Tot Inter Bch  Dsk Unit   Mch User ID      Excp
 _  06/02   07:34  1394     .8   67    43  18   12 0003    0     5 05     17626
 _  06/02   07:49  1812     .8   72    51  15    9 0003    0     6 05     16101
 1  06/02   08:04  1797    1.5   99    59  30   30 0010    0    11 06     17810
 _  06/02   08:18  1645    1.1   85    51  26   13 0017    1    12 05     22127
 _  06/02   08:33  1983    1.3   89    62  20   13 0003    0    14 05     26450
 _  06/02   08:48  1988    1.3   92    65  21   14 0003    1     9 05     25196
 _  06/02   09:03  1613    2.2   96    68  21   16 0012    1    10 05     24750
 _  06/02   09:18  1861     .9   96    48  42   13 0003    1     9 05     22439

                                                                          Bottom

 F3=Exit                  F5=Refresh          F12=Cancel
 F13=Sort (date/time)     F14=Sort (count)    F24=More keys
```

The **User ID** category is helpful if you suspect a particular user or group of users is using more system resources than they should. To track performance by subsystem — QINTER, QBATCH, or any valid subsystem you are using — first select the category by typing a 1 next to **Subsystem** and pressing Enter, and then put these subsystems' names into the blank **Subsystem** fields. The **Pool**, **Communications line**, and **Control unit** categories all work in the same way.

The **Functional area** category works a little differently. You must set up a functional area before you can select it. You can put any or all of the categories we've discussed (except the interval) in a functional area so that each time you run the reports, you simply select your defined functional area. Because they allow you to choose only the categories you're interested in and they use these same categories every time you run the reports, functional areas are a nice way be sure you're consistently reporting on pertinent data over a certain period.

For example, let's say that every time you run your reports, you want only particular jobs run by particular users in a particular subsystem. By setting up a functional area with this information in it, you can select all of these parameters with one keystroke for the functional area, as opposed to entering each of these parameters every time you run the reports. This approach also helps eliminate input errors that can lead to inconsistency among the samples. You set up functional areas using Option 6, Configure and manage tools, on the Performance Tools menu. Then you select Option 1, Working with functional areas. For more information about Option 6, see Chapter 14.

Now that you have selected the categories for your report, you will see the Specify Report Options screen in Figure 12.10. Here, you can perform two main functions: you can enter a Report Title and you can limit the report's scope. If you captured data for a long period, you can limit what the system will use in the performance report. Some programmers run the monitor 24 hours a day, all week, to have one very large sample. Then, using this option, they print several reports based on particular start and stop days and times. Although this is a valid approach, we don't recommend it because it produces very big performance file members. The bigger these files, the more time it takes to run the reports and the more overhead the system needs to process these reports.

To submit the performance reports to run in batch, press Enter. You can verify that your job is running using the WRKSBMJOB command.

As we said earlier, we have just brought you through the most complex of the scenarios for running a performance report. If you understand this process, you can run any of the performance reports.

Reading the Reports

Because reading the reports can be a difficult process, we'll take you step-by-step through the System and Component Reports in Chapter 13. These reports give you performance information about several components. For these components,

FIGURE 12.10

Specify Report Options

```
                        Specify Report Options

Type choices, press Enter.

  Report Title ......... Report for Tuesday's Busy Processing

  Start:
     Day  ...............     *First         *First, MM/DD/YY
     Time ...............     *First         *First, HH:MM:SS
  Stop:
     Day  ...............     *Last          *Last, MM/DD/YY
     Time ...............     *Last          *Last, HH:MM:SS
  Measured Profile:
     Profile ............      *None         *None, name
     Replace ............     N              Y=Yes, N=No




  F3=Exit       F12=Cancel
```

Table 12.2 shows percent utilization guidelines for three categories of performance: good, acceptable, and poor.

TABLE 12.2

Guidelines to Match to System and Component Performance Tools Reports

		Good (%)	Acceptable (%)	Poor (%)
Processor	High-priority jobs, 1 processor	< 70	70–80	> 80
	High-priority jobs, 2 processors	< 75	75–85	> 85
	High-priority jobs, 3 processors	< 79	79–89	> 89
	High-priority jobs, 4 processors	< 81	81–91	> 91
Disk Arm	9332/9335/Internal disk	< 40	40–50	> 50
	9336/9337	< 50	50–60	> 60
IOP	Disk	< 35	45	> 50
	Local Workstation	< 25	35	> 40
	Multifunction	< 35	45	> 50
	Communications	< 35	45	> 50
Remote Line Utilization		< 30	35	> 40

If any of your components' performance numbers are less than the "good" guidelines, they are probably not contributing to a performance problem and you need to concentrate your efforts elsewhere. If any of your components fall within the "acceptable" range, you probably don't have a problem with that component now, but you need to monitor that component closely and start planning how to handle it in the future. If any of your components are equal to or greater than the "poor" number, you need to address the problem immediately. A component in this range is probably contributing to a major performance problem on your system.

OPTION 4: CAPACITY PLANNING/MODELING

The next option from the Performance Tools menu that belongs in this group of options is Option 4, Capacity planning/modeling, which allows you to use a tool called BEST/1. BEST/1 lets you build performance models, either from scratch or based on information from the Performance Monitor files. Because using the Performance Monitor files your system generates simplifies the process of modeling your system's components, this is the method we prefer.

A couple of warnings about using this tool: First, some functions of BEST/1 use a lot of CPU cycles, so be careful. You don't want to create new performance problems, so try to use BEST/1 during periods of low system activity. Second, IBM recommends a minimum processor size of D60 to run this tool. In our experience, you can run the tool on smaller systems, but some functions take a long time to run. Again, be careful not to let this tool be the cause of your system's performance problems.

A popular use of BEST/1 is projecting "what if" scenarios. For example, if you estimate that your business will grow by 50 percent over the next twelve months, you can let this tool calculate what your approximate transaction throughput and response time will be. BEST/1 can also tell you what size processor and other hardware components you will need to support the growth in workload.

Another use for this tool is to see how system component changes — CPU, disk IOPs, workstation IOPs, and disk drives — will affect performance. Each of these components affects performance, some more than others. You can learn a great deal by changing these components to see how the change affects your performance. For example, we often use this tool to see how a different CPU on a system would affect a system's performance. You can see the effect of changing disk technology, for example, if you move from 9335 disk drives to 9337 drives. You can also see what different protection schemes, such as checksum, mirroring, or RAID, will do to your performance.

BEST/1 is much too complex for us to cover in detail here. In fact, we could probably write a book on this subject by itself. For more information about this tool, see IBM's *AS/400 BEST/1 User's Guide* and IBM's *BEST/1*

Redbook. We recommend that you have both manuals available when you work with BEST/1.

Option 7: Display Performance Data

The Display Performance Data option presents the Performance Monitor data interactively. This display summarizes much of the performance data and provides detailed job information. Looking at the data interactively before printing a report can help you determine what you want to include or avoid in the report. For example, if you want a report over a peak period that included specific jobs, you could use the interactive view of the data to determine the intervals to include in the report. However, you need to be careful about using this option: the interactive view uses queries to select the data, which can eat up system resources. If you are running on a production system, you may want to lower the priority of this work or reschedule it to reduce its impact on the more-critical production work that might be running.

When you select Option 7 from the main Performance Tools menu, the screen in Figure 12.11 appears. This screen lets you select a previously collected performance sample. Place a 1 next to the performance member that you want to process and press Enter. If you have many samples, you can sort them by name, text, or date/time.

Figure 12.11
Select Performance Member Screen

```
                         Select Performance Member

Library . . . . . .    QPFRDATA

Type option, press Enter.
  1=Select

Option   Member       Text                                          Date       Time
  1      TU0602AM     Sample during high Activity                 06/02/94   08:30:00
  _      TU0602PM     Sample during high Activity                 06/02/94   13:28:34
  _      WE0603AM     Sample during high Activity                 06/03/94   08:30:00
  _      WE0603PM     Sample during high Activity                 06/03/94   13:30:00
  _      Q942940733   Sample during high Activity                 10/21/94   07:33:12

                                                                              Bottom

F3=Exit      F12=Cancel          F15=Sort By Name          F16=Sort By Text
F19=Sort by Date/Time
```

The next screen is the Display Performance Data screen, which you can see in Figure 12.12. Depending on how big the sample is and how busy your system is, this screen sometimes can take a while to display. Remember that this command runs interactively, so be careful not to create a performance problem by running this command at busy processing times. Let's look at some important fields on this display.

FIGURE 12.12
Display Performance Data Screen

```
                         Display Performance Data

Member  . . . . . . TU0602AM   F4 for list
Library . . . . . . QPFRDATA

Elapsed Time . . . . . . :   3:54:27      Version . . . . . . . :   2
System . . . . . . . . . :   PERF1        Release . . . . . . . :   3.0
Start date . . . . . . . :   06/02/94     Model . . . . . . . . :   F60
Start time . . . . . . . :   08:30:00     Serial Number . . . . :   10-99999

CPU utilization (interactive) . . . . . . . : 65%
CPU utilization (other) . . . . . . . . . . : 29%
Job count . . . . . . . . . . . . . . . . . : 2900
Transaction count . . . . . . . . . . . . . : 1500
Transactions per hour . . . . . . . . . . . : 375
Average response (seconds)  . . . . . . . . :   .7
Disk utilization (percent)  . . . . . . . . : 12.56
Disk I/O per second . . . . . . . . . . . . :  5.6




F3=Exit   F4=Prompt   F5=Refresh   F6=display all jobs   F10=Command entry
F12=Cancel            F24=More Keys
```

The top section provides performance-sample overview information. The **Elapsed Time** field tells how long the sample ran. In Figure 12.12, the elapsed time is 3 hours, 54 minutes, and 27 seconds.

The next field shows the name of the **System** the sample was taken on. This field will help users with multiple systems identify which system the sample came from.

Next comes the **Start date** and **Start time** for the sample. The date field is in mm:dd:yy format, and the time is in hh:mm:ss format.

The **Version** and **Release** fields display the release of the operating system on which you took the sample. The **Model** number is the AS/400 model. The **Serial Number** of the CPU on which you took the sample also appears. You cannot alter the serial number, so it will always be unique. However, you can change the system name through network values. The default system name is the serial number. Most installations change the name of their AS/400 to something meaningful. For example, our system is named PERF1.

The next part of the screen shows performance data summarized from the performance member selected. These fields are averages of all the samples taken, so it is important to realize the activity characteristics of your sample data. If you have one high-activity hour and three low-activity hours, the performance member may appear to be all right, when in reality, you have an hour that needs some analysis work. The shorter the sample period, the less likely it is that your performance samples are skewed.

The first field is the interactive work's **CPU utilization**. You can find guidelines for high-priority jobs in Table 8.2 on page 114. An F60 has one processor, so for this sample, the high-priority CPU utilization guideline is 70 percent. Because this sample shows 65 percent utilization for interactive jobs, and because most high-utilization jobs are interactive job, we probably don't have a problem.

The **Job count** field shows the number of jobs that ran during the sample. The **Transaction count** field keeps track of the interactive workload. Both of these fields are important for trend analysis.

Average response time in seconds is a good indicator of what kind of performance your interactive users see. Compare this number to your company's response time performance objective.

The **Disk utilization** appears as a percent. You can measure this percentage against the guidelines.

You can also look at job performance information by pressing F6 to display all jobs.

Option 9: Performance Tools Graphics

From the Performance Tools Graphics menu, you can choose to work with graph formats and packages, work with historical data, and display graphs and packages. When you select Option 9 from the Performance Tools menu, the Performance Tools Graphics screen appears, as in Figure 12.13.

Let's look at each option on the Performance Tools Graphics menu.

- Option 1 - Work with graph formats and packages. This option lets you create, change, copy, or delete graph formats and packages. From this option, you can also display sample graphs and graph package contents.
- Option 2 - Work with historical data. This option lets you create or delete historical data. You need this data to display historical data graphs. This option is also useful with trend analysis.
- Option 3 - Display graphs and packages. This option lets you display performance and historical data graphs. Performance data graphs show

FIGURE 12.13
Performance Tools Graphics Menu

```
PERFORMG
                      Performance Tools Graphics
                                                          System: PERF1

 Select one of the following:

      1. Work with graph formats and packages
      2. Work with historical data
      3. Display graphs and packages
      70. Related Commands




 Selection or command
 ===>____________________________________________________

 F3=Exit   F4=Prompt   F9=Retrieve   F12=Cancel
```

the performance for a specific data collection. Historical data graphs use data for several data collections and show performance trends.

OPTION 10: THE ADVISOR

The final option in this group of Performance Tools is the Advisor. The Advisor interprets and analyzes the data in your Performance Monitor files and suggests ways to improve your performance.

Why use the Advisor? Well, this tool is like having your own resident performance expert. You can use it to help you understand what is happening with your system. The Performance Tools can be very complex, and the Advisor makes it easier to understand the results of the Performance Tools. For example, one task that the Advisor performs very well is identifying communications problems and suggesting ways to fix them. We suggest that you use the Advisor to check your work. It is an easy way to get a (cheap) second opinion.

We will show you how to run the Advisor interactively. However, the results from the Performance Advisor can also be generated in batch, which will minimize its impact on other users and still give you the information you need. It is our choice when we need to get Advisor recommendations. The Analyze Performance Data (ANZPFRDTA) command can be put in a batch job stream specifying OUTPUT(*PRINT). Running this job will give you the same messages and recommendations shown here in the interactive displays.

To run the Advisor interactively, select Option 10, Advisor, from the Performance Tools menu to display the screen in Figure 12.14.

FIGURE 12.14
Select Member for Analysis Screen

```
                        Select Member For Analysis

Library . . . . . .   QPFRDATA

Type option, press Enter.
  1=Select   2=Display

Option    Member     Text                                      Date      Time
   1      TU0602AM   Sample during high Activity             06/02/94  08:30:00
   _      TU0602PM   Sample during high Activity             06/02/94  13:28:34
   _      WE0603AM   Sample during high Activity             06/03/94  08:30:00
   _      WE0603PM   Sample during high Activity             06/03/94  13:30:00
   _      Q942940733 Sample during high Activity             10/21/94  07:33:12

                                                                          Bottom

F3=Exit     F12=Cancel          F15=Sort By Name         F16=Sort By Text
F19=Sort by Date/Time
```

When you see the Select Member For Analysis screen, you place a 1 next to the sample against which you want to run the Advisor and press Enter. The size of the sample will determine how long it takes for the screen in Figure 12.15 to appear.

At this point, you select the time interval you want to analyze by placing a 1 next to it. You may also press F13 to select all the samples. We suggest you process only the periods that have high activity in transactions counts, response time, total CPU utilization, interactive utilization, or faulting. When you run this function interactively, be careful when selecting all the intervals on large samples, because it will use a lot of CPU.

When you press Enter to process the intervals you have selected, you will get a message at the bottom of the screen telling you that the Advisor is working. The size of your sample, the number of intervals you select, and how busy your system is will determine how long this process takes. We have seen

FIGURE 12.15
Select Time Intervals on Performance Reports

```
                          Select Time Intervals To Analyze

Member  . . . . :TU0602AM                               Library . . . .: QPFRDATA

 Type option, press Enter.
  1=Select                                 CPU              Hig             Pool
                     Transaction      ---Utilization--- --- Util --- -- Fault / Sec --  Excp
 Opt  Date   Time    Count  Resp    Tot  Inter  Bch    Dsk   Unit   Mch   User  Id     Util
     06/02  07:34    1394    .8     67    43     18     12   0003    0      5   05     1762
     06/02  07:49    1812    .8     72    51     15      9   0003    0      6   05     1610
  1  06/02  08:04    1797   1.5     99    59     30     30   0010    0     11   06     1781
     06/02  08:18    1645   1.1     85    51     26     13   0017    1     12   05     2412
     06/02  08:33    1983   1.3     89    62     20     13   0003    0     14   05     2645
     06/02  08:48    1988   1.3     92    65     21     14   0003    1      9   05     2519
     06/02  09:03    1613   2.2     96    68     21     16   0012    1     10   05     2475
     06/02  09:18    1861    .9     96    48     42     13   0003    1      9   05     2243

                                                                                   Bottom

 F3=Exit     F5=Refresh     F11=Display Histogram      F12=Cancel      F13=Select All
 F14=Deselect All
```

samples take more than 30 minutes. This is why it is important not to have large performance samples. If you do have large samples, make sure you narrow the scope of what you are asking the Advisor to examine.

When the Advisor is finished processing the sample, a screen similar to the one in Figure 12.16 will appear. This screen is a sample. Every system will produce different screens based on the data the Advisor examined.

To display the detailed recommendations, conclusions, or interval conclusions, place a 5 next to the item you want to display and press Enter. In Figure 12.16, we have placed a 5 next to the **Separate batch from interactive jobs** recommendation. By doing this and pressing Enter, we get the screen in Figure 12.17.

As you can see in Figure 12.17, the Display Detailed Recommendation screen gives you a lot of very useful information. However, you know your system best and you should carefully consider the Advisor's suggestions before following them. For example, in Figure 12.16 and 12.17, it advises ways to prevent two different types of jobs from running in the same subsystem. However, you may not always be able to separate all your different types of work. If you don't have enough memory or other system resources to separate your job types, or if the Advisor is telling you to move a batch job that you run only once a month, you cannot justify creating a separate pool for the job. The point here is to be

FIGURE 12.16

Advisor Display Recommendations Screen

```
                          Display Recommendations
                                                           System: PERF1
Member . . . . . : TU0602AM          Library . . . . . . : QPFRDATA
System . . . . . : PERF1             Version/Release . . : 2/ 3.0
Start Date . . . : 06/02/94          Model       . . . . : F60
Start Time . . . : 07:19:05          Serial Number . . . : 10-99999

Type Options, Press Enter.
      5=Display Details

   Option     Recommendations and Conclusions
                      Recommendations
     5      Separate batch from interactive jobs.
                        Conclusions
            ASP space capacity approached guideline of 80.0%.
            Disk service time exceeded guideline.
                    Interval Conclusions
            No performance problems found in pools data.
            Total disk I/O was 93214.  (56163 reads and 37051 writes)
            No performance problems on listed SDLC lines



                                                               Bottom
F3=Exit      F6=Print      F9=Tune System      F12=Cancel      F21=Command Line
```

FIGURE 12.17

Display Detailed Recommendation Screen

```
                    Display Detailed Recommendation

Recommendation:

Separate Batch From Interactive jobs.

Detailed Recommendation:
PFR2660
Cause. . . . . :   Batch and interactive jobs were concurrently active
in the same pool.  This may cause degraded performance by causing
increased paging and increased waiting for an activity level.
Recovery . . . :   Move the batch jobs into their own pool by changing
the batch subsystem description (CHGSBSD) or the batch routing entry
(CHGRTGE).  Refer to the work management guide to determine how large the
initial batch pool size should be for good performance.  Roughly 200-500K
per job is recommended.
Technical Description . . :   The following table shows the
identifier of the pool that had both interactive and batch jobs, and the
date and time this occurred.


                                                         More...
Press Enter to Continue.

F3=Exit       F12=Cancel
```

careful to not let the Advisor run your system. Use it to check your work, or use it as a starting point to validate any information that it gives you. ***Do not blindly follow the advice given by this tool!***

One last note about the Advisor: In Figure 12.16, you may have noticed a function key to tune your system. This function key will work only if you collected the performance sample on the same system on which you are running the Advisor. If this is the case, you may press F9, and the Advisor will adjust the system according to its recommendations (when possible). Make sure that you read the recommendations before you use this function key. You may not want to follow all the recommendations.

The Advisor

In my experience, most AS/400 users are not familiar with the Advisor. This tool has been around for a while and continues to be improved. Use this tool as your performance assistant. I also use the Advisor to find communications and network errors, which are usually difficult to find and correct. The recommendations the Advisor gives are a good starting point for fixing these kinds of problems. Try it . . . You'll like it! ■

Alan Arnold

CHAPTER 13

The System and Component Reports

In the last chapter, you learned to run the reports and saw some guidelines for the numbers you'll see. Now we'll consider in detail the two most important reports: The System Report and the Component Report. These two reports contain the performance data that will help you thoroughly analyze your system's performance. The other reports contain additional detail about the information on these two key reports.

THE SYSTEM REPORT

You should start your performance analysis with the System Report, as shown in Figures 13.1 through 13.5. The length of this report will vary, depending on the size of your sample and the size of your intervals. Our sample report is five pages long, which is the report's minimum size.

The five sections of the System Report are Workload, Resource Utilization, Resource Utilization Expansion, Storage Pool Utilization, and Disk Utilization. Let's look at each of these sections.

Workload

The report's heading in Figure 13.1 shows that this page is the Workload section of the System Report. The heading also contains the date and time that the report ran. The Report Title that we defined in the Specify Report Options screen is on the third line of the heading.

TABLE 13.1
Performance Reports Member and System Information

Field Name	Field Description
Member	Name of the member you specified in the Performance Monitor
Library	Name of the library the performance member was stored in
Model/Serial	Model and serial number of the system the member was captured on
System Name	System name associated with the system the member was captured on
Main Storage	Amount of main storage (memory) on the system when the member was captured
Version/Release	Version and release that the system was at when the member was captured
Started	Start date and time included on this report
Stopped	Stop date and time included on this report

FIGURE 13.1
Workload Section of the System Report

```
System Report                                                                    7/01/96  15:06:19
                                          Workload                                    Page 0001
Performance Report Sample

Member . . . : TU0602AM     Model/Serial  . . :  320-2050/10-XXXXX  Main storage . . :   32.0 M  Started  . . . . : 06/02/96 08:56:43
  Library . . : QPFRDATA    System name . . . :  PERF1              Version/Release  :   3/ 2.0  Stopped  . . . . : 06/02/96 15:55:55
```

Interactive Workload

Job Type	Number Transactions	Average Response	Logical DB I/O Count	Printer Lines	Printer Pages	Communications I/O Count	MRT Max Time
Interactive	15,483	2.48	1,339,082	5,519	116	0	
DDM Server	8	.00	8	0	0	442	
Client Access	673	1.52	10,156	10,616	234	500	
PassThru	988	2.71	52,173	2,287	49	0	
Total/Average	17,152	2.45	1,401,419	18,422	399	942	

Interactive Transactions

Non-Interactive Workload

Job Type	Number of Jobs	Logical DB I/O Count	Printer Lines	Printer Pages	Communications I/O Count	CPU Per Logical I/O	Logical I/O /Second
Batch	24	19,709	6,854	339	11	.02	.7
Spool	2	1,333	0	0	0	.02	.0
AutoStart	2	8,321	318	53	0	.12	.3
Evoke	4	0	0	0	0	.00	.0
Total/ Average	32	29,363	7,172	392	11	.05	1.1

Total CPU Utilization . . . . : 67.4

How busy the system was during the sample

Every performance report shows two lines of Performance Monitor and system data after the heading. Table 13.1 describes the information in these two lines.

The Workload section of the System Report is divided into two subsections: Interactive Workload and Non-Interactive Workload. The interactive subsection categorizes jobs by the number of transactions and the average response time for each transaction. This part of the report gives you an idea of how much interactive work was done on the system during the collection period. Remember that the AS/400 shows transaction counts only for interactive work. If you always keep this in mind, when you look at any performance report you will know immediately whether the job is interactive or batch.

The **Total CPU Utilization** field at the bottom of the page shows the average CPU utilization during the sample period for the interactive and non-interactive workloads.

In the interactive subsection, the number of transactions are categorized by the type of job — **Interactive**, **DDM Server**, **Client Access** or **PCS Support**, and **Passthru**. The job type determines whether the job's statistics are included in this section or the batch section of the report. If you normally track interactive users' transactions and response time, this subsection gives you the data you need. You should be familiar enough with your business to know the usual number of interactive transactions and the response time your users usually get and can expect to get at different transaction rates. We recommend that you track transaction counts, transaction rates, and average response time so that you have a historical record of what your system is doing.

The non-interactive work is important to track, as well. You should also be familiar with the usual number of non-interactive jobs that run on your system. In particular, you should concentrate on batch jobs and track the number of jobs and the logical DB I/O count. If you print a lot of reports in the normal course of your business day, you may also want to track the number of pages printed.

For both interactive and non-interactive workloads, you need to understand the trends of your company's use of your system — when the work is running and what work is running.

By hour, day, week, month, and quarter, when is your system the busiest? Do you know? Use this report to build a trend analysis so that you understand when your system is busy or slow.

What mixture of jobs is running on your system — heavy or light interactive, heavy or light non-interactive? Do you know whether you run more batch work or interactive work? Use this report to build a high-level view of the workloads on your system for all the time periods we've discussed.

Resource Utilization

Figure 13.2 is the Resource Utilization section of the System Report. This section displays additional detail about interactive workload, including a great deal of disk I/O information, and you can use it as an indicator of how busy your auxiliary storage is. This report divides these read and write I/Os into database and non-database.

On this report, you need to be familiar with two values on the Total/Average line: **CPU Util** (CPU Utilization), and **Tns/Hour Rate** (transactions per hour). The **CPU Util** field shows the total interactive CPU utilization. This value is different from that on the workload section of the System Report, which shows the total interactive and non-interactive CPU utilization. If you subtract the **CPU Util** field in this section of the System Report from the **Total CPU Utilization** on the Workload section, you have the percentage of CPU used for non-interactive work.

In addition, you can use the Total/Average CPU Util value as a guideline to gauge whether your system is handling your interactive workload. In Table 8.2, we gave you a chart of guidelines for CPU utilization (page 114). Strictly speaking, these guidelines are for high-priority work, but because your interactive jobs usually will make up most of your high-priority work (the system jobs that run at a high priority usually use from 6 to 12 percent of the CPU), you can use these same guidelines. For example, in Figure 13.2, the **Total/Average CPU Util** value is 54.1 percent. If we add that value to the normal system usage and then measure the total against the guidelines for high-priority work on a single-processor system (B45 at 70 percent), we can see that this example is well within a reasonable range. (To obtain a value for the normal system usage, you can apply a standard 10 percent, or some other percentage between 6 percent and 12 percent; you can also find the CPU utilization for priority 000 work in Figure 13.3. Figure 13.3 is discussed in detail below.)

The **Tns/Hour Rate** (transactions per hour (TPH)) field is an excellent workload indicator for trend analysis. This value is the total number of interactive transactions divided by the number of hours the sample was taken for.

Resource Utilization Expansion

Figure 13.3 shows the Resource Utilization Expansion section of the System Report. This section displays additional detail about system workload, including disk information such as synchronous and asynchronous reads and writes. These read and write I/O values are categorized as database and non-database, and you can use them as an indicator of how busy your system is.

The most useful areas of this report are the **CPU Util** (CPU utilization) and **Cum Util** (cumulative CPU utilization) columns. Interactive or high-priority work (any job with a priority of 20 or lower) should use only a certain amount of the processor, depending on how many processors the system has. Of the

FIGURE 13.2
Resource Utilization Section of the System Report

```
                                     System Report                                        07/01/96 15:06:19
                                  Resource Utilization                                          Page 0002
                                Performance Report Sample

Member . . . : TU0602AM     Model/Serial . . : 320-2050/10-XXXXX   Main storage . . :  32.0 M  Started . . . . : 06/02/96 08:56:43
  Library . . : QPFRDATA     System name . . . : PERF1               Version/Release  :  3/ 2.0  Stopped . . . . : 06/02/96 15:55:55
```

Job Type	Response Seconds	CPU Seconds	Sync Disk I/O	Async Disk I/O	DB I/O
	Average Per Transaction				
Interactive	2.4	.81	13.0	28.4	86.4
DDM Server	.0	2.45	150.1	12.8	1.0
Client Access	1.5	.54	21.2	5.2	15.0
PassThru	2.7	.69	23.0	16.9	52.8
Total/Average	2.4	.79	14.0	26.9	81.7

Job Type	CPU Util	Tns /Hour Rate	Active Jobs Per Interval	Disk I/O Per Second: Total I/O	Synchronous DBR	Synchronous DBW	Synchronous NDBR	Synchronous NDBW	Asynchronous DBR	Asynchronous DBW	Asynchronous NDBR	Asynchronous NDBW
Interactive	49.9	2,217	33	25.6	3.7	1.0	2.9	.3	17.2	.2	.0	.0
DDM Server	.0	1	2	.0	.0	.0	.0	.0	.0	.0	.0	.0
PCS Support	1.4	96	14	.7	.1	.0	.2	.0	.0	.0	.0	.0
PassThru	2.7	141	13	1.5	.1	.0	.6	.1	.5	.0	.0	.1
Total/Average	54.1	2,456	63	27.9	4.0	1.0	3.9	.5	17.8	.3	.0	.1

Total interactive CPU utilization

Transactions per hour during sample period

Figure 13.3

Resource Utilization Expansion Section of the System Report

System Report
Resource Utilization Expansion
Performance Report Sample

7/01/96 15:06:19
Page 0003

Member . . . : TU0602AM
Library . . : QPFRDATA
Model/Serial . . : 320-2050/10-XXXXX
System name . . . : PERF1
Main storage . . : 32.0 M
Version/Release : 3/ 2.0
Started . . . . : 06/02/96 08:56:43
Stopped . . . . : 06/02/96 15:55:55

Job Type	Average Per Transaction: Physical Disk I/O, Synchronous: DBR	DBW	NDBR	NDBW	Physical Disk I/O, Asynchronous: DBR	DBW	NDBR	NDBW	Logical Data Base I/O: Read	Write	Other	Communications I/O: Get	Put
Interactive	6.0	1.6	4.8	.5	27.9	.4	.0	.0	83.6	.4	2.4	.0	.0
DDM Server	2.1	.0	124.6	23.3	1.0	.0	1.0	10.8	1.0	.0	.0	26.8	28.3
Client Access	6.0	2.3	11.1	1.7	3.1	1.0	.0	1.0	13.5	.2	1.3	.7	.0
PassThru	3.4	.7	16.2	2.5	13.4	.7	.0	2.6	51.5	1.1	.0	.0	.0
Total/Average	5.9	1.6	5.7	.7	26.1	.4	.0	.2	79.0	.4	2.2	.0	.0

Priority	Job Type	CPU Util	Cum Util	Disk I/O Sync	Disk I/O Async	CPU Per I/O Sync	CPU Per I/O Async	DIO /Sec Sync	DIO /Sec Async
000	Batch	.6	.6	4,044	3,717	.0426	.0463	.1	.1
	System	5.6	6.3	105,637	2,175	.0133	.6500	4.2	.0
010	Batch	.0	6.3	154	34	.0086	.0393	.0	.0
015	Spool	.0	6.3	4,696	300	.0041	.0643	.1	.0
020	Interactive	49.9	56.2	202,496	441,141	.0619	.0284	8.0	17.5
	DDM Server	.0	56.3	826	61	.0193	.2616	.0	.0
	PCS Support	1.4	57.7	13,832	3,397	.0259	.1056	.5	.1
	Passthru	2.7	60.5	22,737	16,719	.0302	.0411	.9	.6
	Batch	.0	60.5	4	0	.0135	.0000	.0	.0
	Evoke	.0	60.5	18	0	.0032	.0000	.0	.0
	System	.0	60.5	573	99	.0070	.0409	.0	.0
026	Batch	.1	60.6	678	53	.0378	.4841	.0	.0
040	Batch	.0	60.6	243	10	.0064	.1579	.0	.0
	Autostart	.0	60.6	4	0	.0125	.0000	.0	.0
050	DDM Server	.0	60.6	375	42	.0098	.0879	.0	.0
	PCS Support	.0	60.6	493	164	.0108	.0326	.0	.0
	Batch	1.1	61.8	9,682	5,920	.0305	.0500	.3	.2
	AutoStart	4.1	65.9	5,926	133,728	.1749	.0077	.2	5.3
	Evoke	.0	65.9	275	45	.0069	.0426	.0	.0
052	Spool	.0	66.0	265	380	.0278	.0194	.0	.0
Total/Average				372,958	607,985			14.8	24.1

This is another place to see how the high-priority workload is being run between the different job types high-priority work, most CPU utilization should be for the interactive work. In Figure 13.3, each job's priority and type appear in the first two columns. The **CPU Util** column shows that the priority-20 interactive work is getting most of the CPU cycles, which is what you want. Use the **Cum Util** column to verify that you have enough CPU for your workload.

In our example, the cumulative CPU utilization for high-priority work (at priority 20 and below) is 60.5 percent. Checking the information in the Model/Serial line at the top of the section of the report against Table 8.2, we can see that the guideline for this system — B45 — is 70 percent, so this example shows no problem with CPU usage. The priority 0 batch work in Figure 13.3 is the Performance Monitor. If you use the Performance Monitor only occasionally, you can factor out its contribution to overall CPU usage for normal production work.

Storage Pool Utilization

Figure 13.4 shows the Storage Pool Utilization section of the System Report. This section provides an overview of each pool's structure (size and activity level) and activity (paging and job state changes) for the times you select. If the pool size or activity level changes during the sample, the report shows this change by putting an asterisk (*) next to the pool that changed.

The data in the Storage Pool Utilization report is very similar to the information you can get using the WRKSYSSTS command. The main differences are that this report covers a longer period than you normally use with WRKSYSSTS, and this report also shows the **CPU Util**, **Number Tns** (number of transactions), and **Average Response** time for the storage pools.

All the information on this report is extremely useful for tuning your system's performance. The definitions for the fields in this section of the System Report are listed below the pool data itself and are covered in Chapter 8. Because the data is averaged over the period you specified when requesting the report, you want to make sure you are looking at a meaningful period. For example, if the period is a one-hour peak period, you will probably get useful information. If the period is three hours and includes the noon hour or some other off-shift work, your data is of questionable value.

Disk Utilization

The Disk Utilization section of the System Report is shown in Figure 13.5. This report provides information similar to the WRKDSKSTS command, discussed in detail in Chapter 9. Besides the information you can get with the WRKDSKSTS command, you can also see **IOP Util** (Input/Output processor utilization), **Average Service Time**, **Average Wait Time**, and **Total Disk Response Time**.

FIGURE 13.4

Storage Pool Utilization Section of the System Report

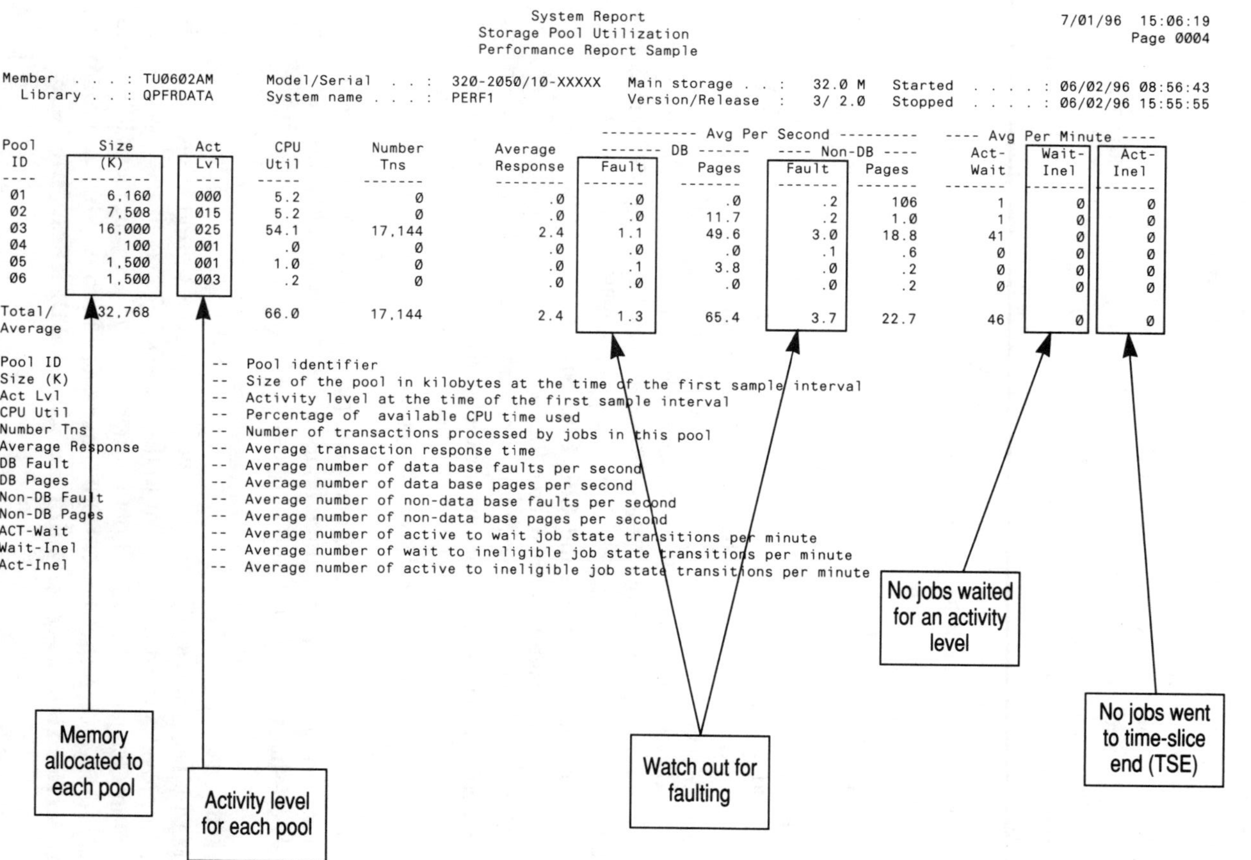

System Report
Storage Pool Utilization
Performance Report Sample

7/01/96 15:06:19
Page 0004

Member . . . : TU0602AM Model/Serial . . : 320-2050/10-XXXXX Main storage . . : 32.0 M Started . . . . : 06/02/96 08:56:43
Library . . : QPFRDATA System name . . . : PERF1 Version/Release : 3/ 2.0 Stopped . . . . : 06/02/96 15:55:55

Pool ID	Size (K)	Act Lvl	CPU Util	Number Tns	Average Response	Avg Per Second: DB Fault	DB Pages	Non-DB Fault	Non-DB Pages	Avg Per Minute: Act-Wait	Wait-Inel	Act-Inel
01	6,160	000	5.2	0	.0	.0	.0	.2	106	1	0	0
02	7,508	015	5.2	0	.0	.0	11.7	.2	1.0	1	0	0
03	16,000	025	54.1	17,144	2.4	1.1	49.6	3.0	18.8	41	0	0
04	100	001	.0	0	.0	.0	.0	.1	.6	0	0	0
05	1,500	001	1.0	0	.0	.1	3.8	.0	.2	0	0	0
06	1,500	003	.2	0	.0	.0	.0	.0	.2	0	0	0
Total/ Average	32,768		66.0	17,144	2.4	1.3	65.4	3.7	22.7	46	0	0

Pool ID -- Pool identifier
Size (K) -- Size of the pool in kilobytes at the time of the first sample interval
Act Lvl -- Activity level at the time of the first sample interval
CPU Util -- Percentage of available CPU time used
Number Tns -- Number of transactions processed by jobs in this pool
Average Response -- Average transaction response time
DB Fault -- Average number of data base faults per second
DB Pages -- Average number of data base pages per second
Non-DB Fault -- Average number of non-data base faults per second
Non-DB Pages -- Average number of non-data base pages per second
ACT-Wait -- Average number of active to wait job state transitions per minute
Wait-Inel -- Average number of wait to ineligible job state transitions per minute
Act-Inel -- Average number of active to ineligible job state transitions per minute

FIGURE 13.5

Disk Utilization Section of the System Report

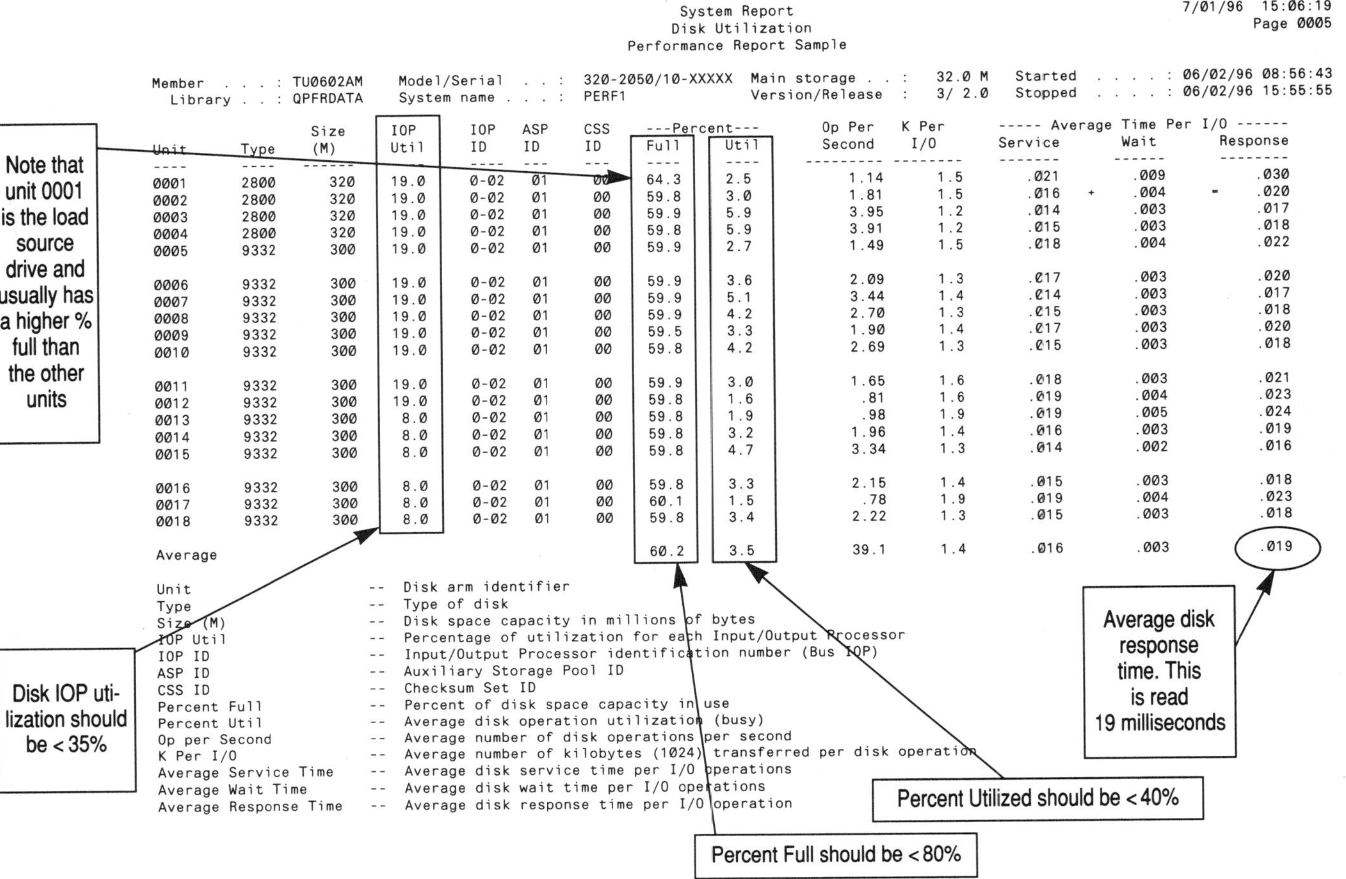

System Report
Disk Utilization
Performance Report Sample

7/01/96 15:06:19
Page 0005

Member . . . : TU0602AM Model/Serial . . : 320-2050/10-XXXXX Main storage . . : 32.0 M Started . . . . : 06/02/96 08:56:43
Library . . : QPFRDATA System name . . . : PERF1 Version/Release : 3/ 2.0 Stopped . . . . : 06/02/96 15:55:55

Unit	Type	Size (M)	IOP Util	IOP ID	ASP ID	CSS ID	Percent Full	Percent Util	Op Per Second	K Per I/O	Average Time Per I/O Service	Wait	Response
0001	2800	320	19.0	0-02	01	00	64.3	2.5	1.14	1.5	.021	.009	.030
0002	2800	320	19.0	0-02	01	00	59.8	3.0	1.81	1.5	.016	.004	.020
0003	2800	320	19.0	0-02	01	00	59.9	5.9	3.95	1.2	.014	.003	.017
0004	2800	320	19.0	0-02	01	00	59.8	5.9	3.91	1.2	.015	.003	.018
0005	9332	300	19.0	0-02	01	00	59.9	2.7	1.49	1.5	.018	.004	.022
0006	9332	300	19.0	0-02	01	00	59.9	3.6	2.09	1.3	.017	.003	.020
0007	9332	300	19.0	0-02	01	00	59.9	5.1	3.44	1.4	.014	.003	.017
0008	9332	300	19.0	0-02	01	00	59.9	4.2	2.70	1.3	.015	.003	.018
0009	9332	300	19.0	0-02	01	00	59.5	3.3	1.90	1.4	.017	.003	.020
0010	9332	300	19.0	0-02	01	00	59.8	4.2	2.69	1.3	.015	.003	.018
0011	9332	300	19.0	0-02	01	00	59.9	3.0	1.65	1.6	.018	.003	.021
0012	9332	300	19.0	0-02	01	00	59.8	1.6	.81	1.6	.019	.004	.023
0013	9332	300	8.0	0-02	01	00	59.8	1.9	.98	1.9	.019	.005	.024
0014	9332	300	8.0	0-02	01	00	59.8	3.2	1.96	1.4	.016	.003	.019
0015	9332	300	8.0	0-02	01	00	59.8	4.7	3.34	1.3	.014	.002	.016
0016	9332	300	8.0	0-02	01	00	59.8	3.3	2.15	1.4	.015	.003	.018
0017	9332	300	8.0	0-02	01	00	60.1	1.5	.78	1.9	.019	.004	.023
0018	9332	300	8.0	0-02	01	00	59.8	3.4	2.22	1.3	.015	.003	.018
Average							60.2	3.5	39.1	1.4	.016	.003	.019

Unit -- Disk arm identifier
Type -- Type of disk
Size (M) -- Disk space capacity in millions of bytes
IOP Util -- Percentage of utilization for each Input/Output Processor
IOP ID -- Input/Output Processor identification number (Bus IOP)
ASP ID -- Auxiliary Storage Pool ID
CSS ID -- Checksum Set ID
Percent Full -- Percent of disk space capacity in use
Percent Util -- Average disk operation utilization (busy)
Op per Second -- Average number of disk operations per second
K Per I/O -- Average number of kilobytes (1024) transferred per disk operation
Average Service Time -- Average disk service time per I/O operations
Average Wait Time -- Average disk wait time per I/O operations
Average Response Time -- Average disk response time per I/O operation

A Write Cache Caution

Note that the **Average Service Time**, **Average Wait Time**, and **Total Disk Response Time** fields in Figure 13.5 give average values for both read and write I/O. The new I/O subsystems that use write cache can throw you a curve here. Recently, I performed a detailed analysis of a specific batch job for a customer who wanted to improve the job's performance. Breaking the job into components of CPU, CPU Wait, Disk, and Other time showed a significant amount of Other time. Finding out what happened during this Other time became a key part of the analysis.

The tool that broke out the time components had used these average service times to calculate the job's disk time. However, the system was running with a 60/40 read-to-write ratio and the specific job's read-to-write ratio was more than 80/20. After many blind alleys in trying to explain the amount of Other time in the job, it dawned on us that the system was using drives with write cache. This feature brings the service time for writes into the 1.5 ms range. This low write service time, when averaged over the 60/40 read-to-write environment, brought the average service time into the 6.0 ms range. But the specific job was doing many more reads than writes (80/20), so 6.0 ms was the wrong service time to be using in the calculations.

Making this adjustment moved the majority of the unexplained Other time back into the Disk component and gave us increased confidence that improving the application's I/O characteristics would improve its performance. ■

Jim Stewart

It is important to keep disk IOP utilization within the recommended guidelines shown in Table 13.2 (page 205), which shows that utilization should be below 35 percent for good performance. In Figure 13.5, the highest disk IOP utilization is 19 percent, so we do not have a disk IOP problem in this sample. IOPs are discussed in detail later in this chapter.

Correcting an IOP bottleneck problem can be as simple as adding IOPs to your system and then moving some disk units from the busy IOP to the new IOP to even out the IOP utilization. However, if you don't have room for an additional IOP, fixing the problem is not as simple. You may have to add an additional bus expansion unit or buy a larger system to support more IOPs.

Average Service Time is the average time the disk unit takes to service disk I/O requests. In our example, this time ranges from 0.014 to 0.021 milliseconds. The **Average Wait Time** is usually associated with IOP queuing. **Total Disk Response Time**, sometimes called Disk Service Time, is the total of Service Time plus Wait Time.

THE COMPONENT REPORT

The Component Report is usually the second report you will use for performance analysis. The length of this report will vary, depending on the size of your sample, the number of interval samples, the number of storage pools defined on your system, and the number of system components (e.g., disk drives, IOPs).

The seven sections of the Component Report are Component Interval Activity, Job Workload Activity, Storage Pool Activity, Disk Activity, IOP Utilization, Local Workstations/Response Time Buckets, and Exception Occurrence Summary and Interval Counts. Let's look at each of these sections in detail.

Component Interval Activity

Figure 13.6 is the Component Interval Activity section of the Component Report. This report gives values for **CPU utilization**, **Disk I/O per second**, **High Utilization**, and **Pool Faults per second** for each interval during which data was captured.

The first field on this report that we focus on is the **Rsp/Tns** (response time per transaction) field, which can help you identify the intervals with the highest response time. If you have an interval with a response time that is much higher than the average, this field is a good starting point for your investigation.

For example, if your response time per transaction values are about 1.5 seconds and one interval has a response time of 8.1 seconds, you may have a problem to investigate. The columns next to the interval with the 8.1-second response time may provide a clue. Directly left of this field is the **Tns/Hour** (transactions per hour) column. This field shows how many transactions were completed during the interval. If the transactions per hour were much higher during this one interval, it's logical to assume that the response time might be longer. However, if the number of transactions per hour for this interval is in the same range as for the other intervals, the problem is probably something else. You next want to look at the CPU utilization, which is shown in the three columns to the right of the response time column.

CPU utilization is divided into **Total**, **Inter** (interactive), and **Batch**. The figure for system CPU utilization does not appear; in fact, if you add total the interactive and batch columns, they will not add up to the total CPU utilization. To figure out system CPU utilization for each interval, you need to do the following calculation:

Total CPU Utilization – Total Interactive Utilization – Total Batch Utilization = Total System Utilization

System CPU utilization can be important. If a system is using a lot of CPU cycles to get its own work done, your work cannot use these cycles. What constitutes "a lot" of system CPU cycles? Good question. And the answer is: It depends on how much and what kind of work you are doing. As a general guideline, watch the normal trend for your system and track this number over a period of two weeks to a month. If your system consistently uses 10 to

FIGURE 13.6

Component Interval Activity Section of the Component Report

```
                                        Component Report                                                  7/01/96  15:10:02
                                  Component Interval Activity                                                   Page    1
                                    Performance Report Sample
Member . . . : TU0602AM      Model/Serial  . . :  320-2050/10-XXXXX   Main storage . . :   32.0 M    Started  . . . . : 06/02/96  08:56:43
  Library . . : QPFRDATA     System name . . . :  PERF1               Version/Release  :   3/ 2.0    Stopped  . . . . : 06/02/96  15:55:55

                                                        ---- Disk I/O ----         High                     Pool
 Itv        Tns      Rsp       ---- CPU Utilization ---  --- Per Second ---    -Utilization-         --- Faults/Sec --
 End       /Hour    /Tns      Total    Inter    Batch    Sync       Async      Disk     Unit       Mch      User   ID       Excp
-----   ---------   ----      -----    -----    -----    -------    -------    ----     ----       ---      ----   --     -------
09:11       3,822    2.5       82.0     68.1 *    4.7      20.0       26.1        8     0004         0         8   03       4,465
09:26       3,832    2.7       88.3     67.7 *   11.6      22.0       26.7        9     0004         0         8   03       2,545
09:41       3,435    1.7       76.3     59.4      8.5      17.5       25.8        8     0008         0         7   03       3,699
09:56       2,806    1.9       61.5     49.5      5.4      12.4       21.8        6     0004         0         5   03       2,016
10:11       4,173    3.6       87.9     78.2      3.6      16.8       29.2       11     0007         0         7   03       2,912

10:26       2,765    2.3       78.0     60.0     10.1      15.3       26.6        8     0004         0         5   03       1,989
10:41       2,862    3.6       79.6     67.8 *    3.8      12.3       32.9        9     0003         0         5   03       2,123
10:56       2,650    2.4       80.7     68.0 *    5.3       9.9       28.3        7     0004         0         3   03       2,010
11:11       2,389    3.1       72.4     59.6      5.2       9.8       28.8        8     0004         0         3   03       2,146
11:26       2,638    1.8       73.0     60.4      5.0       8.5       30.8        7     0004         0         3   03       2,370

11:41       2,048    3.1       70.0     58.4      5.2       9.5       23.9        6     0004         0         3   03       1,917
11:56       2,621    2.4       82.5     70.4 *    3.2      13.7       32.3        9     0004         0         5   03       2,372
12:11       1,507    5.9       63.3     49.7      7.2      11.6       26.3        7     0004         0         4   03       1,730
12:26       1,057    1.8       48.3     36.9      6.3       3.2       21.5        4     0007         0         1   03       1,243
12:41       1,719    2.3       64.8     53.6      4.6       7.2       20.2        5     0004         0         3   03       1,673

12:56       2,124    1.5       50.5     41.4      4.3       5.7       14.4        4     0004         0         2   03       1,798
13:11       1,371    2.5       46.2     34.4      6.4       4.4       13.8        5     0004         0         1   03       1,820
13:26       2,725    1.7       69.4     57.5      4.8       8.6       18.5        6     0004         0         3   03       2,272
13:41       2,354    2.4       69.8     58.1      4.6       7.7       24.5        7     0003         0         2   03       2,148
13:56       2,297    2.1       66.8     55.1      5.3       6.2       22.8        5     0004         0         1   03       2,133

14:11       2,425    1.6       49.5     38.7      4.9       9.0       18.0        6     0004         0         4   03       1,805
14:26       2,400    1.7       55.1     44.5      5.1      10.6       14.7        6     0004         0         4   03       1,518
14:41       2,120     .7       45.5     23.0     16.1       9.4       16.2        4     0004         0         2   03       1,331
14:56       2,196    2.5       72.8     59.5      5.7       8.2       29.9        7     0004         0         3   03       1,721
15:10       1,539    2.4       63.3     50.8      5.3       7.1       27.6        7     0004         0         2   03       1,419

15:25       2,923    2.2       73.0     59.7      5.7       9.1       27.7        8     0004         0         3   03       1,799
```

Remember, CPU utilization for high-priority jobs should not exceed 70%

15 percent of the system for system work, this may be your norm. If your performance analysis shows a large discrepancy, you need to investigate. We have discovered system problems that require PTFs or other corrective action from IBM by tracking the system CPU utilization.

If the **Total CPU Utilization** column is always close to 100 percent, you obviously have a busy system. This percentage can be acceptable under certain circumstances; for example, when interactive CPU utilization is within the guidelines in Table 8.2 on page 114. Again, because interactive jobs usually make up most of your high-priority jobs (allowing for 6 to 12 percent for system jobs), you can use this chart as a rough guideline for interactive jobs.

According to the guidelines, for a single-processor AS/400 the CPU utilization for high-priority work should be below 70 percent. As long as the figure in this column is not above 70 percent, you are probably leaving enough CPU cycles for the remainder of the workload (i.e., batch and other low-priority work). Batch work will use all remaining CPU cycles. If your interactive CPU is running at 60 percent and you have enough batch work running to use the remaining 40 percent of CPU, it can use that much, thus making your total CPU utilization 100 percent.

Use the batch column to identify patterns during the day, week, or month when you usually run heavy batch work. If you notice that you constantly have high batch activity during periods of slow response time, reschedule the batch work to run at other times. This report shows not only the busy periods, but also the periods when your system's activity is low. If possible, schedule work so that you are using most of your system at all times.

The **High Utilization**, **Disk**, and **Unit** fields identify the disk that was the busiest during the interval. Because the AS/400 spreads its data evenly across all disk units, you want to see all disk units in use. Disk utilization is a concern only if you consistently see the same disk in this column. This pattern could indicate one of two situations: a disk unit may be going bad, and a service person needs to look at your drive as soon as possible; or a file or program that is very busy has been associated with a disk unit, either through an ASP or the contiguous option on the create file command. The second situation is not bad, as long as the percent of time the disk is busy is within guidelines.

The **Pool Faults/Sec** columns help you identify the faults occurring in the machine and user pools. Remember that the machine pool is always pool 01, and it can cause the most performance problems. The importance of the user pools varies, but you need to monitor them and keep them within their guidelines. The report shows the user pool with the highest fault rate per interval.

Job Workload Activity

Figure 13.7 shows the Job Workload Activity section of the Component Report. This report provides information about each job and task that ran during the

FIGURE 13.7
Job Workload Activity Section of the Component Report

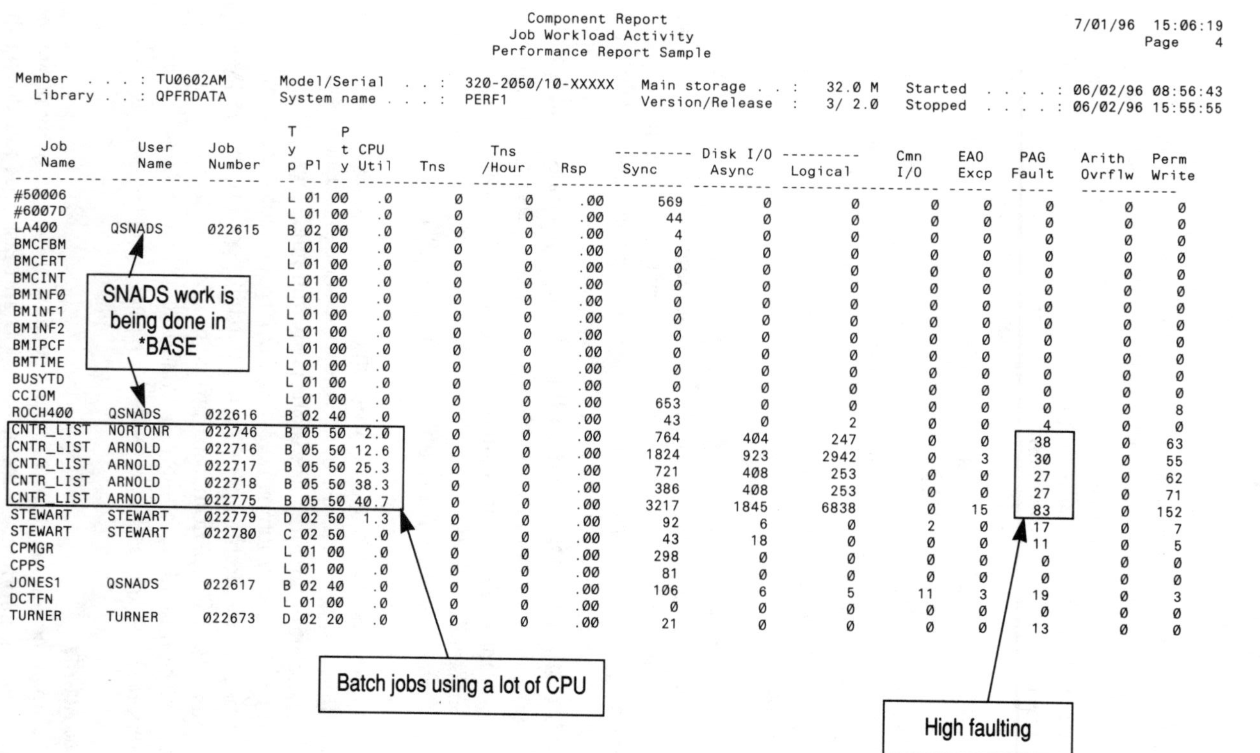

Component Report
Job Workload Activity
Performance Report Sample

7/01/96 15:06:19
Page 4

Member . . . : TU0602AM
Library . . : QPFRDATA
Model/Serial . . : 320-2050/10-XXXXX
System name . . . : PERF1
Main storage . . : 32.0 M
Version/Release : 3/ 2.0
Started . . . . : 06/02/96 08:56:43
Stopped . . . . : 06/02/96 15:55:55

Job Name	User Name	Job Number	Typ	Pl	Pty	CPU Util	Tns	Tns /Hour	Rsp	Disk I/O Sync	Disk I/O Async	Disk I/O Logical	Cmn I/O	EAO Excp	PAG Fault	Arith Ovrflw	Perm Write
#50006			L	01	00	.0	0	0	.00	569	0	0	0	0	0	0	0
#6007D			L	01	00	.0	0	0	.00	44	0	0	0	0	0	0	0
LA400	QSNADS	022615	B	02	00	.0	0	0	.00	4	0	0	0	0	0	0	0
BMCFBM			L	01	00	.0	0	0	.00	0	0	0	0	0	0	0	0
BMCFRT			L	01	00	.0	0	0	.00	0	0	0	0	0	0	0	0
BMCINT			L	01	00	.0	0	0	.00	0	0	0	0	0	0	0	0
BMINF0			L	01	00	.0	0	0	.00	0	0	0	0	0	0	0	0
BMINF1			L	01	00	.0	0	0	.00	0	0	0	0	0	0	0	0
BMINF2			L	01	00	.0	0	0	.00	0	0	0	0	0	0	0	0
BMIPCF			L	01	00	.0	0	0	.00	0	0	0	0	0	0	0	0
BMTIME			L	01	00	.0	0	0	.00	0	0	0	0	0	0	0	0
BUSYTD			L	01	00	.0	0	0	.00	0	0	0	0	0	0	0	0
CCIOM			L	01	00	.0	0	0	.00	653	0	0	0	0	0	0	8
ROCH400	QSNADS	022616	B	02	40	.0	0	0	.00	43	0	2	0	0	4	0	0
CNTR_LIST	NORTONR	022746	B	05	50	2.0	0	0	.00	764	404	247	0	0	38	0	63
CNTR_LIST	ARNOLD	022716	B	05	50	12.6	0	0	.00	1824	923	2942	0	3	30	0	55
CNTR_LIST	ARNOLD	022717	B	05	50	25.3	0	0	.00	721	408	253	0	0	27	0	62
CNTR_LIST	ARNOLD	022718	B	05	50	38.3	0	0	.00	386	408	253	0	0	27	0	71
CNTR_LIST	ARNOLD	022775	B	05	50	40.7	0	0	.00	3217	1845	6838	0	15	83	0	152
STEWART	STEWART	022779	D	02	50	1.3	0	0	.00	92	6	0	2	0	17	0	7
STEWART	STEWART	022780	C	02	50	.0	0	0	.00	43	18	0	0	0	11	0	5
CPMGR			L	01	00	.0	0	0	.00	298	0	0	0	0	0	0	0
CPPS			L	01	00	.0	0	0	.00	81	0	0	0	0	0	0	0
JONES1	QSNADS	022617	B	02	40	.0	0	0	.00	106	6	5	11	3	19	0	3
DCTFN			L	01	00	.0	0	0	.00	0	0	0	0	0	0	0	0
TURNER	TURNER	022673	D	02	20	.0	0	0	.00	21	0	0	0	0	13	0	0

sample period. You can use this report to find out what pool a particular job or task is running in and its priority.

The first field on this report is the **Job Name** field. This field lists tasks and jobs that ran during the sample period in alphabetical order. You can easily identify the tasks because they start with a pound sign (#) and appear first.

The next field is the **User Name** field, which contains the name of the user who ran the job. For system tasks and LIC jobs, you will not see a user name.

The third field is **Job Number**, which is the job's system-assigned job number. If the same user runs multiple jobs from the same device the system sorts the different jobs by the job number. For system tasks and LIC jobs, you will not see a job number.

The next field, **Typ**, shows the type of job. This field is a one-character code that represents the kind of job or task. The most common jobs are L (licensed internal code), B (batch jobs), C (communications), and I (interactive jobs).

The next field, **Pl**, contains the number of the storage pool the job ran in. You may have up to 16 storage pools on your system, so this number will be between 1 and 16.

The **Pty** (priority) field shows the job or task's priority. If the priority changed during the job, the original priority appears on this report. Any valid priority between 00 and 99 can appear here. Priority 00 is reserved for system tasks and jobs.

The **CPU Util** (CPU utilization) field shows the CPU utilization during the sample period for the job or task for the intervals in which the job was active.

Let's examine some of the uses of the fields we just described. First, these fields let you audit the setup of your subsystems. For example, you can see whether a priority 50 batch job is running in an interactive pool, which could adversely affect performance. You can also check what types of jobs are running in your *BASE subsystem — because pool 02 is always the *BASE pool, you simply look for the value 02 in the **Pl** field. Although the default system configuration runs all jobs in this pool, we suggest that you separate different types of work into different storage pools. This report can help you do so.

A second use for this section of the Component Report is to see how much CPU each job is using. A job that is consistently using a lot of CPU cycles may point to an application that is not written efficiently. This area can be a good starting point to identify an application problem.

The **Tns** (transactions), **Tns/Hour** (transactions per hour), and **Rsp** (average response time) fields are also handy for evaluating interactive jobs. Zeros in these columns indicate the jobs are some type other than interactive — you will see numbers in these columns only if an I is in the **Typ** field. We use the average response time field to look for batch-like work that is running in an interactive pool. For example, when a compile runs interactively, this column will display a high number, such as 95.59. This type of work will adversely affect the other work being done within the same pool. Look for such jobs and move them to keep response time consistent within the interactive pools.

The three types of Disk I/O displayed are Sync (synchronous), Async (asynchronous), and Logical. The main performance consideration here is that if interactive transactions have high I/O rates, chances are good that non-interactive work is being done interactively. You need to eliminate such situations whenever possible.

Also, check the PAG Fault column for page faults. They are usually an indication that not enough main storage existed to run the job, or the job was competing with too many other jobs to get the optimal amount of main storage to process the job.

Storage Pool Activity

The next section of the Component Report is the Storage Pool Activity section. This report contains information about each storage pool defined to the system. Every system has a minimum of two storage pools: pool 01, the machine pool, and pool 02, the *BASE pool. The report starts a new page for each pool. We have included three separate pages of this section of the report — one for the machine pool, one for *BASE, and one for the Interactive pool — in Figures 13.8a, 13.8b, and 13.8c.

The **Pool identifier** field, under the first two rows, shows the name of the pool that the report is displaying. Pool information, similar to the information you get from the WRKSYSSTS command, appears for each interval.

The first field we will examine on this report is **Size (KB)**, which shows how much storage is in the pool at the end of each interval. This value can change if you are using an auto-tuner that changes the amount of storage allocated to each pool. Some auto-tuners, such as IBM's, also adjust the **Act Level** (activity level) field. We recommend that you leave auto-tuners off during the collection of performance data.

Remember that you will see numbers in the **Total Tns** (transactions) and **Avg Rsp Time** (average response time) fields only if the pool you are looking at ran interactive jobs. Watch the database and non-database faults and the transitional data: Act-Wait, Wait-Inel, Act-Inel. Follow the guidelines for these fields, which are in Chapter 8.

Disk Activity

Figure 13.9 is the Disk Activity section of the Component Report. This report gives you information about your disk units. Because disk drives are usually the slowest component of your system, you want to optimize their performance in any way possible. This report shows you most of the key areas related to disk performance.

FIGURE 13.8A

Machine Pool Page of the Storage Pool Activity Section of the Component Report

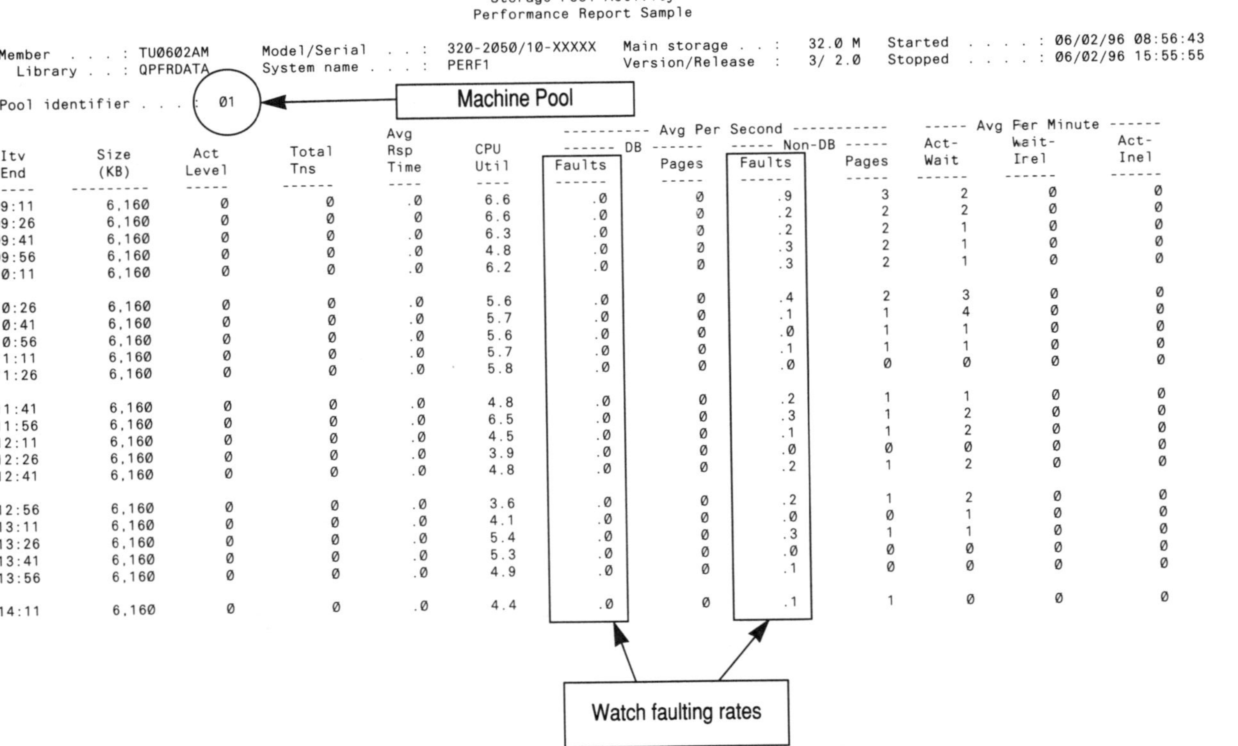

Component Report
Storage Pool Activity
Performance Report Sample

7/01/96 15:10:02
Page 10

Member . . . : TU0602AM   Model/Serial . . : 320-2050/10-XXXXX   Main storage . . : 32.0 M   Started . . . . : 06/02/96 08:56:43
Library . . : QPFRDATA   System name . . . : PERF1   Version/Release : 3/ 2.0   Stopped . . . . : 06/02/96 15:55:55

Pool identifier . . . : 01

Itv End	Size (KB)	Act Level	Total Tns	Avg Rsp Time	CPU Util	Avg Per Second: DB Faults	DB Pages	Non-DB Faults	Non-DB Pages	Avg Per Minute: Act-Wait	Wait-Inel	Act-Inel
09:11	6,160	0	0	.0	6.6	.0	0	.9	3	2	0	0
09:26	6,160	0	0	0	6.6	.0	0	.2	2	2	0	0
09:41	6,160	0	0	.0	6.3	.0	0	.2	2	1	0	0
09:56	6,160	0	0	.0	4.8	.0	0	.3	2	1	0	0
10:11	6,160	0	0	.0	6.2	.0	0	.3	2	1	0	0
10:26	6,160	0	0	.0	5.6	.0	0	.4	2	3	0	0
10:41	6,160	0	0	.0	5.7	.0	0	.1	1	4	0	0
10:56	6,160	0	0	.0	5.6	.0	0	.0	1	1	0	0
11:11	6,160	0	0	.0	5.7	.0	0	.1	1	1	0	0
11:26	6,160	0	0	.0	5.8	.0	0	.0	0	0	0	0
11:41	6,160	0	0	.0	4.8	.0	0	.2	1	1	0	0
11:56	6,160	0	0	.0	6.5	.0	0	.3	1	2	0	0
12:11	6,160	0	0	.0	4.5	.0	0	.1	1	2	0	0
12:26	6,160	0	0	.0	3.9	.0	0	.0	0	0	0	0
12:41	6,160	0	0	.0	4.8	.0	0	.2	1	2	0	0
12:56	6,160	0	0	.0	3.6	.0	0	.2	1	2	0	0
13:11	6,160	0	0	.0	4.1	.0	0	.0	0	1	0	0
13:26	6,160	0	0	.0	5.4	.0	0	.3	1	1	0	0
13:41	6,160	0	0	.0	5.3	.0	0	.0	0	0	0	0
13:56	6,160	0	0	.0	4.9	.0	0	.1	0	0	0	0
14:11	6,160	0	0	.0	4.4	.0	0	.1	1	0	0	0

FIGURE 13.8B

*BASE Pool Page of the Storage Pool Activity Section of the Component Report

```
                                   Component Report                                   7/01/96  15:10:02
                                 Storage Pool Activity                                   Page   12
                               Performance Report Sample
Member  . . . : TU0602AM    Model/Serial  . . :  320-2050/10-XXXXX  Main storage . . :  32.0 M  Started  . . . . : 06/02/96 08:56:43
  Library . . : QPFRDATA    System name . . . :  PERF1              Version/Release  :  3/ 2.0  Stopped  . . . . : 06/02/96 15:55:55
Pool identifier . . . : 02   <--  *BASE
```

Itv End	Size (KB)	Act Level	Total Tns	Avg Rsp Time	CPU Util	Avg Per Second – DB – Faults	DB – Pages	Non-DB – Faults	Non-DB – Pages	Avg Per Minute – Act-Wait	Wait-Inel	Act-Inel
09:11	7,508	15	0	.0	5.2	.0	17	1.0	4	5	0	0
09:26	7,508	15	0	.0	4.1	.0	15	.2	0	1	0	0
09:41	7,508	15	0	.0	5.2	.0	23	.1	0	0	0	0
09:56	7,508	15	0	.0	5.0	.0	19	.1	0	0	0	0
10:11	7,508	15	0	.0	3.2	.0	11	.3	1	0	0	0
10:26	7,508	15	0	.0	5.8	.0	14	.7	4	5	0	0
10:41	7,508	15	0	.0	4.7	.0	6	.3	1	3	0	0
10:56	7,508	15	0	.0	5.4	.0	8	.1	0	2	0	0
11:11	7,508	15	0	.0	5.4	.0	11	.1	0	2	0	0
11:26	7,508	15	0	.0	5.0	.0	14	.0	0	0	0	0
11:41	7,508	15	0	.0	5.4	.0	7	.2	0	0	0	0
11:56	7,508	15	0	.0	4.0	.0	6	.1	0	3	0	0
12:11	7,508	15	0	.0	4.3	.0	11	.1	0	2	0	0
12:26	7,508	15	0	.0	6.3	.0	11	.0	0	0	0	0
12:41	7,508	15	0	.0	5.0	.0	6	.1	0	0	0	0
12:56	7,508	15	0	.0	4.9	.0	6	.1	0	5	0	0
13:11	7,508	15	0	.0	6.6	.0	7	.2	1	0	0	0
13:26	7,508	15	0	.0	4.9	.0	6	.1	0	1	0	0
13:41	7,508	15	0	.0	4.7	.0	8	.0	0	0	0	0
13:56	7,508	15	0	.0	5.3	.0	8	.0	0	0	0	0
14:11	7,508	15	0	.0	5.0	.0	13	.2	1	0	0	0

FIGURE 13.8C

Interactive Pool Page of the Storage Pool Activity Section of the Component Report

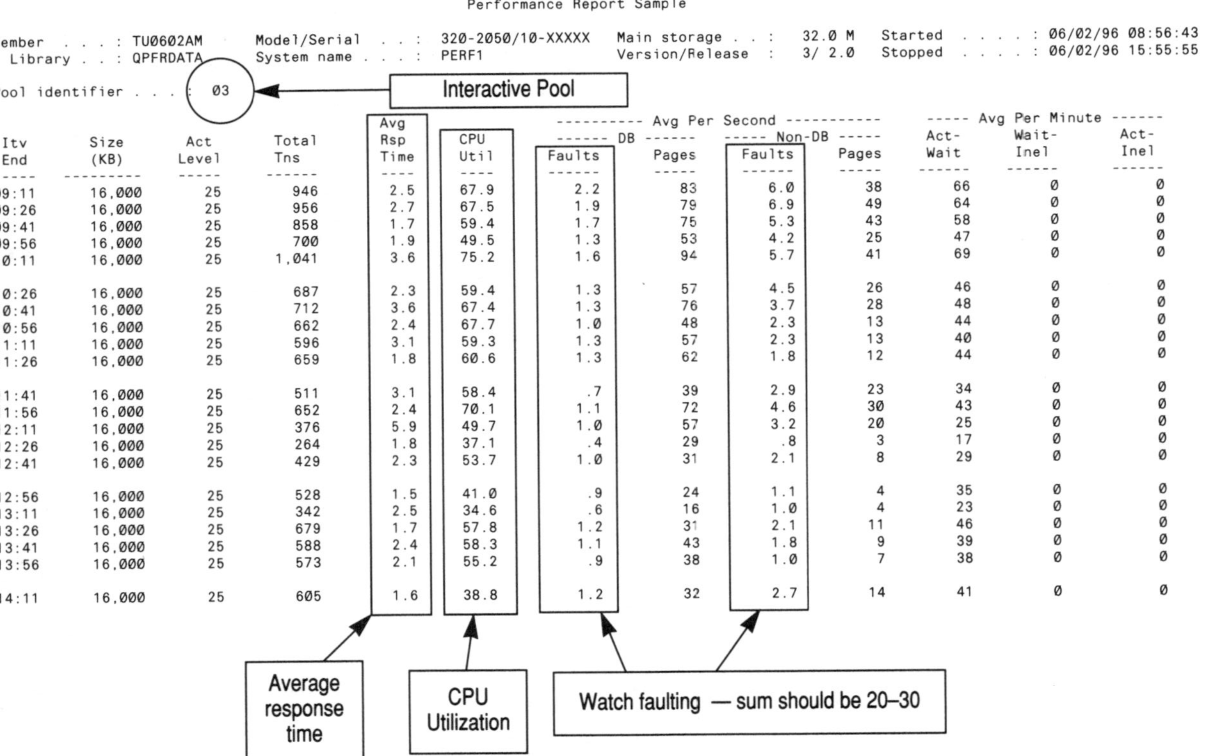

Component Report
Storage Pool Activity
Performance Report Sample

7/01/96 15:10:02
Page 13

Member . . . : TU0602AM   Model/Serial . . : 320-2050/10-XXXXX   Main storage . . : 32.0 M   Started . . . . : 06/02/96 08:56:43
Library . . : QPFRDATA   System name . . . : PERF1   Version/Release : 3/ 2.0   Stopped . . . . : 06/02/96 15:55:55

Pool identifier . . . : 03

Itv End	Size (KB)	Act Level	Total Tns	Avg Rsp Time	CPU Util	DB Faults (Avg Per Second)	DB Pages (Avg Per Second)	Non-DB Faults (Avg Per Second)	Non-DB Pages (Avg Per Second)	Act-Wait (Avg Per Minute)	Wait-Inel (Avg Per Minute)	Act-Inel (Avg Per Minute)
09:11	16,000	25	946	2.5	67.9	2.2	83	6.0	38	66	0	0
09:26	16,000	25	956	2.7	67.5	1.9	79	6.9	49	64	0	0
09:41	16,000	25	858	1.7	59.4	1.7	75	5.3	43	58	0	0
09:56	16,000	25	700	1.9	49.5	1.3	53	4.2	25	47	0	0
10:11	16,000	25	1,041	3.6	75.2	1.6	94	5.7	41	69	0	0
10:26	16,000	25	687	2.3	59.4	1.3	57	4.5	26	46	0	0
10:41	16,000	25	712	3.6	67.4	1.3	76	3.7	28	48	0	0
10:56	16,000	25	662	2.4	67.7	1.0	48	2.3	13	44	0	0
11:11	16,000	25	596	3.1	59.3	1.3	57	2.3	13	40	0	0
11:26	16,000	25	659	1.8	60.6	1.3	62	1.8	12	44	0	0
11:41	16,000	25	511	3.1	58.4	.7	39	2.9	23	34	0	0
11:56	16,000	25	652	2.4	70.1	1.1	72	4.6	30	43	0	0
12:11	16,000	25	376	5.9	49.7	1.0	57	3.2	20	25	0	0
12:26	16,000	25	264	1.8	37.1	.4	29	.8	3	17	0	0
12:41	16,000	25	429	2.3	53.7	1.0	31	2.1	8	29	0	0
12:56	16,000	25	528	1.5	41.0	.9	24	1.1	4	35	0	0
13:11	16,000	25	342	2.5	34.6	.6	16	1.0	4	23	0	0
13:26	16,000	25	679	1.7	57.8	1.2	31	2.1	11	46	0	0
13:41	16,000	25	588	2.4	58.3	1.1	43	1.8	9	39	0	0
13:56	16,000	25	573	2.1	55.2	.9	38	1.0	7	38	0	0
14:11	16,000	25	605	1.6	38.8	1.2	32	2.7	14	41	0	0

FIGURE 13.9
Disk Activity Section of the Component Report

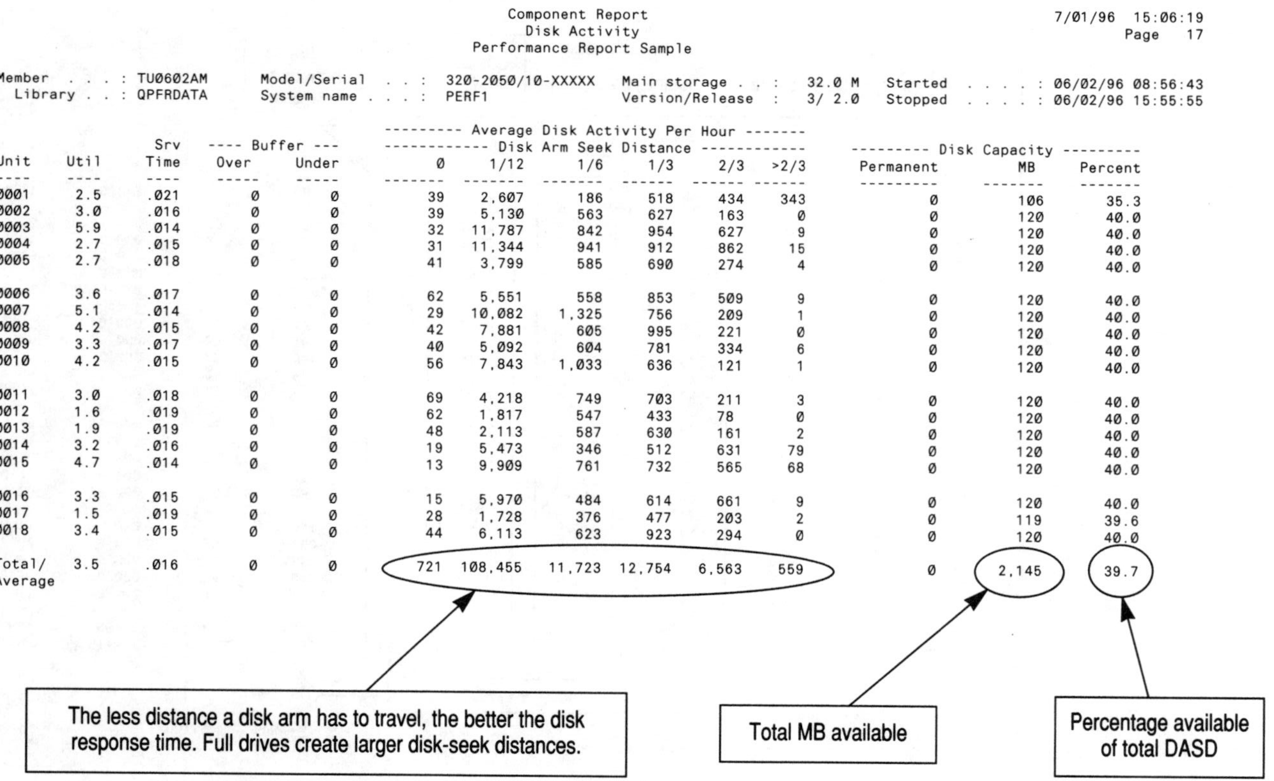

```
                                   Component Report                                  7/01/96  15:06:19
                                     Disk Activity                                        Page    17
                                Performance Report Sample

Member . . . . : TU0602AM    Model/Serial . . :  320-2050/10-XXXXX  Main storage . . :  32.0 M  Started  . . . . : 06/02/96 08:56:43
  Library  . . : QPFRDATA    System name . . . :  PERF1             Version/Release  :  3/ 2.0  Stopped  . . . . : 06/02/96 15:55:55
```

Unit	Util	Srv Time	Buffer Over	Buffer Under	Average Disk Activity Per Hour – Disk Arm Seek Distance 0	1/12	1/6	1/3	2/3	>2/3	Disk Capacity Permanent	MB	Percent
0001	2.5	.021	0	0	39	2,607	186	518	434	343	0	106	35.3
0002	3.0	.016	0	0	39	5,130	563	627	163	0	0	120	40.0
0003	5.9	.014	0	0	32	11,787	842	954	627	9	0	120	40.0
0004	2.7	.015	0	0	31	11,344	941	912	862	15	0	120	40.0
0005	2.7	.018	0	0	41	3,799	585	690	274	4	0	120	40.0
0006	3.6	.017	0	0	62	5,551	558	853	509	9	0	120	40.0
0007	5.1	.014	0	0	29	10,082	1,325	756	209	1	0	120	40.0
0008	4.2	.015	0	0	42	7,881	605	995	221	0	0	120	40.0
0009	3.3	.017	0	0	40	5,092	604	781	334	6	0	120	40.0
0010	4.2	.015	0	0	56	7,843	1,033	636	121	1	0	120	40.0
0011	3.0	.018	0	0	69	4,218	749	703	211	3	0	120	40.0
0012	1.6	.019	0	0	62	1,817	547	433	78	0	0	120	40.0
0013	1.9	.019	0	0	48	2,113	587	630	161	2	0	120	40.0
0014	3.2	.016	0	0	19	5,473	346	512	631	79	0	120	40.0
0015	4.7	.014	0	0	13	9,909	761	732	565	68	0	120	40.0
0016	3.3	.015	0	0	15	5,970	484	614	661	9	0	120	40.0
0017	1.5	.019	0	0	28	1,728	376	477	203	2	0	119	39.6
0018	3.4	.015	0	0	44	6,113	623	923	294	0	0	120	40.0
Total/ Average	3.5	.016	0	0	721	108,455	11,723	12,754	6,563	559	0	2,145	39.7

The **Unit number** is the actuator number. Some disk units, such as IBM's 9335, have two unit numbers, one for each actuator. So, if you are looking at the number of units displayed on this report and they don't match up to the physical number of disk drives you count on your system, chances are that you have some disk drives on your system with multiple actuators.

The **Util** (utilization) field indicates how busy the drives are. Compare the value in this field with the guidelines in Table 13.2 on page 205. **Srv Time** (service time) shows the raw speed of the disk unit. This value is in milliseconds, so for example, you read a value of 0.014 in this column as 14 milliseconds. All disk drive models have different service time characteristics.

The **Buffer Under/Over** fields show the synchronization of the disk drive and the disk IOP. If the disk IOP cannot keep up with the data transferred from the disk drive to disk IOP, you have an overrun condition. The opposite situation creates an underrun condition. Most modern disk IOPs are fast enough that this field is usually not busy. However, on some systems with high disk activity, or if you have an LIC or disk IOP problem, you will see numbers in these columns.

The **Disk Arm Seek Distance** indicates how far the disk arm has to travel to get the data. This information is divided into six buckets. For optimum performance, most of your disk seeks should be in the first five buckets, because the arm does not have to travel more than the distance of the disk platter to read data. However, because the system optimizes itself, you cannot control where your data is on the disk drives. To ensure that you are getting optimum disk seeks, keep your disk utilization in the 80 to 90 percent range and periodically perform a scratch-reload of your system. A scratch-reload is the process of backing everything off your system, re-initializing the disk drives, and then restoring everything. This process will let the system optimize the placement of the objects on the disk drives and eliminate fragmentation that may have occurred.

The Disk Capacity section has two main fields you need to monitor: **MB** (megabytes) and **Percent**. These two fields show how much disk storage capacity is allowed and how much is available. For a complete discussion of disk drive utilization, see the discussion of the WRKDSKSTS command in Chapter 9.

IOP Utilization

Figure 13.10 is the IOP Utilization section of the Component Report. This report displays information about your system's IOPs and is the only place where you can find this information. IOPs are mini-processors, feature cards that plug into your system's bus and bus expansion units. It is important that you monitor the utilization of your IOPs, because they often become a bottleneck to performance that is easy to fix. Table 13.2 provides the guidelines for the various IOPs on the system.

FIGURE 13.10

IOP Utilization Section of the Component Report

```
                                     Component Report                                        7/01/96  15:06:19
                                     IOP Utilizations                                             Page    18
                                 Performance Report Sample

Member . . . : TU0602AM    Model/Serial  . . :  320-2050/10-XXXXX   Main storage . . :   32.0 M   Started  . . . . : 06/02/96 08:56:43
  Library . . : QPFRDATA   System name . . . :  PERF1               Version/Release  :   3/ 2.0   Stopped  . . . . : 06/02/96 15:55:55

Communications                        --- OPSTART Msg ---    --- Bytes Transmitted ---   Restart       BNA        Available
IOP/s                   Utilization    Reverse     Normal      IOP            System     Queues     Received      Storage
--------------------    -----------    -------     ------   -----------   -----------   -------     --------     ---------
BUS 0  IOP 06 (2623)        1.0              0         84             0        14,784         0            0       833,946
BUS 0  IOP 07 (2623)        1.0              0         84             0        14,784         0            0       835,034
BUS 0  IOP 08 (2623)        4.0              0     13,962     6,129,460     4,851,384         0            0        98,204

DASD IOP'S              Utilization    Ops Per Sec
--------------------    -----------    -----------
BUS 0  IOP 02 (6112)           19.0        27
BUS 0  IOP 03 (6112)            8.0        11

Multi-function
IOP's                   Utilization
--------------------    -----------
BUS 0  IOP 01 (2615)            5.0

Local Work                Controller   -- OPSTART Msg --   Bytes   Transmitted Restart     BNA     ----- Queue Average -----    Twinaxial
Staion IOP's      Util    Name         Reverse     Normal  IOP          System Queues   Received   Wait   Suspend   Active        Util
-------------     ----    ----------   -------     ------  -------    -------- -------  --------  ------  -------   ------     ---------
BUS 0  IOP 04     24.0    CTL01              0      20678  9965016    17274433       0         0     .0       .0        .0           .1
       (6140)
BUS 0  IOP 05     19.0    CTL02              0       7814  2993107     7917655       0         0     .0       .0        .0           .0
       (6050)
```

<35%

Less than 35%

Less than 25%

TABLE 13.2

IOP Utilization Guideline Chart

	Good	Acceptable	Poor
Disk IOP	< 60%	70%	> 80%
Local Workstation IOP	< 25%	35%	> 40%
Multifunction IOP	< 35%	45%	> 50%
Communication and Network IOPs	< 35%	45%	> 50%
LAN IOP	<35%	40%	>50%
FSIOP Read/Write Cache Hit*	>90%	90%	<90%
FSIOP OS/2 CPU Utilization*	<80%	80%	>80%

*Obtain these values by querying QAPMIOPD

Watch the Utilization field for each IOP and compare these numbers to the guidelines in Table 13.2. If an IOP goes into the "poor" range, you need to add an IOP to the system and move part of the workload from the poor-performing IOP to the new IOP. The communications and local workstation IOPs tend to go beyond acceptable guidelines more often than other IOPs.

The number of disk drives you put on an IOP is also a performance consideration. For example, although the system can support up to eight 9335 disk drives per IOP, AS/400s are rarely configured with more than four 9335 drives per IOP. Reducing the number of drives per IOP reduces the IOP's utilization and reduces the queuing multiplier for this resource, thus improving performance. Table 13.3 provides guidelines for optimal disk and IOP performance.

TABLE 13.3

Disk-IOP Optimal Performance Guidelines

Disk Drive	Disk IOP	Maximum Number of Drives
9332	6110/6112	4
9335 A01	6110/6112	2
9335 B01	6110/6112	4
9336	6111/6112	2 (1 on busy systems)
9337	6500/6501/6502	1

Local Work Station - Response Time Buckets

Figures 13.11a and 13.11b show the Local Work Station - Response Time Buckets section of the Component Report. This section indicates response times for each locally attached display station on your system. These response times are divided by controllers. The controller number is displayed in the left column,

FIGURE 13.11A

Page 1, Local Work Station-Response Time Buckets Section of the Component Report

```
                                   Component Report                                            7/01/96  15:06:19
                        Local Work Stations - Response Time Buckets                                   Page 0019
                                Performance Report Sample

Member . . . : TU0602AM    Model/Serial . . : 320-2050/10-XXXXX  Main storage . . :  32.0 M  Started  . . . . : 06/02/96 08:56:43
  Library . . : QPFRDATA   System name . . . : PERF1             Version/Release  :  3/ 2.0  Stopped  . . . . : 06/02/96 15:55:55

   Ctl/Device     Util      Bus   IOP
---------------   ----      ---   ---
CTL01             24.0       0     4
```

Ctl/Device	0-001	001-002	002-004	004-008	>>008
DSP02	85	74	39	22	11
DSP03	63	40	34	25	14
DSP04	482	301	196	59	17
DSP05	60	27	30	22	34
DSP06	362	219	171	69	25
DSP07	123	43	47	27	17
DSP08	130	63	27	23	8
DSP10	245	196	120	43	6
DSP11	158	80	82	50	16
DSP12	178	115	93	51	12
DSP13	201	107	74	50	11
DSP14	227	128	72	31	11
DSP15	159	103	89	64	26
DSP16	80	111	76	35	4
DSP17	120	76	76	59	14
DSP18	138	189	115	44	13
DSP19	77	67	59	52	12
DSP22	26	37	22	10	5
DSP23	24	15	17	17	8
DSP24	184	175	93	47	16
DSP25	143	106	74	60	27
DSP28	920	317	185	60	9
DSP30	1,318	183	44	18	6
DSP31	33	22	17	7	5
DSP33	70	33	20	4	4
DSP34	29	5	6	2	12
DSP49	498	175	120	48	12
DSP50	181	164	98	30	17
DSP51	96	65	69	43	14

FIGURE 13.11B

Page 2, Local Work Station-Response Time Buckets Section of the Component Report

```
                                  Component Report                                         7/01/96  15:06:19
                       Local Work Stations - Response Time Buckets                              Page 0020
                                Performance Report Sample

Member  . . . : TU0602AM    Model/Serial  . . :  320-2050/10-XXXXX  Main storage . . :   32.0 M  Started  . . . . : 06/02/96 08:56:43
  Library . . : QPFRDATA    System name . . . :  PERF1              Version/Release  :   3/ 2.0  Stopped  . . . . : 06/02/96 15:55:55

   Ctl/Device     Util       Bus    IOP
---------------   ----       ---    ---
CTL02             19.0        0      5
```

Ctl/Device	0-001	001-002	002-004	004-008	>>008
DSP35	62	38	22	13	5
DSP36	249	139	40	23	4
DSP38	91	48	28	22	2
DSP39	304	218	141	38	13
DSP40	206	131	99	82	33
DSP41	247	200	107	38	11
DSP42	192	119	100	64	21
DSP52	2	11	8	3	2
DSP54	693	259	26	17	5
DSP56	54	54	14	1	0
DSP58	206	99	8	3	1
DSP59	215	84	15	3	7
MARY1	326	151	24	3	3
MARY2	15	13	6	3	2
Total Responses	9,272 +	4,800 +	2,803 +	1,385 +	495 = 18,755
	49%	26%	15%	7%	3%

FIGURE 13.12

Exception Occurrence Summary and Interval Counts Section of the Component Report

```
                                   Component Report                                        7/01/96  15:06:19
                      Exception Occurrence Summary and Interval Counts                          Page 0021
                                Performance Report Sample

Member  . . . : TU0602AM      Model/Serial  . . :  320-2050/10-XXXXX    Main storage . . :   32.0 M    Started  . . . . : 06/02/96 08:56:43
  Library . . : QPFRDATA      System name . . . :  PERF1                Version/Release  :   3/ 2.0    Stopped  . . . . : 06/02/96 15:55:55
```

Exception Counts

Exception Type	Description	Total
Size	Size	942
Binary Overflow	Binary overflow	0
Decimal Overflow	Decimal overflow	942
Flp Overflow	Floating point overflow	0
Decimal Data	Decimal data	0
Aut Lookup	Authority lookup	44
PAG Fault	Process Access Group fault	50,257
Seize Conflict	Seize conflict	2,310
Lock Conflict	Lock conflict	92
Verify	Verify	17,745
EAO Total	Effective Address Overflow total	31,742

Usually program issues

Security issue

Memory will reduce these

Program issues

Exceptions Per Second

Itv End	Size	Binary Overflow	Decimal Overflow	Flp Overflow	Decimal Data	Aut Lookup	PAG Fault	Seize Conflict	Lock Conflict	Verify	EAO Total
09:11	.0	.0	.0	.0	.0	.0	4.2	.1	.0	1.1	2.9
09:26	.0	.0	.0	.0	.0	.0	4.1	.1	.0	1.0	1.2
09:41	.0	.0	.0	.0	.0	.0	4.1	.1	.0	.9	2.5
09:56	.0	.0	.0	.0	.0	.0	2.5	.0	.0	.8	1.0
10:11	.0	.0	.0	.0	.0	.0	2.9	.5	.0	.9	1.4
10:26	.0	.0	.0	.0	.0	.0	3.2	.1	.0	.8	1.0
10:41	.0	.0	.0	.0	.0	.0	3.0	.1	.0	.7	1.2
10:56	.0	.0	.0	.0	.0	.0	2.0	.0	.0	.6	1.2
11:11	.0	.0	.0	.0	.0	.0	1.8	.1	.0	.8	1.1
11:26	.0	.0	.0	.0	.0	.0	1.3	.0	.0	.7	1.5
11:41	.0	.0	.0	.0	.0	.0	1.8	.0	.0	.5	1.2
11:56	.0	.0	.0	.0	.0	.0	3.0	.1	.0	.7	1.4
12:11	.0	.0	.0	.0	.0	.0	2.5	.0	.0	.4	1.1
12:26	.0	.0	.0	.0	.0	.0	.5	.0	.0	.3	.8
12:41	.0	.0	.0	.0	.0	.0	1.1	.0	.0	.6	.9
12:56	.0	.0	.0	.0	.0	.0	.7	.0	.0	.6	1.1
13:11	.0	.0	.0	.0	.0	.0	.6	.0	.0	.6	1.1
13:26	.0	.0	.0	.0	.0	.0	1.4	.0	.0	.8	1.4
13:41	.0	.0	.0	.0	.0	.0	1.3	.0	.0	.8	1.2
13:56	.0	.0	.0	.0	.0	.0	.6	.0	.0	.6	1.4

with each device listed in order beneath. The five buckets — response times of less than 1 second, response times of from 1 to 2 seconds, and so on — are listed to the right of the devices. The numbers in the columns represent the number of responses in a particular time interval.

The last page of this report shows the totals for all the workstation controllers on the system. This information is extremely useful when you're trying to find what percentage of your users are experiencing different response times. For example, in Figure 13.11b, we see that 9,272 responses occurred in the 0-001 bucket. By adding the total number of responses for each bucket and dividing by the number of responses in this particular bucket, we can see that 49 percent of the time the users experience subsecond response time.

Exception Occurrence Summary and Interval Counts

Figure 13.12 is the Exception Occurrence Summary and Interval Counts section of the Component Report. This section provides information about the exceptions that occurred on your system, grouped by interval and total occurrences. Having some exceptions is normal for every system. However, when your system goes beyond a normal number of exceptions, your system overhead increases to handle these exceptions.

Check for exception tables in the IBM Redbook *AS/400 Performance Management V3R1*. These tables show how much CPU each different type of exception error rate is using. The types of exception errors are explained below.

Size exceptions occur when the result field is too small to hold the result of an arithmetic operation. Size exceptions can cause higher CPU usage as well as possible user concern — are the applications properly programmed? Are the final values for dollar amounts or inventory correct? The most common reason for size exceptions, in 99.9 percent of the documented cases, is reformatting a date from MMDDYY to another format by multiplying the value by 10000.01 (or some minor variation on this scheme). The solution is to use MOVE instructions to correct the error.

Binary, **Decimal**, and **Flp** (floating point) overflow exceptions occur when the results of an arithmetic operation are out of the range of acceptable values. The sum of Binary and Decimal overflow exceptions equal the value in Size exceptions above.

Decimal Data exceptions occur when data values do not match the AS/400 specifications. They most often occur in applications migrated from a S/36. They may or may not be a problem. You can use the IBM Programmer's Tool Kit PRPQ to correct invalid data.

Aut Lookup (authority lookup) counts aren't really exceptions. They indicate additional processing that was performed during object access and are caused by using private authority on objects. Review your object authorizations for objects with private authority that isn't necessary.

PAG Faults also are not exceptions. They represent the number of page faults that occurred on the system and are related to the number of jobs and the memory resource available to these jobs.

Seize/Lock Conflict counts vary by application. The counts don't necessarily indicate a performance problem. If 50 conflicts last for 30 seconds each, you have a problem; or if 5,000 conflicts last for 2 milliseconds each, you don't have problem. To see whether there is a seize/lock contention problem, run the Performance Monitor with trace data collection and then use the transaction report (PRTTNSRPT) and lock report commands. These reports will help you identify the seize/lock conflicts that are longest in duration and will give you an indication of their frequency.

Verify exceptions occur when a pointer is not resolved (such as calling another program), a referenced object doesn't exist (as in a test for object existence), or when a domain violation occurs (executing a blocked MI instruction under other than level 40 security). If these exceptions are caused by using blocked MI instructions, your machine will have many VLOG entries of type 0B00 0007. You can find how to get additional information by using the OS/400 Security Journal. Consult IBM's *Security Reference Manual* (SC41-8083) for information on using this journal.

Extended Address Overflow (EAO) exceptions occur in LIC or LIC-generated code. They are the result of internal address arithmetic operations that overflow. The system automatically recovers from them. If the EAO CPU usage consistently exceeds 10 percent of your overall CPU percentage, check with IBM's Level 2 or your system maintainer for assistance.

Trace Data Required

The System and Component Reports cover most of the information you need to get started on performance analysis. However, you should also investigate other reports and methods, such as using trace data, that give you more detailed information.

In contrast to sample data, which provides information at the job level, trace data lets you analyze individual transactions. You can select trace data when you run the STRPFRMON command. Generally, you collect trace data when you need to figure out what is causing a performance problem.

The PRTTNSRPT (Print Transaction Report) command prints the main reports related to Performance Monitor trace data. The PRTTNSRPT command provides three types of reports: system and job summaries, job transaction report, and transition detail report.

System and Job Summaries

The System and Job summaries contain very useful information. Because trace data allows characterization of individual transactions, you can use this report to determine resource utilization per transaction, which lets you analyze application-level performance problems. The Job Summary section includes top-10 lists for the programs, jobs, and transactions with highest resource usage, such as

- CPU per transaction
- Disk I/O per transaction
- Response time per transaction
- Database reads/writes per transaction
- Non-database reads/writes per transaction

You can compare information from this report with Tables 43 and 45 in Appendix A of IBM's International Technical Support Center's document, *AS/400 Performance Management* (GG24-3723). This comparison can highlight application transactions that exceed resource guidelines in these tables.

The Job Summary section also includes transaction frequency information. This information gives you a good idea of the application areas that are costing the most in resources and therefore represent the best areas to work on for improved performance.

Job Transaction and Transition Detail Reports

You request the Transaction and Transition reports with the select/omit options on the PRTTNSRPT command. Be sure to narrow the request to a particular job and/or interval, because these reports can be very, very large.

The Job Transaction report lists each transaction that your end users enter. The report assigns a program name, derived from the trace data, to each transaction. The program that is named is the program issuing the workstation GET that causes the application to wait on the interactive user's next input from the display. Although this program may not be the one using all the resources attributed to the transaction, it is a good starting point. Someone familiar with the application can usually take this information and find out where the real problem is, either in the named program or in programs it calls.

The Transition Detail report expands the amount of detail for each transaction. This report shows information collected at each job-state transition that occurs during the transaction. Thus, whenever a job transitions between the active state and wait state, you get information about the programs and objects involved at the time of the transition. This information can provide valuable clues about the transaction and can help in determining what the end user was doing in the transaction.

Using trace data and the PRTTNSRPT report to analyze your applications goes beyond the scope of this book. A good example of how to use this command in analyzing applications is in the *AS/400 Performance Tools* document (SC41-8084), in the section "Using the PRTTNSRPT Command."

You should become familiar with ways to use trace data alone and in combination with other tools. Such knowledge will help you go into more detail when examining performance problems — from the job using the most resources to the programs using the most resources to the individual instructions that are the most costly. This very powerful set of tools lets you zero in on application performance problems.

Providing Feedback to Management

Earlier in the book we described the performance methodology. In Step 6, you provide feedback to management. For this purpose, information from the Component Interval Activity report (Figure 13.6) is excellent. I use this information and a PC graphics package (any package will do) to create the Detail Transaction Analysis chart in Figure 13.A. This chart is a great way to show graphically how many transactions you are processing during different times of the day.

FIGURE 13.A
Detail Transaction Analysis Chart

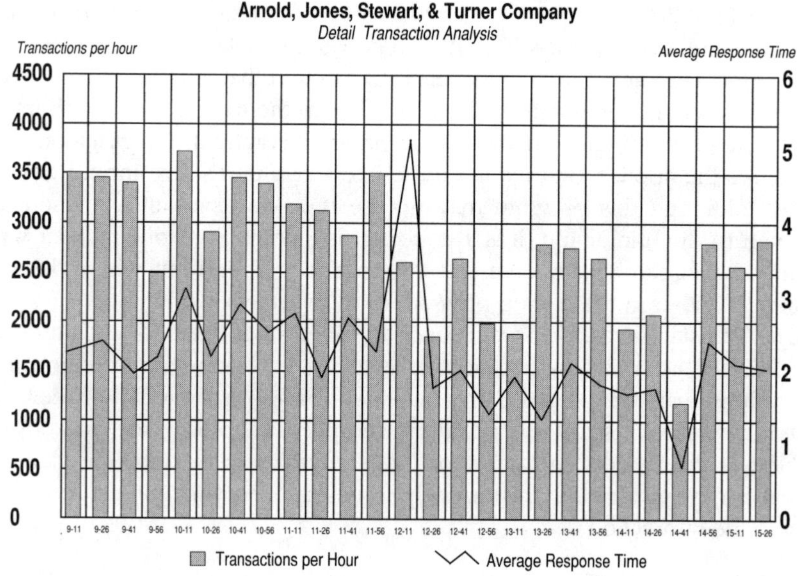

Providing Feedback to Management *continued*

To create my chart, I look at the TNS/Hour column in the Component Interval Activity report and use the transactions counts for each interval as one axis. I like to add a secondary axis for response time, using the response-time values from the Rsp/Tns column. This arrangement lets me contrast response time to the number of interactive transactions that are running for this sample.

A second chart that can provide information useful for managers is the CPU Utilization Analysis chart, shown in Figure 13.B, which uses the CPU Utilization information from the Component Interval Activity report. This chart uses a stacked bar to show the System, Interactive, and Batch CPU Utilization amounts for each interval. (I have to calculate the System CPU Utilization.) As in the previous chart, I have contrasted these numbers with response time. With this information, the chart can show patterns of the times particular types of work run and how each type affects response time. Remember, the way you present the performance information is important. Be creative with all of the great information the Performance Tools provide. ■

Alan Arnold

FIGURE 13.B
CPU Utilization Analysis Chart

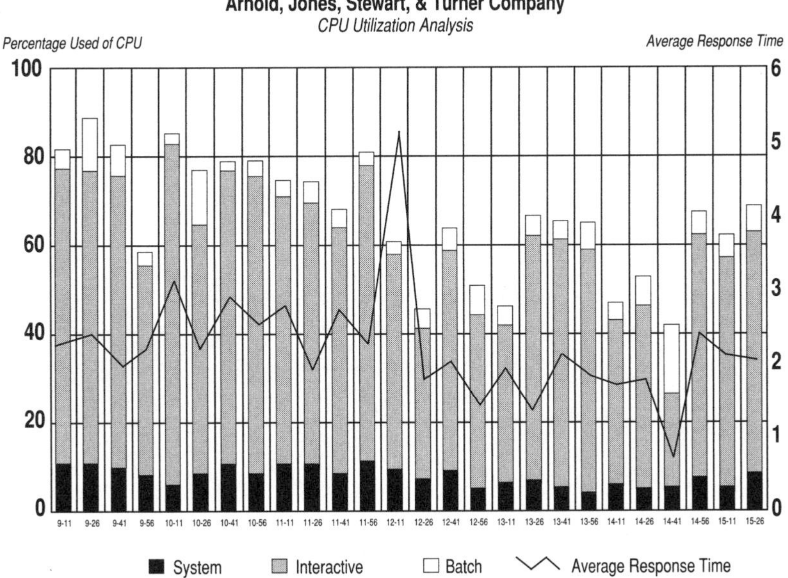

CHAPTER 14

Groups Three and Four: Performance Tools Utilities and Miscellaneous Functions

GROUP THREE: PERFORMANCE TOOLS UTILITIES

The Performance Tools Utilities let you analyze an individual application's performance. The other Performance Tools we have discussed look at the entire system. They can identify that a problem exists, and the PRTTNSRPT command can provide performance characteristics for individual transactions. The Performance Utilities take you to the next level, where you can find the specific application coding techniques that are causing the problem. In addition, using these tools on the transactions that you have identified as complex or very complex can tell you what is causing the transaction complexity.

Many application programmers do not realize that these utilities are a part of the Performance Tools. Nor do they know that the utilities are very powerful for analyzing why an application is performing poorly. But programmers also need to understand that the Performance Tools Utilities can be even more useful in avoiding problems if you integrate them into the development process for new applications. By using these tools, you can analyze alternatives in application coding techniques to find the best approach from a performance point of view.

We will consider these utilities as they appear on a basic CISC machine. If you work on a RISC machine, these same functions are available to you in a different format.

Using the Programmer Performance Utilities

You access these utilities by choosing Option 5 at the main Performance Tools menu. The Programmer Performance Utilities menu, which is in Figure 14.1, allows you to collect job traces and program instruction statistics, list file and key structures that programs use, and see information about a job's PAG. From this menu, you can also analyze disk activity at the object level.

Looking at Figure 14.1, you notice that the utilities are divided into four options: Work with job traces, Work with program run statistics, Select file and access group utilities, and Analyze disk activity. The following is a brief discussion of each option.

Figure 14.1
Programmer Performance Utilities Menu

```
                    Programmer Performance Utilities

Select one of the following:

     1. Work with job traces
     2. Work with program run statistics
     3. Select file and access group utilities
     4. Analyze disk activity









Selection or command
===>____________________________________________________________
F3=Exit   F4=Prompt   F9=Retrieve   F12=Cancel
```

Option 1: Work with Job Traces

This option lets you start and stop the collection of job trace information and create reports from the collected information. Do not confuse this job trace information with the trace data associated with the STRPFRMON command. This option traces an individual job, which you specify on the STRJOBTRC command.

Tracing a specific job lets you learn exactly what the job is doing at the program call level. You can use the trace job output to learn the following information:

- Number of application program calls
- Number of application program initializations
- Relative CPU time each program used
- Number of DB and NDB disk I/Os per program call
- Number of full and shared file opens/closes
- Number of subfile reads and writes
- Number of messages each program received

The utilities report this information for each transaction in the trace period. With this information, you can see what portion of the job is using the most resources. By comparing previous trace data with trace data obtained after you make changes, you can also measure the effect of program changes.

Option 2: Work with Program Run Statistics

This option lets you set up and run SAM, the Sampled Address Monitor. It performs analysis at the individual instruction level within the programs that you define to the SAM environment. SAM finds the hot spots in a program.

Usually, you use SAM after the PRTTNSRPT or the trace job tools. These tools find the programs that are using the most CPU. Then, SAM can locate the specific instructions that are being executed most frequently in the programs. As part of its reporting function, SAM produces a histogram showing the amount of time spent in individual high-level-language instruction execution in the program.

The SAM functions are a powerful way to find the instructions in a program that have the greatest potential for performance improvement. Knowing this, you can focus efforts to improve the program's performance on these instructions. You often can improve performance by changing the algorithms, redefining data types, changing array indexing, etc. For more information about SAM, see Chapter 4.

Option 3: Select File and Access Group Utilities

Option 3 provides information about an application's program-to-file use and relationships between the physical and logical files. For active jobs, you can obtain the following PAG information:

- All the files the job opened and how they are opened (I, O, IO)
- Logical I/O count for each file
- Whether SHARE(*NO) is specified on the files
- All the programs activated in the job
- Which programs the job is leaving active

This information is useful in separating the high-use files, which you need to pre-open when first entering the application, from low-use files, which you need to open only when the application needs them. This information can also signal a problem if you see frequently called programs that the job is not leaving active.

These utilities determine the following program and file relationships.

- Number of logical files dependent on each physical file
- Name of each dependent logical file
- Names of all files and record formats a given program uses

- Names of all programs that use a particular file
- Key fields and select/omit criteria each logical file uses

This information may suggest ways of combining logical files. By reducing the total number of logical files that must be maintained, you can improve the application (and overall system) performance.

Option 4: Analyze Disk Activity

You select Option 4, Analyze disk activity, when one or two disk units are consistently more than 50 percent busy and other disk units are less busy. This option lets you find out what objects are being accessed with a frequency that is causing the imbalance in disk utilization.

If you find that the high activity is primarily because of database file I/O, you may be able to balance the use and improve performance by offloading the files involved and reloading the files, which will redistribute them. The *Performance Tools/400 Guide* gives details on how to best reload such files.

Group Four: Miscellaneous Functions

The last group of commands available from the Performance Tools main menu is the group we call Miscellaneous Functions. This group has only one menu option, Option 6, Configure and manage tools. This option lets you display and change functional area definitions, delete file members containing previously collected performance data, copy performance data members, and change the format or update performance data files into the formats the current release requires.

When you select Option 6 from the Performance Tools menu, the Configure and Manage Tools menu appears, as in Figure 14.2. Let's examine each option on this menu.

Option 1: Work with Functional Areas

With Option 1, you can create, copy, and delete functional areas and change who and what is in the functional areas. Remember that functional areas define groups of performance characteristics that you can use to run the performance tools reports. For example, if you always want to run the system report for users JIM01 and RICK01, you set up a functional area to include these users.

If your company is going to run the performance reports regularly (which it should), you will want to look at your performance data from different perspectives. For example, if you suspect that the accounting applications are causing some kind of performance problem, you may want to create functional areas that group the accounting applications by programs or users. You could then use these functional areas each time you run the performance reports.

FIGURE 14.2
Configure and Manage Tools Menu

```
                        Configure and Manage Tools

Select one of the following:

       1. Work with functional areas
       2. Delete performance data
       3. Copy performance data
       4. Convert performance data









Selection or command
===> ________________________________________________________
F3=Exit   F4=Prompt          F9=Retrieve               F12=Cancel
```

Setting up functional groups is not difficult, but you will need some information such as program names and user names. This information-gathering is well worth the investment. Once a particular group is set up, you never have to change it; just select the function group name as you run the reports and you are all set.

Option 2: Delete Performance Data

Option 2 lets you delete file members that contain previously collected performance data. Each time you collect performance data, the system adds a new member to twelve performance files. This option goes to each of these files and deletes the member that you specify. You can do this process manually by going to each performance file and deleting the specified member, but it is easier to use this option.

Don't make the mistake of overlooking this process. If you are collecting performance data regularly (and you should), you are going to start using a lot of disk space storing performance samples. We recommend that you back up the samples weekly or monthly, and then delete the samples from your main storage with this option. Don't forget to back up the samples before you delete them — as we have mentioned before, historical data is often useful in solving performance problems.

Option 3: Copy Performance Data

Option 3 lets you copy selected members in the performance files. With this option, you can move only specific members of a file instead of the whole QPFRDATA file or another data library that contains your performance data. Although you may not use this option often, it is sometimes appropriate to set up procedures for your organization that allow you to copy performance members between systems, and this option makes that copying easier.

Option 4: Convert Performance Data (Head 2)

With Option 4, you can change the format of old performance samples to your system's current format. You usually select this option when you install a new release of your operating system and you have performance data that you want to use from the previous release. To use the previous data, you must run it through this option. Most users of the Performance Tools discover this option because they try to run the Performance Tools against a previous release's data sample, and an error message appears in the job log that tells them to run this option. You may also need to run this option to move performance data between systems if you're moving data to a system with a different version of the Performance Tools.

Glossary

Active-Ineligible (A-I) Transitions
The number of jobs that are moving from the active state to the ineligible state. Jobs exceed the time slice value and become ineligible when they use more CPU time than is defined in the job class. A high number of A-I transitions can indicate that the activity level in the storage pool or subsystem is too low.

Active State
One of three states — Active, Ineligible, and Wait — that a job can be in. A job in the active state has everything it needs to use the CPU.

Activity Level
A value you set that determines the number of jobs that are eligible to compete for the CPU in a storage pool.

Asynchronous Disk I/O
Disk I/O that is performed by a LIC task at the same time that the job is processing. Contrast with synchronous disk I/O.

Auxiliary Storage Pool (ASP)
A logical unit of disk storage. Disk units can be dedicated to a particular use by including them in an auxiliary storage pool.

Batch Job
A type of job that requires little or no interaction with the user. Several batch jobs can usually run concurrently in a subsystem.

Class description
An object that contains the run-time attributes of a job, such as time slice, priority, and purge.

CPU Seconds Per Disk I/O Operation (Batch)
The number of seconds of CPU each disk I/O uses during a batch job. This value should be consistent from day to day. If not, the program's processing may be highly data dependent, errors or exceptions may be occurring in the job, or disk I/O may be higher than usual.

CPU per Transaction, Average
The average number of seconds of CPU that each transaction uses. The interactive time slice should be two to three times this value. CPU per transaction values for individual transactions may vary considerably from the average.

CPU Utilization
The percent of CPU that a particular program uses. You can find this value using PRTTNSRPT and TPST and investigate it with SAM commands.

CPU Utilization, Cumulative
The percent of CPU all your applications are using. You can find this value with TPST. If this value is high, look in your applications to eliminate such practices as full open/close and lots of external calls.

Database (DB) Operations per Job or Transaction
The number of database operations required by each job or transaction. This value should be consistent from one transaction to another within one job. A large variation may indicate changing the environment from application to another. Each database operation lasts an average of 20 to 50 milliseconds. A large number of database operations per job or transaction can be a large contributor to high interactive response time.

Devices, Number of Active
The number of different jobs that entered transactions within a sample period.

Disk I/O (DIO) per Job or Task
The number of database and non-database reads and writes for each job or task.

Disk I/O (DIO) Per Second
The number of database and non-database reads and writes per second. The total number is limited to the number of devices on system. This value should stay at 40 percent of capacity or less (or the base disk service time divided into 1).

Disk Percent Busy
The percent of time that your disk is busy. Keep your disk busy less than 45 percent of the time to avoid queuing.

Disk Percent Space Utilized
The percent of your disk space that's utilized. As this value gets above 90 percent, system performance can degrade because the extents that store data are smaller and more read/write operations are required to get data.

Disk Performance Terms

As the disk resource becomes more complex than just a standard auxiliary hard drive, new disk performance terms are coming into use. Some of the new performance terms are listed below:

Cache, buffer: In this context, an amount of electronic memory (RAM) that holds data that would otherwise be on DASD. You can set up a cache, or buffer, to assist on reads or writes. RAM can process or access data much faster than DASD (nanoseconds versus milliseconds). A cache accelerates performance because the system can access the data more quickly.

Cache directories: A portion of cache allocated to keep track of what data is in cache (and by extension, on DASD), to make looking for data that may reside in RAM or on DASD more efficient.

Cache tuning algorithms: The process a disk subsystem uses to adjust the amount of data brought into a cache through a look-ahead buffer, depending on the pattern of I/Os.

Latency: The average time necessary for the appropriate file to spin under the head so the head can read the data once the actuator has moved the disk into position.

Look-ahead buffering (or caching): The process of pulling more data into a cache or buffer than is requested by a particular read from DASD, in the hope that the next request will be for contiguous data. Because of the AS/400's method of storing data across multiple DASD units, this practice has only intermittent success in helping improve performance.

LRU (Least-Recently Used) cache algorithm: Removes the data used least recently so that higher-priority data remains in cache, thereby optimizing the cache's efficiency.

LFU (Least-Frequently Used) cache algorithm: Prioritizes the data in cache by eliminating that data used least frequently.

Seek Time: The average time it takes for actuators to move the heads to the appropriate track on the drive to read the data.

Write Assist Device (WAD): An extra HDA in the 9337 1xx models that holds data that is a duplicate of data held in a write buffer, thereby releasing the system from waiting for the controller to complete a RAID 5 transaction. It also provides redundancy in case the write buffer fails or loses power before the write with penalty is complete.

Write penalty: The cost that results from using RAID 5 or checksum because a write includes four I/O operations instead of one: The subsystem must 1) read old data, 2) read old parity or check data, 3) write new data, and 4) write new parity for each write to DASD. A write cache or write assist device (WAD) usually masks the write penalty.

Distributed Data Management (DDM)
A way of accessing data. DDM files allow the user to access remote files as if they were on a local system.

Errors, Communications
Errors in the communications component. These errors can occasionally cause significant slowdowns; to find them, review the error log with STRSST (Start System Service Tools) and use a query to review device errors.

Errors, Disk
Errors in the disk component. Unrecoverable disk errors are logged in ERRLOG. Recoverable errors cannot be tracked; however, one indication of recoverable errors is that the system may quiesce (no DIO and no CPU) though disk IOP processing is high.

EXCS ACTM Per Transaction
A value calculated by PRTTNSRPT that estimates the CPU and DIO queuing effect. Excess Active Time is one of the response time components that make up the Exceptional Wait breakdown given in the Job Summary Report produced by the PRTTNSRPT command.

Exceptions, Program
When the result of an operation exceeds a set value — for example, size exceptions occur when the **Result** field in a database is too small to hold the result of an arithmetic operation. Exceptions may cause significant performance degradation. Find the suspected job in PRTCPTRPT Exception Counts or Trace and look for messages.

Fault
When data needed by the processor is not in main storage.

Faults Per Second
The number of times per second that a fault occurs. In general, you should keep the total of database and non-database faults per pool per second to fewer than 20. Larger systems can have more faults without affecting performance.

Faults per Transaction or Job
The number of database and non-database faults that a transaction or job incurs.

I/O per Unit Time, Batch
In a batch job, the number of I/O operations that occur per unit time. This value is a measure of batch throughput, especially if the I/O is in the form of database reads and writes. If batch jobs get a lot of non-database I/O, try putting each job in its own pool.

Ineligible Wait Time
Time a job or transaction spends waiting until it is eligible to access the CPU. The system runs best when the ineligible wait time per transaction is 5-10 percent of the response time, as long as throughput stays up.

Interactive Job
A job that requires constant interaction between the user and the computer.

IOP (Input/Output Processor)
Miniprocessors or feature cards that plug into your system's bus and bus expansion units; can be disk, local workstation, multifunction, or communication IOPs. You should monitor the percent of your IOPs that are utilized.

IOP (I/O Processor) Utilization, Communications
The percent of your communications IOP that's utilized. A high IOP utilization, which can lead to queuing and degraded communication performance, can be caused by temporary line errors or, in the case of token ring, other systems on the token ring.

IOP (I/O Processor) Utilization, Disk
The percent of your disk IOP that is utilized. High utilization can cause queuing and degraded performance.

Licensed Internal Code (LIC)
The machine-level microcode that drives the hardware.

Logical Disk I/O (LDIO)
The movement of data between the user program and the system's LIC buffer area. The number of LDIO operations is a measure of job progress and system-useful workload (as opposed to paging). If an application's blocking and file size remain constant from one run to the next, the LDIO will remain the same, too. Contrast with physical disk I/O.

Machine Pool
System storage pool 1. You should be sure to allocate enough memory to the machine pool. If you are using the QPFRADJ IPL tuning adjustment function and you add main storage, make sure you reset the pool sizes either from the IPL storage pool adjustment functions or from the guidelines in the AS/400 Work Management Guide.

Machine Interface (MI)

The point that determines whether the user or the system controls transactions. **Tasks** carried out by the system below the MI are beyond the user's control. **Jobs** at the operating system and applications levels can be controlled by users.

N-Way Architecture

Architecture that allows for multiple processors in an AS/400.

Non-Database Reads, Average per Transaction

The average number of times per transaction the system reads non-database information. You should strive to minimize this value, not necessarily reduce it to zero.

PAG (Process Access Group)

An internal job structure that keeps active job information, such as file buffers and program valuables. PAGs exist only while a job is active.

Page

The smallest amount of data transferred between disk and main storage. On the AS/400, the page size is 512 bytes.

Page Frame

A main storage area used to contain a page of data. Page frames are the same size as a page.

Physical Disk I/O

Data read by the system from or to the disk device. The system does physical disk I/O below the MI; one example is moving data between the disk and the LIC buffer area. Physical I/O will vary between runs of a job, depending on paging, activity in other jobs, or changes in how the system physically stores data on a disk. Contrast with Logical I/O.

Pool Database Faults Per Second

The rate at which pages are brought into a pool.

Priority

A numeric value from 1 to 99 that a user assigns to a job that indicates the job's relative importance to the system. Highest-priority jobs should be assigned a 1, and lowest-priority jobs should be assigned a 99.

Private Pool

A storage pool in which OS/400 allows only one subsystem to run.

Program DIO

Shown with PRTNSRPT and TPST. Investigate with PRTTNSRPT transition detail, trace job, code review.

Program DIO, Cumulative
Shown with TPST. Investigate with PRTTNSRPT transition detail, trace job, code review, etc.

Program Temporary Fix (PTF)
An interim fix, developed by IBM, for program bugs.

Purge Attribute
The class attribute that allows the system to determine whether to move a job's PAG data from main storage to disk after it completes the transaction.

Queuing
Placing something in line, where it waits to execute or receive service.

Response Per Transaction, Average
The average time it takes your system to respond to a transaction's request; shown with PRTTNSRPT and PRTCPTRPT. The value is an average; you should look for times when a value is extremely high or extremely low.

Sampled Address Monitor (SAM)
Part of Performance Tools on CISC machines; identifies which program instructions are using the most CPU. The same function is available in the Performance Explorer on RISC machines.

Seize / Lock
The protection of an object from use by others. Below the MI, the protection is called a **seize**. Above the MI, the protection is called a **lock**. You can find the number of seizes and locks with PRTTNSRPT and PRTLCKRPT.

Shared Pool
A storage pool in which OS/400 allows many subsystems to run.

Short Wait, Short Wait Extended
Activity levels. A job goes into a **short wait** when it's likely that the job can be completed in a short time. If a job exceeds the 2-second limit on short waits, the system moves the job to the wait state. This process is a **short wait extended**. You can find the number of jobs in these states using PRTTNSRPT; they're usually associated with remote I/O.

Sign-On/Off
The process used to gain or relinquish access to a system. Users signing on and signing off systems can use a lot of system resources, especially when many occur at the same time. Consider using DSCJOB as an alternative to SIGNOFF and assigning program passwords for workstation security. This approach is much less disruptive to system performance.

Subsystem
An operating environment through which OS/400 coordinates work flow and resource usage. Subsystems can be tailored to process different types of jobs efficiently.

Synchronous Disk I/O
When a job issuing an I/O request must wait for the operation to finish before it can continue processing. Contrast with asynchronous disk I/O.

Task Dispatching Queue (TDQ)
A queue into which the system places all jobs that need CPU time. The TDQ is maintained by job priority and the order of arrival on the queue.

Thrashing
A pool paging condition. A number of pages are stolen for use by another program, and the data in those pages is overwritten by the stealing program. Then, the first job needs the pages that were overwritten, so the system must rewrite that data.

Time Slice, Time Slice End
A class attribute set by the user that specifies the amount of time a job can use the processor before it must give it up to another job of equal priority in the queue. It must also give up its activity level if an ineligible job has a priority equal to or greater than this job. The TSE causes A-I and A-W job transitions. If your interactive jobs often reach TSE, you should consider performing the function in batch. Keep this interval short in interactive jobs to minimize wait time for other jobs.

Timing and Paging Statistics Tool (TPST)
A program RPQ for CISC machines (2799-EER) that identifies which programs are using a lot of CPU time. The same function is available on RISC machines in the Performance Explorer.

Wait-Active (W-A) Transitions
The number of jobs moving from the wait state to the active state. The jobs may have been waiting on external input, an object (for example, data area), or a database record lock.

Wait-Ineligible (W-I) Transitions
The number of jobs moving from the wait state to the ineligible state. If this value is always zero, the activity level is set too high, and all transactions immediately start competing for CPU and memory with work already in the system. This setup can cause severe performance problems. Strive to keep the number of W-I transitions at about 10-20 percent of A-W transitions. Let the old work finish first.

Appendix A

Documenting Your System

Because almost every aspect of your system affects performance, it is important to document your system completely. Thorough system documentation is a must for comparing your system's performance before and after changes. This list shows all the commands necessary to document your system and other steps you need to take to ensure that you have all the information you need.

1. WRKSYSVAL *ALL *PRINT. This command lists all system values on the system.
2. WRKHDWPRD. This command lists the rack configuration of your system's hardware.
3. PRTDEVADR. This command lists the addresses of all your system's devices.
4. DSPNETA *PRINT. This command prints all your system's network attribute parameters.
5. WRKSBSD *ALL. This command and its print screens capture all your subsystem description information.
6. WRKCLS *ALL. This command and its print screens capture all your class entries.
7. DSPLCLHDW *PRINT. This command prints your system's hardware listing.
8. DSPSFWRSC *PRINT. This command print the system software installed on your system.
9. DSPS36. This command and its print screens print your system's S/36 environment settings.
10. WRKRPYLE *PRINT. This command prints all your system's reply lists.
11. WRKEDTD. This command and its print screen prints all your system's edit descriptions.
12. WRKOBJ QSYS/*ALL *LIB. This command prints all libraries on the system.
13. Document any user objects that you are keeping in libraries such as QGPL, QUSRSYS, etc.
14. RTVCFGSRC. This command provides a source listing of your configuration objects.

15. SAVCFG. This command saves configuration objects.
16. Maintain a source listing of your system's startup program(s).
17. Maintain a list of all alterations your company has made to IBM objects, such as commands.
18. DSPFD *ALL QP* TYPE(*ALL) *PRINT FILEATR(*PRTF). This command lists all your system's print file changes.
19. List system and user profiles.
20. List folders and documents.
21. Print out the system service tools (SST) information about ASP sizes, disk configurations in each ASP, protection used in each ASP, threshold of each ASP, etc.
22. Determine PTF status, including the latest cumulative tape applied.
23. Run the Performance Monitor on a daily basis.
24. Run the System and Component reports on a daily basis.

Update all of this documentation on a regular, recurring basis, such as once a quarter. Don't do it once and forget about it. This information is useful only when it is up-to-date and accurate. Keep a copy of this information off site with your backup tapes. This information can also help you with availability planning as well as performance management.

APPENDIX B

The Timing and Paging Statistics Tool

If your machine is pushing the processor to the limit, or if you wonder what the performance difference would be between two ways of programming a function, TPST could be the right tool for the job. TPST is very useful for finding out the CPU time for a specific application function and for learning what portion of the CPU time you can attribute to each program in the function. Although PRPQs like TPST don't have official long-term support from IBM, TPST is a mainstay for gathering data and is likely to remain available. In V3R6, TPST became part of the Performance Explorer, which is loaded in the base OS/400.

The most obvious reason for monitoring CPU usage is to see how much CPU time a program is using so you can evaluate whether it's using too much. A less obvious, but perhaps more important, reason is not **how much** CPU time the program is using but **why** it's using that time.

TPST gathers information by simply intercepting each call to a program and the corresponding return. When a job calls a program you're testing, TPST initializes a number of collection values that track CPU time, the number of disk I/O operations, and other information until the program returns. TPST associates a set of collection values with each job that calls a program you want measured. TPST then gathers all these separate job-level measurement values for each measured program into a single, system-wide value it prints in its report. For example, if 10 jobs each call program XYZ 50 times, the TPST report will show that program XYZ was called 500 times in the time period. The report doesn't show program data by job, only by total program activity — something to keep in mind as you evaluate the report.

In addition to recording the time spent in the primary program, TPST records the CPU time used by programs called by the program you're monitoring. If program XYZ calls program ZZZ, TPST adds the CPU time used in ZZZ to the time used by program XYZ and records the result as Cumulative CPU Usage Time (CCPU) for program XYZ. The TPST report, then, shows two values: the CPU time spent in program XYZ and the CPU time spent in program XYZ plus all the programs XYZ called.

With TPST, you can monitor all programs in all libraries on the system, or you can monitor subsets. The ENTTPST (Enter TPST) command lets you enter generic names to select a category of program. For example, if all your accounts receivable program names start with "AR," you could monitor all accounts receivable programs in an application library by specifying APPLLIB/AR* or on all AR programs in every library by specifying *LIBL/AR*.

Using TPST is straightforward. First, you specify on the ENTTPST command the programs you want monitored. You start TPST using the STRTPST (Start TPST) command, which has no parameters. Depending on what you want to measure, you then run the program or programs or just let the system do whatever it's supposed to be doing. When the test is complete or the system has run long enough for you to see what kind of activity it's been performing, you stop TPST and specify where to save the data using the STPTPST (Stop TPST) command. You can then run one or both TPST report programs — LSTTPST (List TPST) and CMPTPST (Compare TPST) — against that data. Table B1 lists all TPST commands and their functions; for details about the command syntax, see the *TPST User's Guide*.

TABLE B1

TPST Commands

Command	Description
ENTTPST	Defines the measurement environment
STRTPST	Starts data collection
STPTPST	Stops data collection and saves measurement data
ENDTPST	Undefines the measurement environment
LSTTPST	Prints TPST reports
CMPTPST	Prints a report comparing measurement data from up to nine runs

RECOGNIZING RED FLAGS

The names of OS/400 programs begin with a Q. The second and third characters of the name usually make up the component code, which identifies the kind of function the program performs. For example, QDBxxxx is an OS/400 database module, QDMxxxx is part of common data management, QQQxxxx is query management, and QRGxxxx is the RPG support. QRGXxxx is runtime support, and QRGRxxx is part of the RPG/400 compiler.

When the TPST CPU data-by-program report shows a lot of calls to OS/400 programs, you should investigate. To determine whether the calls are causing a performance problem or whether you could improve performance by eliminating some calls or otherwise modifying your program, you need to ask yourself some questions: Is the runtime environment interactive or batch? Are lots of different functions being performed at each workstation? What is the menu and application call structure?

OS/400 database create and query programs are necessary parts of any data processing operation. However, used frequently, they use a lot of CPU and disk I/O resources, thereby reducing the resources available for other processing. There is often a better way to perform the processing that will reduce the use of creates and queries — and their resource usage.

Here is a list of OS/400 programs that, if seen often on a TPST report, might signal a performance problem:

QDBCRTFI	Create database file
QDBCRTME	Create database member
QDBDLTFI	Database delete file
QDBDLTME	Delete database member
QDBDUPFI	Duplicate file
QDBOPEN	Database open
QDDCLF	Create logical file command processing program (CPP) (must read entire physical file)
QDDCLFM	Create logical file member CPP (must read entire physical file)
QDDCPF	Create physical file CPP (QDDxxx commands usually require high disk I/O for a short time)
QDDCPFM	Create physical file member CPP
QDDDMBR	Delete member CPP
QDMCRODP	Create prototype open data path (part of the full database open)
QDMRCLSE	Reclaim close (CL Reclaim Resources or Cobol STOP processing)
QLBPDSD	Cobol symbolic dump
QLICRDUP	Create duplicate object CPP
QPRCRTPG	Create user program (should run in batch)
QPRxxx	Create user program modules (should run in batch)
QQQIMPLE	Query initialization (watch out for index creation)
QQQOPTIM	Query optimizer (use debug mode to find out what the optimizer is doing
QRGRTxxx	RPG/400 compiler (should run in batch)
QRGXDUMP	Dump RPG variables in symbolic form
QRGXERR	Set up object time error information
QRGXINIT	Initialize object program (rule of thumb: once per program log-on

APPENDIX C

Sample Query

The following query lists all of the transactions that consumed greater than or equal to 0.5 CPU seconds per transaction (transition from Tnx Start to Tnx End). The 0.5 CPU seconds is controlled by the "Select record tests" coded in the query.

The query provides a large set of candidate jobs that can be further analyzed using the methodology described in Chapter 4 in the discussion of reducing transaction complexity.

```
Query                                                    TRCQRY
    Library                                              TSTLIB
    Query text                                           Interactive
Tnx Pgms - Sorted CURPGM,PRVPGM,CPU/Tnx
    Query CCSID                              37
    Query language id
    Query country id

        *** . is the decimal separator character for this query ***
    Collating sequence . . . . . . . . . . Hexadecimal

    Processing options
      Use rounding                           Yes (default)
      Ignore decimal data errors             No (default)
      Ignore substitution warnings           Yes
      Use collating for all compares         No
```

Selected files

ID	File	Library	Member	Record Format
T01	QTRTSUM	QPFRDATA	Q953521559	TSUMREC

Result Fields

Name	Expression	Column Heading	Len	Dec
SYNCIO	tsdbrd + tsdbwrt + tsndbrd + tsndbwrt		6	0
ASYNCIO	tadbrd + tadbwrt + tandbrd + tandbwrt		6	0
TIME	(trnhour * 10000) + (trnmin * 100) + trnsec + (trnsecd * .001)		9	3
ENDTIME	(trnhour * 3600) + (trnmin * 60) + trnsec + (trnsecd * .001) + trsp		9	3
WNLTIME	tinelw + tinela	INLWT	7	3

Select record tests

AND/OR	Field	Test	Value (Field, Numbers, or 'Characters')
	TTYPE	EQ	'I'
AND	TCPU	GE	.5

Ordering of selected fields

Field Name	**Sort Priority**	**Ascending/ Descending**	**Break Level**	**Field Text**
TPVPGM	20	A	1	PREVIOUS PROGRAM NAME
TPGM	10	A	1	PROGRAM WHICH CAUSED TNS
TIME				
TSKJOB				JOB NAME
TSKUSR				USER NAME
TSKNUM				JOB NUMBER SYSTEM ASSIGNED
TTYPE				JOB TYPE AND SUBTYPE
TSPOOL				POOL NUMBER JOB RAN IN
TPRTY				JOB PRIORITY
TRSP				TNS RESPONSE TIME (SEC)
TCPU	30	D		TNS CPU TIME (SEC)
SYNCIO				
ASYNCIO				
TSZTM				TNS SEIZE WAIT TIME (SEC)
TLCKTM				TNS LOCK WAIT TIME (SEC)
TSWTM				SHORT WAIT TIME (SEC)
TSWXTM				TNS SHORT WAITX TIME (SEC)

Field Name	**Sort Priority**	**Ascending/ Descending**	**Break Level**	**Field Text**
TBMPL				BEG NUM ACTIVE IN MPL SLOTS
TIMPL				BEG NUM WAITING FOR MPL SLOT
TPGM1				FIRST PROGAM NAME IN STACK
TPGM2				SECOND PROGAM NAME IN STACK
TPGM3				THIRD PROGAM NAME IN STACK
TPGM4				FOURTH PROGAM NAME IN STACK
TDELTM				DELAY TIME (SEC)

Report column formatting and summary functions

Summary functions: 1-Total, 2-Average, 3-Minimum, 4-Maximum, 5-Count

						Overrides			
Field Name	Summary Functions	Column Spacing	Column Headings	Len	Dec Pos	Null Cap	Len	Dec Pos	Numeric Editing
TPVPGM		0	PGM @Tnx Start	10					
TPGM		2	PGM @Tnx End	10					
TIME		2	Tnx Start HH:MM:SS.mmm	9	3				Yes
TSKJOB		2	Job Name	10					
TSKUSR		1	User Name	10					
TSKNUM	5	1	Job Number	6					
TTYPE		0	TY	2					
TSPOOL		1	PL	2					
TPRTY		1	PTY	3	0				
TRSP	2	0	RSPsec	7	3				
TCPU	2	0	CPUsec	7	3				Yes
SYNCIO	2	1	SynDIO	6	0				Yes
ASYNCIO	2	0	AsyDIO	6	0				Yes
TSZTM	2	0	Szsec	7	3				Yes
TLCKTM	2	0	Lksec	7	3				Yes
TSWTM	2	0	Swsec	7	3				Yes
TSWXTM	2	0	SWXsec	7	3				Yes
TBMPL	2	0	B MPL	3	0				
TIMPL	2	0	I MPL	3	0				Yes
TPGM1		1	TPGM1	10					
TPGM2		1	TPGM2	10					
TPGM3		1	TPGM3	10					
TPGM4		1	TPGM4	10					
TDELTM	2	1	DLYsec	7	3				

Report breaks

Break Level	New Page	Suppress Summaries	Break Text
1	No	No	

Selected output attributes

Output type .... Printer
Form of output .... Detail
Line wrapping .... No

Printer Output

Printer device .... *PRINT
Report size
Length .... 66 (default)
Width 205
Report start line 6
Report end line 60
Report line spacing .... Single space
Print definition .... No

Printer Spooled Output

Spool the output .... (Defaults to value in print file, QPQUPRFIL)
Form type .... (Defaults to value in print file, QPQUPRFIL)
Copies 1
Hold .... (Defaults to value in print file, QPQUPRFIL)

Cover Page

Print cover page .... Yes
Cover page title

Page headings and footings

Print standard page heading . . Yes

Page heading
Selected Interactive Tnx - Sorted by CURPGM, PRVPGM, and CPU/Tnx

Page footing
***** END OF QUERY PRINT *****

Sample Output

The following is a portion of the output from the sample query provided in this appendix. The "PGM @ Tnx Start" entry specifies the transaction program the user was in when he or she pressed Enter (or selected a function key, roll key, etc.). The "PGM @ Tnx End" entry is the transaction program the user is in when the application does the next get to the workstation (QWSGET) screen.

FILE	LIBRARY	MEMBER	FORMAT
QTRTSUM	QPFRDATA	Q953521559	TSUMREC

09/02/96 08:54:15

Selected Interactive Tnx - Sorted by CURPGM, PRVPGM, and CPU/Tnx

PGM @Tnx Start	PGM @Tnx End	Tnx Start HH:MM:SS.mmm	Job Name	User Name	Job Number	TY	PL	PTY	RSPsec	CPUsec	SynDIO	AsyDIO	Szsec	Lksec . . .
MP080R	LX121R	16:48:24.262	ML1X2047	YNDGL01	889136	I	04	20	2.101	1.963	1			
		16:52:47.377	ML1X2047	YNDGL01	889136	I	04	20	2.048	1.896	2			
		16:25:11.976	ML1X2047	YNDGL01	889136	I	04	20	2.106	1.880	7			
		16:21:50.235	ML1X2047	YNDGL01	889136	I	04	20	2.042	1.871	5	1		
		16:49:53.640	ML1X2047	YNDGL01	889136	I	04	20	2.008	1.863				
		16:29:03.394	ML1X2047	YNDGL01	889136	I	04	20	1.944	1.831				
		16:31:32.366	ML1X2047	YNDGL01	889136	I	04	20	1.943	1.828				
		16:54:43.491	ML1X2047	YNDGL01	889136	I	04	20	1.936	1.818				
		16:07:04.806	ML1X2047	YNDGL01	889136	I	04	20	1.933	1.801	1	1		
		16:30:40.266	ML1X2047	YNDGL01	889136	I	04	20	1.877	1.758				
		16:29:49.145	ML1X2047	YNDGL01	889136	I	04	20	1.859	1.741				
		16:36:07.170	ML1X2047	YNDGL01	889136	I	04	20	1.779	1.662	1	3		
				AVG			1.965		1.826	1				
				COUNT 12										
DU900R	MP490R	17:23:20.767	DP647S2	CCMO	889051	I	04	20	2.164	1.763	25	19		
		16:51:29.198	FI220S2	DAVIDA	896153	I	04	20	1.235	.742	23	15		
		16:25:44.404	FI223S2	ALANC	890352	I	04	20	1.774	.673	40	13		
		17:45:16.903	FI217S2	SILKH01	889509	I	04	20	.850	.617	4	15		
		17:41:52.930	FI217S2	SILKH01	889509	I	04	20	.696	.561		15		
		18:12:32.361	FI217S2	SILKH01	889284	I	04	20	.817	.508	6	13		
				AVG					1.256	.811	16	15		
				COUNT 6										

SAMPLE TRANSACTION REPORT

Transaction Report

Member . . . :	Q953560849	Model/Serial . :	F97 /10XXXXX	Main storage . . :	1536.0 M	Started . . . . :	12 22 96 08:50:39
Library . . :	QPFRDATA	System name . . :	S101	Version/Release :	3/ 1.0	Stopped . . . . :	12 22 96 10:44:40
Job name . . :	SMPLJOB	User name . . . :	Turner	Job number . . . :	153109	TDE/PI/Pty/Prg . :	0842/08/20/YES

					Physical I/O Counts						***** Transaction Response Time (Sec/Tns)				
					Synchronous				Async		******	- Activity Level Time -			Inel
Time	Excp	Program Name	Type	CPU Sec Per Tns	DB Read	DB Wrt	NDB Read	NDB Wrt	Sum	Disk I/O	****	Active	Short Wait	Seize Cft	Time A-I/W-I
08.50.47		HMP049P		.005					0	0	.005	.005			
08.50.53		HMP049P		.006					0	0	.006	.005			
08.50.59	Y	MN00		.073			7	9	16	7	3.105	.318	2.076		.710
08.51.05		HMP049P		.121					0	0	6.107	.137	2.097		3.872
08.51.14		HMP049P		.007					0	0	.006	.005			
08.51.17		MN00		.069		3	9		12	6	3.581	.549	2.097		.935
08.51.25		MN00		.001					0	0	.002	.001			
08.51.40		MN00		.229			2		2	0	.284	.284			
08.51.46		MN00		.196					0	0	.205	.205			
08.51.48		MN00		.498			1		1	0	.539	.539			
08.51.51		HMP301R		.167					0	0	2.721	.179	2.100		.441
08.51.58	Y	HMP301R		.066	18		1		19	6	.400	.400			
08.55.33		MN01		.002					0	0	.002	.002			
08.55.33		HMP301R		.001					0	0	.001	.001			
08.55.34		HMP301R		.007					0	0	.006	.006			
08.55.44		MN00		.036			2		2	0	3.303	.065	3.238		
08.58.03		MN00		.239			2		2	0	.277	.277			
08.58.10		HMP549P		.125			2		2	0	4.337	.182	2.098		2.056
08.58.23		HMP549P		.006					0	0	.006	.004			
08.58.31		MN00		.023					0	0	5.911	.022	2.097		3.791

Sample Interactive Program Statistics Report

Job Summary Report
Interactive Program Statistics

1/05/97 10:04:18
Page 0085

Member . . . : Q953560849 Model/Serial . : F97/10-XXXXX Main storage . . : 1536.0 M Started . . . . : 12 22 96 08:50:39
Library . . : QPFRDATA System name . . : S101 Version/Release : 3/ 1.0 Stopped . . . . : 12 22 96 10:44:40

					Cum	—— Sync Disk I/O Rqs/Tns ——					Async		Short	Seize		Cum
	Number	Program	CPU	CPU	CPU	DB	DB	NDB	NDB	DIO	Rsp	Wait	Wait	Pct	Pct	
Rank	Tns	Name	/Tns	Util	Util	Read	Write	Read	Write	Sum	/Tns	/Tns	/Tns	/Tns	Tns	Tns
1	7092	MN00	.160	4.1	4.1	2	2	7	1	12	2	1.971	1.283	.003	9.6	9.6
2	6302	HMP330R	.091	2.1	6.2	8		3		11	1	.837	.302	.002	8.5	18.2
3	4515	HMP3001R	.092	1.5	7.7			9	2	12	11	1.284	.388	.001	6.1	24.3
4	3071	PIP235R	.055	.6	8.3	2		1	1	4	1	.289	.072	.043	4.2	28.4
5	2802	APSMSS	.125	1.2	9.6	5	2	7	4	17	4	2.482	1.114	.010	3.8	32.2
6	2752	PIP019R	.040	.4	10.0	3	1	1	1	7		.200	.038	.001	3.7	36.0
7	2372	MRP1RW	.052	.4	10.5	4		1		5	1	.453	.177	.001	3.2	39.2
8	2312	MRP30R	.122	1.0	11.5	5		3	1	8	3	.374	.058	.001	3.1	42.3
9	2085	PIP101R	.036	.2	11.8	2	1			3	1	.249	.028	.001	2.8	45.1
10	2054	PIP100R	.063	.4	12.2	3		1		4	2	.438	.149	.002	2.8	47.9
11	1987	RBH10R1	.093	.6	12.9	7	1	1		9	3	.546	.216	.001	2.7	50.6
12	1898	ISS003R	.042	.3	13.2	2		1		3		.314	.118	.001	2.6	53.2
13	1679	HMP543R	.023	.1	13.3	1	1	1	2	5	2	.237	.093	.001	2.3	55.5
14	1622	APS6RW	.091	.5	13.9	8	7	3	3	21	6	.340	.008	.002	2.2	57.7

APPENDIX D

AS/400 RAMP-C Charts

The following charts are helpful when doing your performance analysis work. The relative system performance ratios are estimated based upon the AS/400 environment RAMP-C workload with a 9404 Model B10 with 8MB of main storage and 945MB of DASD equaling 1.0. The ratios were estimated at maximum configurations running at 70 percent utilization.

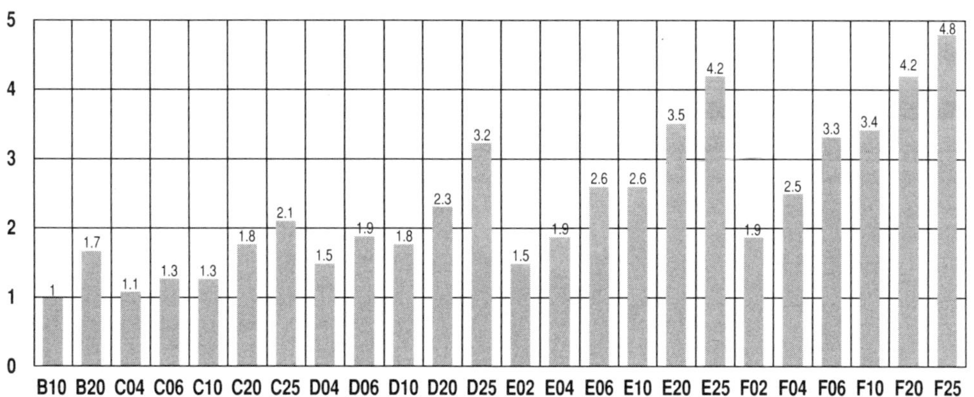

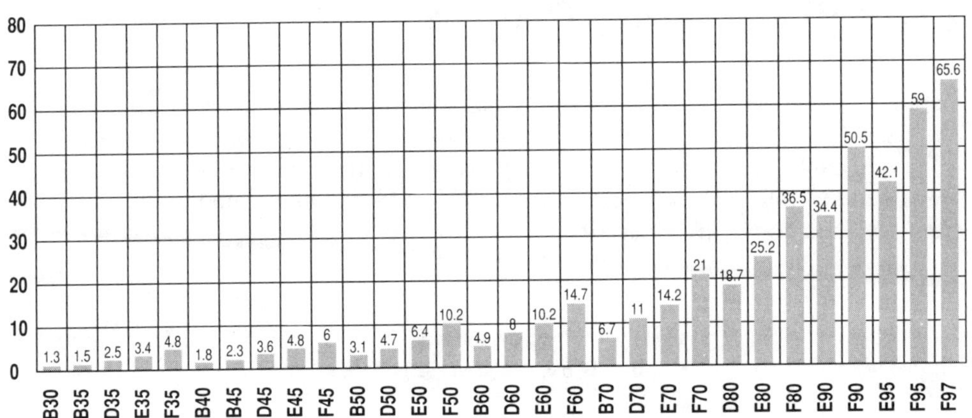
AS/400 RAMP-C
B, C, D, E & F 9206 Models
80
70
60
50
40
30
20
10
0
1.3
1.5
2.5
3.4
4.8
1.8
2.3
3.6
4.8
6
3.1
4.7
6.4
10.2
4.9
8
10.2
14.7
6.7
11
14.2
21
18.7
25.2
36.5
34.4
50.5
42.1
59
65.6
B30
B35
D35
E35
F35
B40
B45
D45
E45
F45
B50
D50
E50
F50
B60
D60
E60
F60
B70
D70
E70
F70
D80
E80
F80
E90
F90
E95
F95
F97

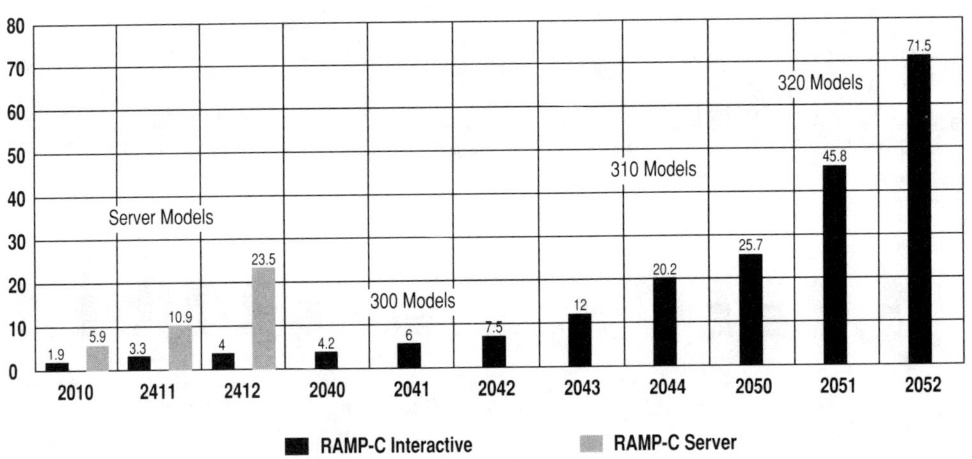
AS/400 RAMP-C
The Advanced Series Models
80
70
60
50
40
30
20
10
0
Server Models
300 Models
310 Models
320 Models
1.9
5.9
3.3
10.9
4
23.5
4.2
6
7.5
12
20.2
25.7
45.8
71.5
2010
2411
2412
2040
2041
2042
2043
2044
2050
2051
2052
RAMP-C Interactive
RAMP-C Server

AS/400 RAMP-C
Server Series

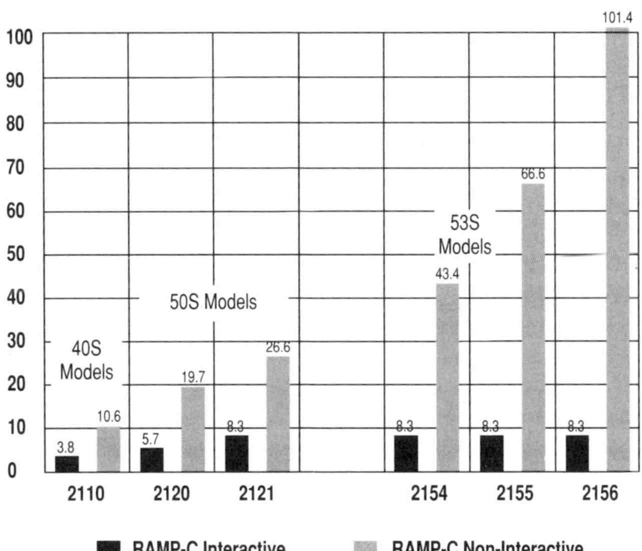

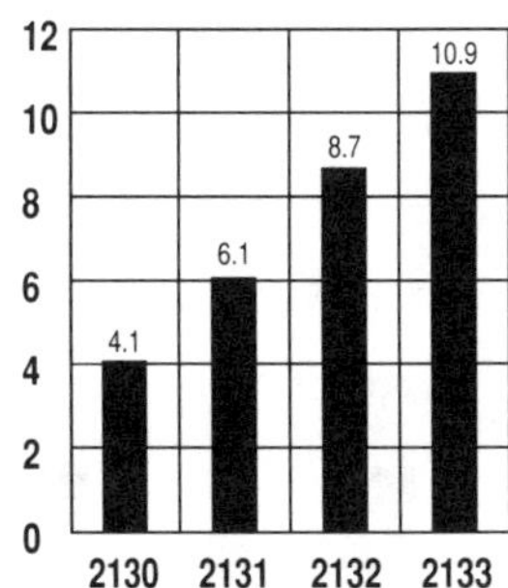

AS/400 RAMP-C
5XXSeries

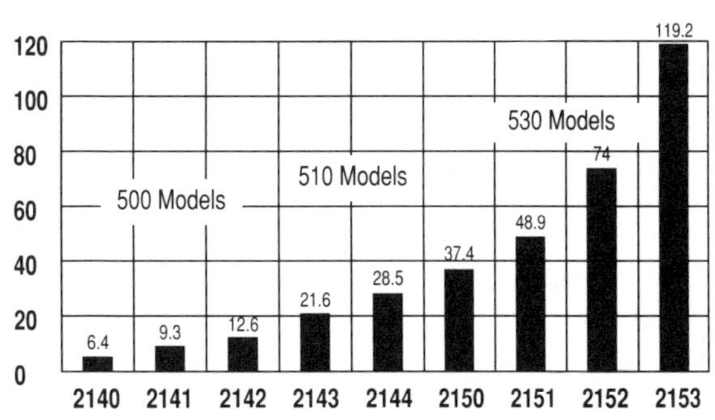

APPENDIX E

Third-Party Performance Tools

Several products on the market or near commercial release will monitor your system and report performance problems in real time. Some of the general features of this type of product include a graphical interface, the ability to monitor jobs or tasks or both, and the ability to monitor system activities.

Many performance monitors are available for the AS/400 from third-party vendors. Using vendor information, we have indicated in the chart below those products that support real-time (dynamic) performance monitoring and a distributed systems environment.

Product Name	Vendor	Vendor Phone	Dynamic Graphical Interface	Multiple Systems Monitor
NetPerfector	Open Universal Software	(514) 344-6040	Yes	Yes
Q System Monitor	CCSS (Europe), Ltd.	(44) 634-281432	Yes	Yes
Dynamic	Baber Information Services	(214) 650-0506	Yes	Yes
The Performance Analyser	Macro 4 plc	(44) 293-886060	No	No
Visual Control	Bytware	(800) 932-5553	Yes	No
Visual Performance Monitor	Midrange Technology Consultancy	(31) 10-4131746	Yes	No
Snapshot/400	Prolific	(800) 875-3380	Yes	No
MasterView Performance Monitor	Software Architects International	(508) 420-5079	Yes	Yes
ISM/CP for OS/400	The Information System Manager, Inc.	(800) 966-6771	No	Yes
SystemScan	Tomisar Systems	(513) 771-3353	No	Yes

Index

O

P

Q

R

S

Also Published by *NEWS/400* and Duke Press

THE A TO Z OF EDI

By Nahid M. Jilovec

Electronic Data Interchange (EDI) can help reduce administrative costs, accelerate information processing, ensure data accuracy, and streamline business procedures. Here's a comprehensive guide to EDI to help in planning, startup, and implementation. The author reveals all the benefits, challenges, standards, and implementation secrets gained through extensive experience. She shows how to evaluate your business procedures, select special hardware and software, establish communications requirements and standards, address audit issues, and employ the legal support necessary for EDI activities. 263 pages.

APPLICATION DEVELOPER'S HANDBOOK FOR THE AS/400

Edited by Mike Otey, a **NEWS/400** *technical editor*

Explains how to effectively use the AS/400 to build reliable, flexible, and efficient business applications. Contains RPG/400 and CL coding examples and tips, and provides both step-by-step instructions and handy reference material. Includes diskette. 768 pages, 48 chapters.

AS/400 DISK SAVING TIPS & TECHNIQUES

By James R. Plunkett

Want specific help for cleaning up and maintaining your disk? Here are more than 50 tips, plus design techniques for minimizing your disk usage. Each tip is completely explained with the "symptom," the problem, and the technique or code you need to correct it. 72 pages.

AS/400 SUBFILES IN RPG

On the AS/400, subfiles are powerful and easy to use, and with this book you can start working with subfiles in just a few hours — no need to wade through page after page of technical jargon. You'll start with the concept behind subfiles, then discover how easy they are to program. The book contains all of the DDS subfile keywords announced in V2R3 of OS/400. Five complete RPG subfile programs are included, and the book comes complete with a 3.5" PC diskette containing all those programs plus DDS. The book is an updated version of the popular *Programming Subfiles in RPG/400.* 200 pages, 4 chapters.

C FOR RPG PROGRAMMERS

By Jennifer Hamilton, a **NEWS/400** *author*

Written from the perspective of an RPG programmer, this book includes side-by-side coding examples written in both C and RPG, clear identification of unique C constructs, and a comparison of RPG op-codes to equivalent C concepts. Includes many tips and examples covering the use of C/400. 292 pages, 23 chapters.

CL BY EXAMPLE

By Virgil Green

CL by Example gives programmers and operators more than 850 pages of practical information you can use in your day-to-day job. It's full of application examples, tips, and techniques, along with a sprinkling of humor. The examples will speed you through the learning curve to help you become a more proficient, more productive CL programmer. 864 pages, 12 chapters.

CLIENT ACCESS TOKEN-RING CONNECTIVITY

By Chris Patterson

Attaching PCs to AS/400s via a Token-Ring can become a complicated subject — when things go wrong, an understanding of PCs, the Token-Ring, and OS/400 is often required. *Client Access Token-Ring Connectivity* details all that is required in these areas to successfully maintain and trouble-shoot a Token-Ring network. The first half of the book introduces the Token-Ring and describes the Client Access communications architecture, the Token-Ring connection from both the PC side and the AS/400 side, and the Client Access applications. The second half provides a useful guide to Token-Ring management, strategies for Token-Ring error identification and recovery, and tactics for resolving Client Access error messages. 125 pages, 10 chapters.

COMMON-SENSE C

Advice and warnings for C and C++ programmers

By Paul Conte, a **NEWS/400** *technical editor*

C programming language has its risks; this book shows how C programmers get themselves into trouble, includes tips to help you avoid C's pitfalls, and suggests how to manage C and C++ application development. 100 pages, 9 chapters.

CONTROL LANGUAGE PROGRAMMING FOR THE AS/400

By Bryan Meyers and Dan Riehl, **NEWS/400** *technical editors*

This comprehensive CL programming textbook offers students up-to-the-minute knowledge of the skills they will need in today's MIS environment. Progresses methodically from CL basics to more complex processes and concepts, guiding readers toward a professional grasp of CL programming techniques and style. 512 pages, 25 chapters.

DDS BY EXAMPLE

By R S Tipton

DDS by Example provides detailed coverage of the creation of physical files, field reference files, logical files, display files, and printer files. It includes more than 300 real-life examples, including examples of physical files, simple logical files, multi-format logical files, dynamic selection options, coding subfiles, handling overrides, creating online help, creating reports, and coding windows. 360 pages, 4 chapters.

DDS PROGRAMMING FOR DISPLAY & PRINTER FILES

By James Coolbaugh

Offers a thorough, straightforward explanation of how to use Data Description Specifications (DDS) to program display files and printer files. Covers basic to complex tasks using DDS functions. The author uses DDS programming examples for CL and RPG extensively throughout the book, and you can put these examples to use immediately. Focuses on topics such as general screen presentations, the A specification, defining data on the screen, record-format and field definitions, defining data fields, using indicators, data and text attributes, cursor and keyboard control, editing data, validity checking, response keywords, and function keys. A complimentary diskette includes all the source code presented in the book. 446 pages, 13 chapters.

DATABASE DESIGN AND PROGRAMMING FOR DB2/400

By Paul Conte

This textbook is the comprehensive guide for creating flexible and efficient application databases in DB2/400. The author shows you everything you need to know about physical and logical file DDS, SQL/400, and RPG IV and COBOL/400 database programming. Clear explanations illustrated by a wealth of examples, including complete RPG IV and COBOL/400 programs, demonstrate efficient database programming and error handling with both DDS and SQL/400. Each programming chapter includes a specific list of "Coding Suggestions" that will help you write faster and more maintainable code. In addition, the author provides an extensive section on practical database design for DB2/400. This is the most complete guide to DB2/400 design and programming available anywhere. Approx. 772 pages, 19 chapters.

DESKTOP GUIDE TO THE S/36

By Mel Beckman, Gary Kratzer, and Roger Pence, **NEWS/400** *technical editors*

This definitive S/36 survival manual includes practical techniques to supercharge your S/36, including ready-to-use information for maximum system performance tuning, effective application development, and smart Disk Data Management. Includes a review of two popular Unix-based S/36 work-alike migration alternatives. Diskette contains ready-to-run utilities to help you save machine time and implement power programming techniques such as External Program Calls. 387 pages, 21 chapters.

THE ESSENTIAL GUIDE TO CLIENT ACCESS FOR DOS EXTENDED

By John Enck, Robert E. Anderson, and Michael Otey

The Essential Guide to Client Access for DOS Extended contains key insights and need-to-know technical information about Client Access for DOS Extended, IBM's strategic AS/400 product for DOS and Windows client/server connectivity. This book provides background information about the history and architecture of Client Access for DOS Extended; fundamental information about how to install and configure Client Access; and advanced information about integrating Client Access with other types of networks, managing how Client Access for DOS Extended operates under Windows, and developing client/server applications with Client Access. Written by industry experts based on their personal and professional experiences with Client Access, this book can help you avoid time-consuming pitfalls that litter the path of AS/400 client/server computing. 430 pages, 12 chapters.

ILE: A FIRST LOOK

By George Farr and Shailan Topiwala

This book begins by showing the differences between ILE and its predecessors, then goes on to explain the essentials of an ILE program — using concepts such as modules, binding, service programs, and binding directories. You'll discover how ILE program activation works and how ILE works with its predecessor environments. The book covers the new APIs and new debugging facilities and explains the benefits of ILE's new exception-handling model. You also get answers to the most commonly asked questions about ILE. 183 pages, 9 chapters.

IMPLEMENTING AS/400 SECURITY, SECOND EDITION

A practical guide to implementing, evaluating, and auditing your AS/400 security strategy

By Wayne Madden, a **NEWS/400** *technical editor*

Concise and practical, this second edition brings together in one place the fundamental AS/400 security tools and experience-based recommendations that you need and also includes specifics on the latest security enhancements available in OS/400 V3R1. Completely updated from the first edition, this is the only source for the latest information about how to protect your system against attack from its increasing exposure to hackers. 389 pages, 16 chapters.

INSIDE THE AS/400

An in-depth look at the AS/400's design, architecture, and history

By Frank G. Soltis

The inside story every AS/400 developer has been waiting for, told by Dr. Frank G. Soltis, IBM's AS/400 chief architect. Never before has IBM provided an in-depth look at the AS/400's design, architecture, and history. This authoritative book does just that — and also looks at some of the people behind the scenes who created this revolutionary system for you. Whether you are an executive looking for a high-level overview or a "bit-twiddling techie" who wants all the details, *Inside the AS/400* demystifies this system, shedding light on how it came to be, how it can do the things it does, and what its future may hold — especially in light of its new PowerPC RISC processors. 475 pages, 12 chapters.

INTRODUCTION TO AS/400 SYSTEM OPERATIONS

by Patrice Gapen and Heidi Rothenbuehler

Here's the textbook that covers what you need to know to become a successful AS/400 system operator. System operators typically help users resolve problems, manage printed reports, and perform regularly scheduled procedures. *Introduction to AS/400 System Operations* introduces a broad range of topics, including system architecture; DB2/400 and Query; user interface and Operational Assistant; managing jobs and printed reports; backup and restore; system configuration and networks; performance; security; and Client Access (PC Support).

The information presented here covers typical daily, weekly, and monthly AS/400 operations using V3R1M0 of the OS/400 operating system. You can benefit from this book even if you have only a very basic knowledge of the AS/400. If you know how to sign on to the AS/400, and how to use the function keys, you're ready for the material in this book. 234 pages, 10 chapters.

AN INTRODUCTION TO COMMUNICATIONS FOR THE AS/400, SECOND EDITION

By John Enck and Ruggero Adinolfi

This second edition has been revised to address the sweeping communications changes introduced with V3R1 of OS/400. As a result, this book now covers the broad range of AS/400 communications technology topics, ranging from Ethernet to X.25, and from APPN to AnyNet. The book presents an introduction to data communications and then covers communications fundamentals, types of networks, OSI, SNA, APPN, networking roles, the AS/400 as host and server, TCP/IP, and the AS/400-DEC connection. 210 pages, 13 chapters.

JIM SLOAN'S CL TIPS & TECHNIQUES

By Jim Sloan, developer of QUSRTOOL's TAA Tools

Written for those who understand CL, this book draws from Jim Sloan's knowledge and experience as a developer for the S/38 and the AS/400, and his creation of QUSRTOOL's TAA tools, to give you tips that can help you write better CL programs and become more productive. Includes more than 200 field-tested techniques, plus exercises to help you understand and apply many of the techniques presented. 564 pages, 30 chapters.

MASTERING THE AS/400

A practical, hands-on guide

By Jerry Fottral

This introductory textbook to AS/400 concepts and facilities has a utilitarian approach that stresses student participation. A natural prerequisite to programming and database management courses, it emphasizes mastery of system/user interface, member-object-library relationship, utilization of CL commands, and basic database and program development utilities. Also includes labs focusing on essential topics such as printer spooling; library lists; creating and maintaining physical files; using logical files; using CL and DDS; working in the PDM environment; and using SEU, DFU, Query and SDA. 484 pages, 12 chapters.

OBJECT-ORIENTED PROGRAMMING FOR AS/400 PROGRAMMERS

By Jennifer Hamilton, a **NEWS/400** *author*

Explains basic OOP concepts such as classes and inheritance in simple, easy-to-understand terminology. The OS/400 object-oriented architecture serves as the basis for the discussion throughout, and concepts presented are reinforced through an introduction to the C++ object-oriented programming language, using examples based on the OS/400 object model. 114 pages, 14 chapters.

PERFORMANCE PROGRAMMING — MAKING RPG SIZZLE

By Mike Dawson, CDP

Mike Dawson spent more than two years preparing this book — evaluating programming options, comparing techniques, and establishing benchmarks on thousands of programs. "Using the techniques in this book," he says, "I have made program after program run 30%, 40%, even 50% faster." To help you do the same, Mike gives you code and benchmark results for initializing and clearing arrays, performing string manipulation, using validation arrays with look-up techniques, using arrays in arithmetic routines, and a lot more. 257 pages, 8 chapters.

POWER TOOLS FOR THE AS/400, VOLUMES I AND II

Edited by Frederick L. Dick and Dan Riehl

NEWS 3X/400's Power Tools for the AS/400 is a two-volume reference series for people who work with the AS/400. *Volume I* (originally titled *AS/400 Power Tools*) is a collection of the best tools, tips, and techniques published in *NEWS/34-38* (pre-August 1988) and *NEWS 3X/400* (August 1988 through October 1991) that are applicable to the AS/400. *Volume II* extends this original collection by including material that appeared through 1994. Each book includes a diskette that provides load-and-go code for easy-to-use solutions to many everyday problems. *Volume I*: 709 pages, 24 chapters; *Volume II*: 702 pages, 14 chapters.

PROGRAMMING IN RPG IV

By Judy Yaeger, Ph.D., a **NEWS/400** *technical editor*

This textbook provides a strong foundation in the essentials of business programming, featuring the newest version of the RPG language: RPG IV. Focusing on real-world problems and down-to-earth solutions using the latest techniques and features of RPG, this book provides everything you need to know to write a well-designed RPG IV program. Each chapter includes informative, easy-to-read explanations and examples as well as a section of thought-provoking questions, exercises, and programming assignments. Four appendices and a handy, comprehensive glossary support the topics presented throughout the book. An instructor's kit is available. 450 pages, 13 chapters.

PROGRAMMING IN RPG/400, SECOND EDITION

By Judy Yaeger, Ph.D., a **NEWS/400** *technical editor*

This second edition refines and extends the comprehensive instructional material contained in the original textbook and features a new section that introduces externally described printer files, a new chapter that highlights the fundamentals of RPG IV, and a new appendix that correlates the key concepts from each chapter with their RPG IV counterparts. Includes everything you need to learn how to write a well-designed RPG program, from the most basic to the more complex, and each chapter includes a section of questions, exercises, and programming assignments that reinforce the knowledge you have gained from the chapter and strengthen the groundwork for succeeding chapters. An instructor's kit is available. 440 pages, 14 chapters.

PROGRAMMING SUBFILES IN COBOL/400

By Jerry Goldson

Learn how to program subfiles in COBOL/400 in a matter of hours! This powerful and flexible programming technique no longer needs to elude you. You can begin programming with subfiles the same day you get the book. You don't have to wade through page after page, chapter after chapter of rules and parameters and keywords. Instead, you get solid, helpful information and working examples that you can apply to your application programs right away. 204 pages, 5 chapters.

THE QUINTESSENTIAL GUIDE TO PC SUPPORT

By John Enck, Robert E. Anderson, Michael Otey, and Michael Ryan

This comprehensive book about IBM's AS/400 PC Support connectivity product defines the architecture of PC Support and its role in midrange networks, describes PC Support's installation and configuration procedures, and shows you how you can configure and use PC Support to solve real-life problems. 345 pages, 11 chapters.

RPG ERROR HANDLING TECHNIQUE

Bulletproofing Your Applications

By Russell Popeil

RPG Error Handling Technique teaches you the skills you need to use the powerful tools provided by OS/400 and RPG to handle almost any error from within your programs. The book explains the INFSR, INFDS, PSSR, and SDS in programming terms, with examples that show you how all these tools work together and which tools are most appropriate for which kind of error or exception situation. It continues by presenting a robust suite of error/exception handling techniques within RPG programs. Each technique is explained in an application setting, using both RPG III and RPG IV code. 164 pages, 5 chapters.

RPG IV BY EXAMPLE

By George Farr and Shailan Topiwala

RPG IV by Example addresses the needs and concerns of RPG programmers at any level of experience. The focus is on RPG IV in a practical context that lets AS/400 professionals quickly grasp what's new without dwelling on the old. Beginning with an overview of RPG IV specifications, the authors prepare the way for examining all the features of the new version of the language. The chapters that follow explore RPG IV further with practical, easy-to-use applications. 500 pages, 15 chapters.

RPG IV JUMP START

Moving ahead with the new RPG

By Bryan Meyers, a **NEWS/400** *technical editor*

Introducing the "new" RPG, in which the columnar syntax has been challenged (all the specifications have changed, some vestigial specifications from an earlier era have been eliminated, and new specifications and data types have been added), this book shows you RPG IV from the perspective of a programmer who already knows the old RPG. Points out the differences between the two and demonstrates how to take advantage of the new syntax and function. 193 pages, 12 chapters.

RPG/400 INTERACTIVE TEMPLATE TECHNIQUE

By Carson Soule, CDP, CCP, CSP

Here's an updated version of Carson Soule's *Interactive RPG/400 Programming*. The book shows you time-saving, program-sharpening concepts behind the template approach, and includes all the code you need to build one perfect program after another. These templates include code for cursor-sensitive prompting in DDS, for handling messages in resident RPG programs, for using the CLEAR opcode to eliminate hard-coded field initialization, and much more. There's even a new select template with a pop-up window. 258 pages, 10 chapters.

S/36 POWER TOOLS

Edited by Chuck Lundgren, a **NEWS/400** *technical editor*

Winner of an STC Award of Achievement in 1992, this book contains five years' worth of articles, tips, and programs published in *NEWS 3X/400* from 1986 to October 1990, including more than 290 programs and procedures. Extensively cross-referenced for fast and easy problem solving, and complete with diskette containing all the programming code. 737 pages, 20 chapters.

STARTER KIT FOR THE AS/400, SECOND EDITION

An indispensable guide for novice to intermediate AS/400 programmers and system operators

By Wayne Madden, a **NEWS/400** *technical editor*

with contributions by Bryan Meyers, Andrew Smith, and Peter Rowley

This second edition contains updates of the material in the first edition and incorporates new material to enhance its value as a resource to help you learn important basic concepts and nuances of the AS/400 system. New material focuses on installing a new release, working with PTFs, AS/400 message handling, working with and securing printed output, using operational assistant to manage disk space, job scheduling, save and restore basics, and more basic CL programming concepts. Optional diskette available. 429 pages, 33 chapters.

SUBFILE TECHNIQUE FOR RPG/400 PROGRAMMERS

By Jonathan Yergin, CDP, and Wayne Madden

Here's the code you need for a complete library of shell subfile programs: RPG/400 code, DDS, CL, and sample data files. There's even an example for programming windows. You even get some "whiz bang" techniques that add punch to your applications. This book explains the code in simple, straightforward style and tells you when each technique should be used for best results. 326 pages, 11 chapters, 3.5" PC diskette included.

TECHNICAL REFERENCE SERIES

Edited by Bryan Meyers, a **NEWS/400** *technical editor*

Written by experts — such as John Enck, Bryan Meyers, Julian Monypenny, Roger Pence, Dan Riehl — these unique desktop guides put the latest AS/400 applications and techniques at your fingertips. These "just-do-it" books (featuring wire-o binding to open flat at every page) are priced so you can keep your personal set handy. Optional online Windows help diskette available for each book.

Desktop Guide to CL Programming

By Bryan Meyers, a **NEWS/400** *technical editor*

This first book of the **NEWS/400** *Technical Reference Series* is packed with easy-to-find notes, short explanations, practical tips, answers to most of your everyday questions about CL, and CL code segments you can use in your own CL programming. Complete "short reference" lists every command and explains the most-often-used ones, along with names of the files they use and the MONMSG messages to use with them. 205 pages, 36 chapters.

Desktop Guide to AS/400 Programmers' Tools

By Dan Riehl, a **NEWS/400** *technical editor*

This second book of the **NEWS/400** *Technical Reference Series* gives you the "how-to" behind all the tools included in *Application Development ToolSet/400* (ADTS/400), IBM's Licensed Program Product for Version 3 of OS/400; includes Source Entry Utility (SEU), Programming Development Manager (PDM), Screen Design Aid (SDA), Report Layout Utility (RLU), File Compare/Merge Utility (FCMU), and Interactive Source Debugger. Highlights topics and functions specific to Version 3 of OS/400. 266 pages, 30 chapters.

Desktop Guide to DDS

By James Coolbaugh

This third book of the **NEWS/400** *Technical Reference Series* provides a complete reference to all DDS keywords for physical, logical, display, printer, and ICF files. Each keyword is briefly explained, with syntax rules and examples showing how to code the keyword. All basic and pertinent information is provided for quick and easy access. While this guide explains every parameter for a keyword, it doesn't explain every possible exception that might exist. Rather, the guide includes the basics about what each keyword is designed to accomplish. The *Desktop Guide to DDS* is designed to give quick, "at your fingertips" information about every keyword — with this in hand, you won't need to refer to IBM's bulky *DDS Reference* manual. 132 pages, 5 major sections.

Desktop Guide to RPG/400

By Roger Pence and Julian Monypenny, **NEWS/400** *technical editors*

This fourth book in the *Technical Reference Series* provides a variety of RPG templates, subroutines, and copy modules, sprinkled with evangelical advice, that will help you write robust and effective RPG/400 programs. Highlights of the information provided include string-handling routines, numeric editing routines, date routines, error-handling modules, tips for using OS/400 APIs with RPG/400, and interactive programming techniques. For all types of RPG projects, this book's tested and ready-to-run building blocks will easily snap into your RPG. The programming solutions provided here would otherwise take you days or even weeks to write and test. 211 pages, 28 chapters.

Desktop Guide to Creating CL Commands

By Lynn Nelson

In this most recent book in the *Technical Reference Series,* author Lynn Nelson shows you how to create your own CL commands with the same functionality and power as the IBM commands you use every day, including automatic parameter editing, all the function keys, F4 prompt for values, expanding lists of values, and conditional prompting. After you have read this book, you can write macros for the operations you do over and over every day or write application commands that prompt users for essential information. Whether you're in operations or programming, don't miss this opportunity to enhance your career-building skills. 164 pages, 14 chapters.

UNDERSTANDING BAR CODES

By James R. Plunkett

One of the most important waves of technology sweeping American industry is the use of bar coding to capture and track data. The wave is powered by two needs: the need to gather information in a more accurate and timely manner and the need to track that information once it is gathered. Bar coding meets these needs and provides creative and cost-effective solutions for many applications. With so many leading-edge technologies, it can be difficult for IS professionals to keep up with the concepts and applications they need to make solid decisions. This book gives you an overview of bar code technology including a discussion of the bar codes themselves, the hardware that supports bar coding, how and when to justify and then implement a bar code application, plus examples of many different applications and how bar coding can be used to solve problems. 70 pages.

USING QUERY/400

By Patrice Gapen and Catherine Stoughton

This textbook, designed for any AS/400 user from student to professional with or without prior programming knowledge, presents Query as an easy and fast tool for creating reports and files from AS/400 databases. Topics are ordered from simple to complex and emphasize hands-on AS/400 use; they include defining database files to Query, selecting and sequencing fields, generating new numeric and character fields, sorting within Query, joining database files, defining custom headings, creating new database files, and more. Instructor's kit available. 92 pages, 10 chapters.

USING VISUAL BASIC WITH CLIENT ACCESS APIs

By Ron Jones

This book is for programmers who want to develop client/server solutions on the AS/400 and the personal computer. Whether you are a VB novice or a VB expert, you will gain by reading this book because it provides a thorough overview of the principles and requirements for programming in Windows using VB. Companion diskettes contain source code for all the programming projects referenced in the book, as well as for numerous other utilities and programs. All the projects are compatible with Windows 95 and VB 4.0. 680 pages, 13 chapters.